MICHAEL PENNINGTON

Michael Pennington first played Hamlet when a student at Cambridge in 1964. Within a year he was Fortinbras for Peter Hall at the Royal Shakespeare Company with David Warner as the Prince, and in 1969 he was Laertes to the Hamlet of Nicol Williamson. Then in 1980 Pennington gave his own Hamlet at the RSC, of which the *Sunday Telegraph* wrote that he 'leads one as near to the heart of the play as one is ever likely to approach.' In 1994, he was Claudius (and the Ghost) for Peter Hall's *Hamlet* which played a long run in London's West End.

Over the last twenty years, Pennington has played a further variety of classical leads for the RSC, the Royal National Theatre and the English Shakespeare Company, of which he was co-founder and joint artistic director, including Macbeth, Leontes, Richard II, Coriolanus, Angelo, Berowne and Henry V. He has also played central roles in the plays of Euripides, Congreve, Chekhov, Brenton, Poliakoff, O'Casey, Rudkin, Pinter, Edgar and Bulgakov.

In 1983 he was Raskolnikov in Yuri Lyubimov's version of *Crime and Punishment* and launched his one-man-show, *Anton Chekhov*, which ran at the National Theatre and has since toured extensively abroad. In the West End he has starred in the work of Peter Shaffer, Ronald Harwood, Tom Stoppard and John Mortimer. As well as pursuing an active television, film and radio career, he has directed *Twelfth Night* in British, Japanese and American versions, and in 1990 he co-wrote (with Michael Bogdanov) *The English Shakespeare Company: The Story of 'The Wars of the Roses'*, published by Nick Hern Books.

Michael Pennington

HAMLET
A User's Guide

LIMELIGHT EDITIONS
New York

First Limelight edition August 1996

Gen Fund - 1-2001. 17⁰⁰

Copyright © 1996 Michael Pennington

Published in the United States by Proscenium Publishers Inc., New York, by arrangement with Nick Hern Books Ltd, London

Typeset by Country Setting, Woodchurch, Kent TN26 3TB, and printed in Great Britain by Mackays of Chatham

Michael Pennington has asserted his right to be identified as the author of this work

Lines from *Rosencrantz and Guildenstern Are Dead* by Tom Stoppard reproduced by courtesy of Grove Atlantic

Lines from *Dr Zhivago* by Boris Pasternak reproduced by courtesy of Pantheon Books

Library of Congress Cataloguing-in Publication Data

Pennington, Michael, 1943-
  Hamlet: a user's guide / Michael Pennington.
  224p. 23cm
  ISBN 0-87910-083-4
  1. Shakespeare, William, 1564-1616. Hamlet.
2. Tragedy   3. Acting   I. Title.
PR2807.P36 1996
822.3'3—dc20   95-48452
                                         CIP

Contents

STARVELING (*as Moonshine*): All that I have to say is to tell you that the lanthorn is the moon, I the man i' the moon, this thorn-bush my thorn-bush, and this dog my dog.

A Midsummer Night's Dream, 5.1

1
INTRODUCTION

1

INTRODUCTION

'It is *we* who are Hamlet' – *William Hazlitt, English writer.*
'Yes, Germany is Hamlet!' – *Ferdinand Freiligrath, German political poet.*
'This is very Slavic' – *Alexander Herzen, Russian thinker.*
'Poland is a Hamlet!' – *Adam Mickiewicz, Polish Romantic poet.*
'Unfortunate family, those Hamlets' – *anonymous Dublin theatregoer.*

The day that Laurence Olivier died I was filming in Tuscany, John Mortimer's adaptation of his novel, *Summer's Lease.* We were working in the dilapidated splendour of the Castello di Meleto near Gaiole, on an after-dinner scene, John Gielgud and Susan Fleetwood drinking coffee on one sofa, myself on another with Fyodor Chaliapin, the son of the legendary singer. Fyodor was then nearly ninety, with a remarkable character face, more patrician even than Gielgud's, which, together no doubt with his exotic pedigree, had lately given him a satisfactory cameo career in movies without obliging him to move far from his Roman home. In the few days of his stay with us, he had slightly upstaged Sir John as raconteur-in-chief.

Colin Rogers, the producer, came onto the set while we were waiting, sorry to break in, but he felt he must inform us that Olivier had died.

Olivier to us was the handsome devil of a second assistant. During the previous two months we had every dawn scuttled and bumped to work along the treacherous back roads between Radda-in-Chianti and Castelnuovo, taken with increasing confidence by the unit drivers – and to some extent by the actors, who used a spare car for days off as they arose, for jaunts: my own confidence had gone into a recent decline when I had crumped into a Fiat on the crown of a hill, inches from a fairly sheer drop. It was the kind of close shave that happened a lot: the one thing you knew was that you didn't want at any time to be driven by Olivier, who reckoned he could do the journey with his eyes closed and sometimes did. He had obviously now met the Great Carabiniere on one of those hairpin bends.

Colin clarified his news and one kind of shock replaced another. Everyone tried not to look at Gielgud. Chaliapin, who was a little hard of hearing, continued to tell me what the painter Ilya Repin had said to him in his father's house in 1913, unaware of what had dropped into our midst: his voice, a shaving off the Great Larynx, sung out in the silent room. I interrupted him. 'Fyodor, I think I should tell you that Laurence Olivier has died.' In fact, I said it to him twice. 'AAAAAAAGH!' cried Chaliapin, on a fierce intake of breath, and, raising his hands before him, clapped them together in dismay. When they separated, a large fly lay horribly crushed in one of his palms. Now, when I think of the passing of Olivier, this crushed fly is what I see. However, what I hear is the voice of John Gielgud later in the day, talking quietly about his own complex relationship with Olivier and his admiration for him that surpassed all rivalry. Generous, humorous, sad, modest, graceful and un-deceived, it was the voice of Hamlet.

When I think of Hamlet, though, I still think of Olivier, because he was my first. The Academy Cinema in Oxford Street, London's prototypical post-war art house, used to do a Shakespeare season in September, and *Hamlet* was what I got first, in my thirteenth year. The film, though well-known, is rather underrated. It was shot in black and white, in contrast to Olivier's earlier brilliant (but time-serving) *Henry V*: this was done to save money, but was thought to reflect the bleak northern tones of the play, which in fact it did. His voice-over introducing the film as the story of a man who 'could not make up his mind' has been much mocked, but it has always seemed to me a pretty accurate summary of the work, whether interpreted literally or, if you wish, poetically. The film was also tutted at for cutting Rosencrantz, Guildenstern and Fortinbras; but it gained a great linear forthrightness thereby, and asserted *Hamlet* as a fast story above all, which it was long before it became the most picked-over *objet* in literary history. Obviously Olivier's direct and active personality was less-suited to the part than Gielgud's, and than it was to Richard III (and the blond rinse was probably a mistake), but he was after all the Ken Branagh of his day, with a precious populist gift that, in those less competitive days, allowed him to miscast himself from time to time. My father, who took me, had little interest in cinema, let alone the techniques of cinema, but observed that there was a continuity problem, that Olivier periodically sprouted, lost and then re-sprouted a spot on his lip: but I felt only routine filial irritation, so taken up was I by the Ghost, a billowing amoebic figure, its face tantalisingly obscure, its heart thumping in the battlement mists, the voice recorded in fact by Olivier himself – it harrowed me as surely as it did the Prince. My father, again veiling his enjoyment of my enjoyment in technical criticism, said that it sounded as if his dentures were loose: later I found that he was quoting a reviewer.[1]

The whole thing was fine by me, William Walton's music, the hero's murderous leap from a balcony onto Basil Sydney's Claudius at the end, the moody soliloquies over the crashing waves: very soon a series of 78 rpms of the big speeches spun ceaselessly in my room, and a miniature version, created from stills of the film, was painfully cut out, glued and mounted on my Pollock's toy theatre (Regency 1946 model) – the Ghost on his little wire by now a very unimpressive two-inch blob indeed. The experience propelled me towards an adolescence which, despite an early preoccupation with Meredith Willson's *The Music Man*, with *Guys and Dolls* and Dylan Thomas's New York recording of *Under Milk Wood*, and a later one with Billie Holiday and Charlie Parker, was full of Shakespeare. It coincided with Michael Benthall's five-year programme of the complete works (except *Pericles*) at the Old Vic in London: I saw, then read and re-read almost all the plays, always aloud (I still can't read Shakespeare in silence), first as a happily piping treble and soon as a crackly pubescent bari-tenor. It was a thoroughly narrow-minded and wasted youth which at fourteen qualified me to win the £64,000 prize on *Double Your Money* on the subject of Shakespeare (had I actually entered, instead of yelling the answers at the television set), and has I suppose saved a lot of time learning the lines later.

I never worked for, under or with Olivier – indeed, didn't meet him until one day at his house when I was playing Hamlet myself,

---

1   He would no doubt have enjoyed the tale I was recently told, that Olivier, experimenting tirelessly with where to place the ghostly microphone for the recording session, was invited by a frustrated sound engineer to try an orifice he hadn't thought of, to which he responded enthusiastically: 'Oh, do you think *that* would work?'

at Stratford-upon-Avon in 1980. Within a split second of sighting me he declared by way of greeting that he saw I had dyed my hair for the part, just as he had: I silently hoped that my highlights were a little more subtle than his had been. He then vouchsafed some interesting stuff on the difficulties of fighting in the grave with Laertes, an episode I was in fact dissatisfied with in my own performance; but he found it odd that my other vexations at that moment were Hamlet's 'wild and whirling words' after the departure of the Ghost in the first Act: he said he was surprised because Nicol Williamson, who was 'only half the actor that you are, dear boy' had, he felt, been successful in that area. The dizzying compliment slowed me up – and by the time I recalled that he had never seen me before, and probably hadn't seen Nicol's Hamlet either, he had gone for a swim. Older Olivier hands would have spotted the mechanism quicker.

Between the Academy Cinema and Olivier's swimming-pool I had had a small lifetime of Hamlets. Soon after seeing the film I acquired, perhaps in the interests of critical balance, a boxed set of three LPs of Gielgud as the Prince, recorded in 1955 with the Old Vic Company. It catches his performance at fiftyish, a breath late for it really, but it has a wonderful Claudius in Paul Rogers, and a standard of verse-speaking very typical of that era – a bit officer-class, but muscular, direct and on the line; and lurking among the supers are John Wood and John Woodvine. The 1960s were to see something of a revolution in the handling of Shakespearian verse: it is interesting to look behind them to this best example of non-archaic, staunchly classic work. At the time I adjudged Gielgud rather plain, and hankered for Olivier's glamorous visuals in the other medium; I now see that the recording exemplified his wonderful swiftness and generosity – no flourishes, just intelligence, feeling and passionate speed. Then I saw Paul Scofield (his second, in 1956), and wish I could see it with older eyes now. John Neville in 1957 was unkindly condemned by the late Robert Atkins, who thought that with a little more sex and a little less sanctity he'd make a very passable Laertes, but I thought him wonderful; and a rumour (I have no idea how true) that he had been physically ill with nerves on the first night, which I was at, startled me as information of a kind I had not considered before – *strain* on the *actor?* This was strange news which I somehow knew it was important to note. I saw Michael Redgrave play

Hamlet at fifty at Stratford in 1958 (some years after his Prospero, Lear and Antony) and Peter O'Toole open Olivier's regime at the National Theatre at the Old Vic in 1963 – I remember of that mainly the difficulties of Anthony Nicholls as the Ghost in climbing up and down Sean Kenny's set, and a remarkable version of the plotting scene between Redgrave as Claudius and Derek Jacobi as Laertes. I thought I enjoyed all these Hamlets because they were romantic: looking back, I suspect I was hooked because the productions had a strong sense of place and the performances were swift and heroic within them, even if some of them were a bit short on introspection.

Before very long I was in *Hamlet* more than I was in front of it. I played my own first one, as a student at Cambridge University in February 1964, for one week at the ADC Theatre. I was under the benign, irascible and always operatic eye of Gabor Cossa, a Hungarian antique dealer and enthusiastic amateur, now gone but for many years a familiar figure wobbling on his bike down Trumpington Street, his thoughts on Great Theatrical Virtuosities. He periodically rented the theatre to do, usually, Jacobean tragedy, closing up his shop for the rehearsal period: and when he asked me to play Hamlet I was glad, in the vicious world of undergraduate theatre, that he wasn't some doctrinal student director but, if not a professional, at least an adult maverick. We cooked up our production in the back room of the shop, first in love and enthusiasm, and then, for some reason I have forgotten, in rancour and distrust – I think it had something to do with my not being prepared to decide on a certain gesture *before* we had started rehearsing. Thus it was that on the first day Gabor explained his view of each character to his undergraduate cast – which included a number of future actors (Robin Ellis, Matthew Scurfield, Roger Gartland, Matthew Walters), a director (Sue Best), and a movie producer (Simon Perry)[2] – in an upstairs room in the Rose pub in Rose Crescent, leaving Hamlet to last: at which point he cast a proud eye heavenward and said that I would explain Hamlet to them, since 'Michael has his own ideas'. Improvising wildly, I experienced for the first time a feeling of intense personal heat that has since

2 A remarkable group played scene-change music composed by Anthony le Fleming: the late David Munrow, Christopher Hogwood, Hugh Macdonald and Naomi Butterworth, Clare Shanks and the late John Fletcher.

accompanied thirty years in the professional theatre. Of the playing of the part, I recall only surprise that it was enjoyable, fun, a release: I in no way associated acting with enjoyment at that stage, only with the direst self-analysis, and I was surprised not to feel more of a failure. In fact, the part had contracted to fit the lineaments of a twenty-year-old, as it will do for all the extraordinary variety of bodies that have climbed into it – which is not to deny that the part takes an actor of any age further down into his psyche, and further outwards to the limits of his technique, than he has probably been before. The production, of which I also remember little,[3] went OK – George Steiner, no less, enthused about what I'd done in *The Guardian*; and a local critic, while feeling that I had done well to abandon 'the static music of Gielgud [what a slur] for the rush and recoil of thought', did note that 'some gestures tended towards monotony'. Heady stuff. Despite or because of all this, I got spotted by Stratford and joined the RSC, most humbly, that June, graduating within a year to Fortinbras in the Peter Hall-David Warner *Hamlet* of 1965. It was much my best part to date, and I reckoned I was cooking.

Becoming professional marks the end of infatuation and the beginning of co-habitation. No longer carried away by the splendidness of Shakespeare, especially of his lyrical heroes, I felt a lifelong grappling begin, being right away brought up short by the variety of possibilities within even the smallest parts of this inexhaustible play. Peter Hall told me in the early rehearsals that Fortinbras was crucial to its *Realpolitik*: a glamorous political opportunist who can hardly believe his luck as he finally walks into an empty kingdom, its crowned heads lying dead all around. Dismissing Elsinore's past with a wave of the arm, he should, cynically rather than with sorrow, 'embrace his fortune', reserving special sarcasm for Hamlet: 'likely, *had* he been put on, To have prov'd most royal'. Designs were put in hand to make me look like some *Junker* Siegfried: brown leather, brazen breastplate, a blazing blond wig. You can imagine the result: a performance of precocious

---

3 Except that one night a stage-hand was caught onstage when the lights came up – these were the days in which the set was elaborately changed in the dark – and Robin Ellis as Claudius had to deal with the next line 'How dangerous is it that this man goes loose'. I have had reason to remember this thirty years later, handling the same line immediately after Stephen Dillane as Hamlet has run from the stage, stark naked except for the Player's crown.

deliberation and self-indulgence that must have been keenly felt by the dead court of Denmark, holding mortally still after four hours' work while I laboured through my Moment. Seeing it coming during the previews, Peter took me on one side and pretended he'd misinterpreted the part, which should now be swift, businesslike and generous to the vanquished – an expert piece of director's pragmatism which at the time I was indignant about. I fear I must have defied him, for I can remember taking us perilously close to midnight in the later stages of the run, and in the last week, afflicted by laryngitis (and lacking the wisdom to stay at home), inaudibly so. My contract was not renewed, and it was ten years before I worked with the RSC again.

All in all, I found my place better on that occasion as the bottom half of the Ghost, a ten-foot figure theoretically played by Patrick Magee, but really a great two-tiered zimmer frame on little wheels. The idea of this apparition, in full armour and gauze cloak, bearing down out of the swirling mist onto his terrified son, was really cinematic, and theatrically it took a bit of doing: a ghost operator inside the metal cage saw his way, supposedly, through a grille punched into the belly of the beast, while behind him Magee stood on the upper deck, his arms inside the great arms of the model, his head in the helmet. I was that operator.

The visual impact of the thing depended crucially on the volume of smoke around it – without enough, it was revealed as the gimcrackery it was – and smoke is notoriously difficult to control in the theatre. At that time it was created by a paraffin-based compound that left a slippery residue on the stage floor, which had a plastic veneer and was tilted at a fair rake. Two huge walls opened and closed upstage just widely and briefly enough to let the Ghost through – and significantly, there was a winching channel running down the centre of the stage (along which the truck carrying the throne was to move on and off): this turned out, to my infinite alarm, to be a few millimetres wider than the wheels of my machine. I thus found myself doing penance in advance for my Fortinbras, my forehead pressed against the grille, the back of my head in the loins of Magee, trying to manoeuvre myself around without sliding, snagging, colliding or suffocating. It was so dark I was eventually equipped with a walkie-talkie and guided from the prompt corner. Peter Hall asks me to point out that the whole gigantist business was a folly of his youth, and indeed by the time the production reached the Aldwych the following year Brewster Mason was doubling the Ghost and Claudius and all the ironmongery was cut, unwisely leaving me free to Prepare for Fortinbras.[4]

The director's second thoughts on the latter part may reflect more than my inadequacies. There is a tension in this play between poetic tragedy and political dialectic. A coherent political image should frame the *Leidenschaft* of the Prince – but what brings us to our feet at the end is the sheer appeal of the man, and it doesn't need undermining at the eleventh hour. Hall's benchmark production conveyed a strong sense of inner and outer Elsinore – a recently re-armed state in taut deadlock with Norway, driven from within by bureaucracy, surveillance and half-truth, lubricated by schnapps – but the show's reputation rested on the impact of Warner himself. This was a red-scarfed student rebel immobilised by a political alienation anticipating the Paris *évènements* and the Berkeley demonstrations, but primarily a romantic not a political figure. The whole event was certainly strong enough to withstand an aggrieved young actor in a zimmer frame and a narcissistic Fortinbras. 'Go bid the soldiers shoot' I croaked on the last night, dimly sensing that I had got something wrong in phase one of my career, but not knowing that the next performance of the play on the Aldwych stage would be sixteen years later with my own neck on the block – and oddly enough with the same Polonius (Tony Church) and Gravedigger (David Waller).

Meanwhile I met the play again in 1969, graduating now to Laertes in a version put together with entrepreneurial flair by Tony

---

4   Nor was this all. When the Ghost disappears it seems to divide:

BARNARDO: 'Tis here!
HORATIO: 'Tis here!
MARCELLUS: 'Tis gone.

and a *Doppelgänger* double-decker was built for this moment, so now there were four of us plunging through the mists. A further plan, to guide the machine onto a trap door which would rapidly open beneath it, was mercifully abandoned, perhaps because at a technical rehearsal somebody quoted *Macbeth:* an instant later the trap opened like Hell for Don Giovanni, and an actor who had been standing at ease on it found himself perched on its edge, legs dangling in a twenty-foot abyss. Then Magee had to leave the cast (to play in the *Marat/Sade* in London), leaving behind a recording of his speeches: another supernumary was brought in to mime the action on the upper deck (a cushy job, I thought), and David Warner popped in his responses, timing them to the tape. There we stood, confined by our mute tasks, while Magee's voice rang out simultaneously in the two theatres.

Richardson, with Nicol Williamson in the lead. This was the first full-scale Shakespeare at the Round House in Camden Town, until recently the home of Arnold Wesker's Centre 42, idealism still battling in the place with patchouli and dankness. One block of seats was sold for five pounds, a great sum, to subsidise students' tickets at five shillings; Harold Wilson came to the opening, later recommending to President Nixon that he take note of this Williamson, who was duly invited to play a one-man show at the White House. The casting ranged from Gordon Jackson and Judy Parfitt in the north to Michael Elphick and Marianne Faithfull in the south, from Roger Livesey and Mark Dignam in the east to Anthony Hopkins and Anjelica Huston in the west, with Nicol in the middle, baleful and tender, an object lesson in passionate commitment. The violence of his performance was much discussed, but not enough its nimble humour and the tentative benevolence that he brought to the scenes with the Players and the Gravedigger. Elsewhere the show was a riot of individualism, and too many of us in the middle ranks were inside either a bottle or a rolled-up banknote for things to stay stable for very long: I myself threatened not to go to New York with it after being publicly rebuked by Tony Richardson, a warning that must have struck him with all the force of a feather. I did go in the end, mainly I fancy because I wanted to sit in Jim Downey's Bar on 8th Avenue and stand on the corner of Bleecker and McDougal in Greenwich Village.[5] All Shakespearian companies carry a bratpack (not enough women's parts), and we were unthinkable. The production that gave rise to this licensed folly was all bones and muscle and not

5   It was an interesting time. While we were in New York the film of the show, shot with most wicked speed at the Round House late in the run, premiered as a major Columbia picture: the poster featured Nicol bent speculatively over a supine Marianne Faithfull, her breasts impossibly cantilevered (it was really an upright photograph turned through ninety degrees), and it yelled 'From the author of *Romeo and Juliet*: the love story of Hamlet and Ophelia.' The company went on to Boston, San Francisco and Los Angeles: we played cricket on Berkeley campus amid the flying frisbees, and, flushed with success, went on to challenge a UCLA team at the same game, forgetting that English actors in the thirties had established cricket in Hollywood to the point that it is now played to minor county standard. The UCLA team was captained by the brother of the great Everton Decoursey Weekes, who, with Frank Worrell and Clyde Walcott, had been for my generation one of the triple pillars of the world. I nearly had Weekes in the slips, but we were trounced. The last evening of the tour I spent with the director George Roy Hill, more or less providing a shoulder for him to cry on as he lamented the fate of the new picture he was editing and re-editing in despair: the studio was out of patience, and he was convinced it marked the end of his useful career and that of his two stars. What was it called, I asked. Gloomier still, he told me

much brain – played on an open Elizabethan stage, it took pride in being unclassifiably anti-intellectual. Tony Richardson presided with a sort of piratical *laissez-faire*, dispensing provocatively incomplete ideas such as incest between Laertes and Ophelia ('just grab his cock, Marianne'). The show, in its scorn for all traditions, had a conventional air, as if it couldn't be troubled to re-think anything (not even balloon pants and tight doublets), and it had no politics, not even of any kind: it could hardly have been in greater contrast to the cold-war preoccupations of 1965.

I was then free of *Hamlet* for ten years – or rather for five, for it was at a British Council party in Copenhagen, shortly after rejoining the RSC in 1975, that I learned that John Barton had the idea to do the play with me: I immediately felt a great peace, which soon gave way to more or less permanent anxiety. The production was scheduled for 1980. The interim was mine: I didn't talk about it, though I thought about it most days, and he didn't change his mind. The readiness was, it was to be hoped, all.

I pause: what can a man say about his own Hamlet? The part is like a pane of clear glass disclosing the actor to a greedy audience, and playing it changes you for good, and for the better. It may not advance a career, often marking the end of a sequence of work rather than the beginning: it may bring eccentric benefits, in my case the freedom of the city of Assisi. My script, now I look at it again for enlightenment, says gnomic things like 'asleep', 'story story story', 'quick quick', 'wait', 'light energy', 'he waxes desperate with imagination', and, best of all, 'not too silly'. Some nights the part felt like slipping on a tailored glove, others it drove me to frenzy. I can remember a spectator calling 'Don't do it!' when Osric brought Laertes's challenge to the duel; and, one wintry evening, sitting on a tomb in costume in the graveyard of Shakespeare's church after a bomb scare cleared the theatre in the middle of the Closet Scene: the rest of the cast joined the audience in the Arden bar across the road. Another night, I realised beyond all doubt that I had food poisoning just after starting the first

they had been through dozens of working titles, and were no more cheerful about the latest – *Butch Cassidy and the Sundance Kid*. Having dropped him off, I got lost in the mountains above Beverly Hills, and spent some time wandering from door to door in search of directions before getting back very late to the city. Waking in the morning to leave for England, I heard the news of the Sharon Tate killings on Cielo Drive, within a mile or so of where I had been lost the previous night.

soliloquy, and begged leave to take ten minutes break. The audience applauded this request (which was worrying), applauded my return, and then applauded unreasonably at the end – it was a triumph of bloodymindedness, but they took it for the Dunkirk Spirit. This was the only time I have seen Tom Wilkinson, a fine and self-confident actor, blench – he started like a guilty thing upon a fearful summons, being the understudy.

John Barton's production concerned itself more with the breakdown of family relationships than with the political *Zeitgeist*. Most characteristically, it offered a self-referring image of the theatre itself: the chance arrival of a troupe of professional players at the court not only prodded the narrative, but precipitated in Hamlet himself a compulsive enquiry into the nature of acting and action. Rehearsing, I didn't at first understand this idea and distrusted it, fearing to be drawn into some acute Pirandellian angle on the play: before long, it sustained me. The distinction between self-dramatisation and real feeling, between theatricality and life, runs right through *Hamlet*, explaining the peculiar imbalances in Hamlet's language: he is not highly poetic in the manner of Lear or Macbeth, but he makes vertiginous switches between the humdrum and the hypermetaphorical as he strains to become an avenging angel in some atavistic melodrama. Essentially Barton wanted a graceful and sensitive Hamlet, a balance to the recent mass of caustic anti-heroes: meanwhile I thumped Ophelia to the floor in the Nunnery Scene. Many kind and unforgettable things were said to me; on the other hand James Fenton, not yet Professor of Poetry, called me Hamlet, Prune of Denmark, and then reprinted his review in an anthology of his prose, so his kindly description long held a place in the lavatories of the land. Between the food poisoning and the Fenton, the good will of the public and the lightheadedness of the letters, I was, like all of us, left with nothing but my own scruples.

Fourteen years later, in the summer of 1994, I found myself on the stage of the Herodes Atticus arena on the Acropolis in Athens, doubling Claudius and a (non-mechanical) Ghost for, once again, Peter Hall – an exotic two-day incident between Leatherhead and Brighton in a touring schedule eventually leading to a season in the West End of London. After playing Claudius for a month, I had found that he has to be done from his own point of view and not from Hamlet's – as a capable and accomplished man whose machiavellian energies intensify as guilt makes its inroads. As the Ghost I could hear my father's maddening chuckle from beyond the grave, and was mindful not to sound as if my dentures were loose. The Herodes Atticus dates from 190 A. D. and so is in fact Roman (it was built, like the Taj Mahal, by a rich man grieving for his dead wife); but still we were in Greece and in touch with the roots of the game, since it was in a theatre very much like this that Aeschylus invented the dramatic conversation (as opposed to protagonist and Chorus), in *The Persians*. We continued to rehearse the still-young production, finding at last a solution to blood for the death of Polonius, which needed be as shocking as possible; the problem had vexed even Donald Sinden, an actor with, normally, an inexhaustible supply of ways and means, culled both from his own imaginings and his wide knowledge of the last two hundred years of stage practice.[6] For this he is always much teased, by me included. Donald's view was that if he concealed a water pistol about him, charged with Kensington Gore, he would be in a position, pointing it upwards from the chest, to discharge upon himself a bloody explosion. It was a very good idea: I did have to ask him whether he didn't have Henry Irving's water pistol at home.

Peter Hall was naturally not much interested in explaining to the press why he had returned to the play for a third shot (he also did it at the National Theatre with Albert Finney in 1975) – it is a very good play. It was I who kept being asked what the differences were from 1965. What that production and this had in common is that both came at the end of long periods of stultifying Conservative government in England – thirteen years in the first case under Churchill, Eden and Macmillan, then fifteen under Thatcher and in the twilight of Major. But whereas political protest seeped into the earlier version as naturally as a river, the peculiar destructiveness of the Thatcher years gradually exhausted the reflex for

---

6   More than anyone, I suppose, Donald believes in the specific traditions of the theatre, in the handing on of ideas, stage business and even properties from one generation of actors to another. He has owned (but wretchedly been robbed of) Kean's jewelled belt from *Sardanapalus*, Irving's Iachimo boots, the hat worn by Sir John Martin Harvey as Sydney Carton, and he can readily trace genealogies in acting styles in boulevard as much as the classics – from J. L. Toole through Charles Hawtrey and Ronald Squire to Kenneth More. Some relics are more potent than others: I have handled John Philip Kemble's Coriolanus sword, which is a fine and completely unmarked piece, suggesting to me that there wasn't a lot of real clashing of swords in the stage fights of his day.

opposition, so that both new writing and the angle of approach to classical texts became in general less politically informed, more personal, wayward and allusive. The 1994 show, commercially funded where the earlier was subsidised, reflected the times in its very unreflexiveness: the design rather brazen and allusive in the topical mix-and-match style, certain gestures made towards sexual ambiguity, and in Stephen Dillane a wayward, brilliant, uneasy Hamlet; but its real guarantee was Hall's ear for the strong beating heart of Shakespeare's verse, his suspicion of the short cut and the extrapolated image: a fine puritanical instinct at work on the boulevard.

It was over a hundred degrees during the day; we played at nine in the evening, finishing at one in the morning, and then cast and audience would go out for supper. Bats flapped from jutty to crevice of the great stone and weed structure behind us, the evening breeze blew at Ophelia's dress as if to take her fragile wits away, and when Gertrude came forward from the central entrance to report her drowning, it was as if the messenger was about to describe the death of Agamemnon.[7] Hamlet called on all the host of heaven, Laertes demanded 'Do you see this, O God', Claudius appealed to the angels: all these cries rose bare-faced into an enormous, empty, ultramarine sky. Actors don't often get the chance to talk directly to God, and he rewards them with a surge of meaning that was not available to Elizabethan actors, since they played in the afternoons, nor to Greek actors, since they wore masks. The austerity of the setting momentarily suited the play; but in truth the distance we have travelled from the formalities of Greek theatre is unbridgeable – everything had to be addressed fullbloodedly outwards to the audience, it was a mistake to be within twenty feet of the character you were acting with, and interplay in our (or Shakespeare's) sense was quite impossible.[8] Our calves ached from the fifty-yard entrances, and some of the voices might not have made a third performance. Although

---

7 And Gina Bellman, playing Ophelia, had broken a toe and was obliged to drag a bandaged foot around in her madness like the wounded Philoctetes.

8 There was also, for all the excitement, an incongruity: Shakespeare knew little of Greek theatre. The Pyrrhus and Hecuba story in this play he got from Book Two of Virgil's *Aeneid*, *Timon of Athens* comes from North's translation of Plutarch, and there is little else Greek apart from what he would have had from Chapman's Homer and Chaucer for *Troilus and Cressida*, and Theseus's name being stolen for the *Dream*. As for Greek dramatic material,

the space turned everybody momentarily into epic heroes, enough was enough.

The only cloud in the Hellenic sky that week, for some of us, was the news of the death of Innokenti Smoktunovsky, perhaps the best Hamlet I ever saw, albeit confined to an adapted medium, the cinema. Grigori Kozintsev's superb film (translation by Boris Pasternak) arrived in England on the eve of Peter Hall's 1965 production. It opens with Smoktunovsky galloping home to Elsinore with an energy that already suggests a knowledge of foul play. Once there, so oppressive is the sense of surveillance that as he moves silently to and fro between the magpies of the court, his precious thoughts, his only freedom in a murderously attentive world, seem almost audible to them.[9] The emotional refrain throughout is of imprisonment and escape – the camera cuts insistently to the sea beating on the incarcerating walls of Elsinore, and the dawn that drives the Ghost away is a hopeful glimmer on its distant horizon. Claudius applauds aghast at the climax of the Play Scene, performed in the castle courtyard by candlelight; Ophelia is tied into her corset like a straitjacket; the horses bolt from their stables moments before Hamlet is nearly blown off his feet by the stunning image of the Ghost. After Ophelia's mad scene the camera lingers on the Gobelin tapestries in her deserted bedroom, then at fog over water, her already ghostly body sinking beneath it – a macabre version of the Millais painting: at the same moment, a bird takes wing and flies eagerly across the sky towards Hamlet standing on the rocky shoreline. This last is a sentimentality rather distinct from Shakespeare's robust romanticism, but it is justified by the conviction behind it, and in any case made up for by the ensuing bleakness of the Graveyard – like the edge of the northern world, refugees moving to and fro, caravans, gravel, a crooked broken tombstone. Finally, as the soldiers climb steeply

though he may have known Euripides, he received more from the later versions of the Roman Seneca. (Caryl Churchill points out, in the introduction to her translation of *Thyestes*, that Seneca's style influenced not only early Shakespeare, like *Titus Andronicus*, but areas of *Lear* and *Macbeth* as well.) Oddly, though Seneca did dramatise both Oedipus and Phaedra, there is no mention of them in Shakespeare – or of the house of Atreus, whose troubles end with the goddess Athena founding the city state of Athens, symbolised by the Acropolis. Right here.

9   Olivier also used voice-over for the soliloquies, but allowed himself to burst out loud on crucial phrases – 'Nay, not so much, not two!', 'And yet, within a month!' – as people who talk to themselves will; but in the English film there are no eavesdroppers to hear him.

with Hamlet's body to the battlements, a small boy kicks a stone aside in their wake, in an image of dogged continuity. The film's lyrical political protest is both Russian and Shakespearian – though it does suffer from an inevitable Russian scruple, presenting Claudius as a one-dimensional dictator barely allowed the redemption of prayer. You don't, after all, plead for Stalin.[10] But it is still a revelation, and Smoktunovsky at the centre was revealed to world audiences as a born Hamlet, of immense intelligence, grace, bitterness and personal beauty. Goodnight, sweet prince.

★

> In the tragedy of Hamlet, the ghost of a king appears on the stage; Hamlet goes crazy in the second act, and his mistress in the third; the Prince slays his mistress's father under the pretence of killing a rat, and the heroine throws herself into the river. Meantime another of the actors conquers Poland. Hamlet, his mother and his father-in-law carouse on the stage, songs are sung at table, there's quarrelling, fighting, killing; it is a vulgar and barbarous drama which would not be tolerated by the vilest populace of France or Italy. – *Voltaire (1694- 1778)*.

No other play attracts such reverence, and at the same time so much of the contempt bred by familiarity, as *Hamlet*. Voices hush over it; the same voices relax by calling it Omelette. There is indeed some reason to knock the play about – in fact, it's probably a necessary ritual. This is a medieval revenge story severely compromised by Renaissance humanism. It is far too long. The Duel

10 Not least perhaps when your leading actor, as it is believed, had been in Stalin's gulag as well as a prisoner of the Germans in World War II. The meaning of Hamlet as questioner, as the one honest man, fatally clear-sighted, has of course meant even more to the Soviets than to us. Indeed, the entire Russian relationship to the play is a book in itself, and a love story – even though Tolstoy did declare that Shakespeare's work was almost as bad as Chekhov's, filling him with 'an overpowering repugnance, a boundless tedium'. Originally, the playwright was so fervently felt to be a sort of Russian that a common translation of his name was *kopye tryaskin*, literally 'spear-shaker'. Stalin was so afraid of *Hamlet* and *Macbeth* that he commented 'Why is this necessary – playing *Hamlet* at the Art Theatre, eh?' and that was the end of the play in his time unless it was burlesqued: Michael Chekhov's anthroposophist version, in which he deliriously spoke the Ghost's lines as well as his own, was set in purgatory, and banned as gloomy. Nikolai Akimov did the play as a comedy, with Hamlet fat and alcoholic (as was Ophelia, who drowned after a drunken binge), Meyerhold wanted two Hamlets, one solemnly reciting the soliloquies, another, comic, making fun of him; a production at the Vakhtangov Theatre in the 1930s had Horatio shouting the Ghost's lines into an earthenware pot to frighten Claudius.

Scene is crudely written by any standard. Shakespeare had great difficulty manipulating his sources, various and wild, into a coherent play. Whether you regard its psychology, its politics, or its simple theatre logic, it is full of holes. In practice it seems impossible for a production finally to make the play frame the man and the man belong in the play, to place the convulsive energies of the Nunnery Scene in the same world as the Dumb Show, the modernity of the gravediggers on a plane with the medievalism of the King's orchard.

For an heroic tragedy, *Hamlet* is packed with political matter quite difficult to accommodate in production; though not hard to understand, it is embarrassing in a play of this length, and references to the national past, the toings and froings of Voltemand and Cornelius, Fortinbras and the Polish wars, all obtrude at moments when our interest in Hamlet's own story is intensifying. Hamlet's involvement with Denmark's political life is zero, so, unlike many heroes, he does not form the bridgehead between a public and private world. Characteristically, Shakespeare is more interested in the psychic effects of breaking the taboo against regicide than in the actual warp and woof of politics (though he is always concerned with the survival tactics of a usurper); but he is expert at suggesting the inter-relationship of private passions and public life, the acute consciousness in one of the other – he does it supremely in the Histories, *Coriolanus* and *Antony and Cleopatra*, very well in *Measure for Measure* and *Julius Caesar*, and well, with some effort, in *Macbeth*. In these plays, almost every gesture goes simultaneously inward and outward; in *Hamlet* (as in *Othello*), human responses themselves are the fascination, and the political circumstances the play initially expounds are suspended and asserted as need arises.

King Lear (five years later) achieves more profound and complex insights into the condition of the 'bare, fork'd animal', into parenthood, the abuse of goodness, the grotesqueness of sexuality linked to power, madness and sanity, how we fail to live with each other. *A Midsummer Night's Dream* (four years earlier) is funnier than *Hamlet*, and in many ways more metaphysical as well; *Antony and Cleopatra* and even *Troilus and Cressida* are broader in scope. In a sense *Hamlet* is neither one thing nor the other, not quite a political epic, nor yet a study of kingship, nor of intimate character and relationships. The logic of the action is problematic: it is very difficult to track the movements of Polonius, Ophelia, the King and

the Queen in the early part of the play, to establish the origin of
Rosencrantz and Guildenstern, or to understand the story of
Horatio. The play's interior is psychologically and sexually vague,
though heavy with implication, its obliquity making for a great
soupe of red herrings. It is rare for Shakespeare not to establish
unequivocally whether his lovers are in a state of courtship or
consummation – but generations of actors have had to labour over
whether Ophelia and Hamlet have slept together. Apart from giving
rise to the hoariest of thespian jokes ('only on tour'), the depressing
conclusion is that you can take your choice on this, arguing back-
wards from whether you prefer to see the sexuality in Ophelia's
madness arising from experience or virginal instinct. The same
mystery hangs over whether Claudius and Gertrude were lovers
before the old King died, and so whether the talk of adultery (not
to mention incest) is emotional rhetoric or acceptable fact. Actors
playing these parts find that half a dozen Shakespeares tell you
more about middle-aged sexual folly than this, which promises
much but then barely allows the two of them a moment together.
Having started with a rich set of relationships and characters (it
was as natural to him as breathing), Shakespeare thins out his
landscape and lets several of the leading figures go hang, selling his
soul to Hamlet, the volume and interest of whose part in the end
knock everything else for six.

The play's most pathologically interesting feature is also its
cheapest effect: Hamlet's madness, a highly negotiable term upon
which air of all heats has been expended. Apart from its dubious
tactical value – assuming an 'antic disposition' is more likely to
draw attention to him than give him an alibi – this 'madness'
almost makes the play unplayable, since it makes fools of the rest of
the cast, many of whom are not supposed to be fools. It also sets
the central actor on an unrewarding search for eccentric dress and
funny voices.[11] In fact, aside from a few moments of calculated
gibberish, Hamlet speaks nothing but searing good sense throughout the play – a lucidity that drives everyone else to distraction,
rage and sorrow – and drops liberal hints about his pretence to all

---

11   It's worth noticing that after his first alarming appearance to Ophelia, nobody makes
any reference to Hamlet's appearance; so if the chosen image is very adventurous, it suggests
a strange conspiracy to overlook the obvious. This is the play in which actors are advised to
'suit the word to the action' and the word is not, after all, 'Look, where sadly the poor
wretch comes reading dressed in his mother's clothes'.

the wrong people. Gertrude keeps changing her mind about his condition, eager to believe that he is mad only 'in craft' but becoming ever more lyrical in her descriptions of his insanity. Polonius, the arch-politician, at first thinks Hamlet *is* mad, and then changes his mind when he finds himself mocked. The only person who sees through Hamlet without effort is Claudius, himself a dissembler. He is the most sceptical – but also the most inconsistent, using terms for madness and assumed madness interchangeably. The most damaging case is that of Ophelia, with whom Hamlet is extremely explicit, rejecting and denouncing her in a *tour de force* of sexual rhetoric which she then describes as the ravings of a noble mind o'erthrown. This makes her stupid or vain – and her lack of vision leaves the part almost unintelligible, depending on a virtuoso performance of the Mad Scene. In fact, Hamlet's 'distraction' is really a fascinating effect, drawn from the sources to make him attractive to an audience who, lacking our sober apprehensions of mental illness, loved this sort of thing, and got very excited by images of melancholia and bedlam. Even in these terms, it is unevenly delivered: as voyeurs, the Elizabethans might have preferred the twelfth-century source in which the Hamlet figure comes to his mother flapping his arms and crowing like a cock, stomps Polonius to death under a mattress, chops up his body and boils the pieces, finally feeding them to the palace pigs. That's what I call madness: Shakespeare replaces it with perhaps the most intelligent man ever written – otherwise we wouldn't have been listening to him all these years.

There is nothing either good or bad, but thinking makes it so; and listing the deficiencies of the play has the effect of drawing attention to the extraordinary hold it has exercised on the imagination, everywhere, for four centuries and continuing. Every reservation above contains the seed of the play's strengths: it is, in practice, a triumph. Believing we should be held by the spiritual conundrums of *Hamlet*, we respond, time after time, to the energetic storytelling, its loose ends raised to the status of enigma, and the haunting, inexplicable hologram of the Prince. Drawing on archetypes as old as the *Oresteia* at one end and passing them forward to Disney's *The Lion King* (which even has a paternal Ghost intoning 'Remember!') at the other, the play has galvanic force in the theatre, an ability, for all its despair, to heal, and an effect on an audience of any age quite unlike any other I know. It is

an image of entrapment sustained by a series of beautiful gestures –
a son with his father's ghost, a theatre within a theatre, a man with
a sword over a praying murderer, a skull and a spade, a wounded
duellist – crystallised by a remarkable narrative to which they are
locked like barnacles: all except To Be Or Not To Be, which
hovers over the play like a great wing, its greatness lying in its very
detachment.

New spectators may remember their first *Hamlet* for life; for
those who know every word, a revival, which always calls out a
nervy sense of expectation, can be extraordinarily helpful,
especially in a time of doubt. Although its characteristic textures
are cold grey and black, iron and stone, the play is a form of white
magic, lucid and useful beyond itself where *Macbeth*, for instance,
is unholy, closed, a ritual from the subconscious; and it gives rise to
many more interesting enquiries than its story calls for, an uncon-
trollable curiosity threatening its own structure. How else can one
of the most exciting adventure stories in literature take nearly four
hours to perform? It barely falters, and its energy short-circuits all
reservations. What if it is sexually unclear – is there a rule that all
these things must be spelt out ? How can it be thought psychologically weak when Ophelia, anticipating Freud by three centuries,
mentally shifts in her madness between her lover, her brother and
her father so that they become one man; when Claudius, in watching her, reverts to the primal imagery of his conscience: 'O this is
the *poison* of deep grief', and immediately afterwards, in panic at
the approach of Laertes, declares that his foe 'wants not buzzers to
infect his ear'? Hamlet's madness may be hard to track, but its
ambiguity gives the play demonic energy: a touchstone for all their
states of mind, it drives everyone else nearly out of their minds.

Metaphysically, the play does exactly what it sets out to do and
no more, and politically it finds a perfect intersection in the
indispensable figure of Fortinbras, standing at the crossroads of the
play. If we have difficulty moving between the diplomatic intrigue
and the intense introspection, it is because we have lost the knack.
Dazed by imagery, our vocabulary truncated, ears bruised by walls
of blank sound, we have lost much of the mental agility of
the Elizabethan audience, who probably moved more swiftly from
head to solar plexus. The illogic of the action is never evident in
the theatre, and structurally the play has strengths that most
Shakespeares don't – many hesitate somewhere in Act IV,

perhaps with endless parleys between the two sides about to fight the climactic battle, perhaps through the absence of the central character; but assuming Claudius, Laertes and Ophelia know their onions, the loss of the fascinating hero isn't a problem here.

As well as depending on performance the play signally survives it. The writing is so powerful that it can sidestep the production, and this is one of the few plays that can still be worth seeing in a disappointing version. You can observe that the Hamlet is not brilliant enough to think of his lines, that Claudius's court is not characterised enough, that Ophelia is not touching and Laertes is an embarrassment, and still not have wasted your time – you will still be thinking about it all the next day. *Hamlet* has a unique springiness. The central figure, emerging from an old cycle of revenge melodrama, is not only a romantic icon but a hero who goes beyond literature and the theatre: although apparently enmeshed in untypical restraints and ancient scruples, he, more than Othello, Macbeth, or Lear, walks the earth with us, asking our questions. By common consent, he and his play, potently on the side of life for all their catastrophes, are a sort of miracle.

★

And here is what the world most needs: another book on them. This is a kind of owner's manual: I'm offering no views on whether you should have left- or right-hand drive or what colour the model should be, but I know the push-bang-suck of the engine by now and how the distributor works – perhaps also which passages call for pure brake horsepower and which deft cornering. This is only in the slightest sense a history of productions: there are quite a few such books about already. Obviously, it is not a book of scholarship, unless it is sawdust scholarship: it has been written in dressing-rooms during the long tour of the latest *Hamlet*. For closer textual analysis, there are shelves and shelves – I particularly recommend Anne Barton's brief but brilliant essay on the play for the 1979 New Penguin edition. Similarly, any good text will explain the obscure words. I am really imitating a rehearsal, when a naive telling of the story will often provoke a discovery; so the starting point is to open the script and follow it line by line, trying not to make assumptions about character until the action proves them – this is a bigger point than it sounds. (For this reason the chapter about the characters comes after the ones about the action of the play.) From then on, the field is open for any kind of imaginative flight; and indeed the play is often used for the wildest experimentation. Real progress in the theatre frequently comes out of this convinced extrapolation – I would rather see Peter Sellars's radical deconstructions of Shakespeare or Yuri Lyubimov's codes than either a concert performance (the text and only the text) or some half-hearted experiment by a director desperate to be distinctive from a predecessor. All the same, there is a score, and if an experiment fails, it may be because some simple rhythm or bar structure in it has been pointlessly ignored. Above all, the following is all based on the idea that Shakespeare is common coin and nobody's little piece of land.

Like all the plays, *Hamlet* is printed in the first Folio edition in five 'Acti' subdivided into 'Scenae'. The word Act is rather confusing, because we now think in terms of two or maybe three of them for the theatre, with intervals between. So I am calling them Days (they are very nearly the same divisions) – also to draw attention to the fact that, while five separate days of action are presented, Shakespeare's manipulation of 'double time' is so skilled that you can believe that several months have passed by between the beginning and the end: even, if you like, for Hamlet to develop from a graduate of Wittenberg (Day One) to a man of thirty (Day Five, the gravediggers).

The play was probably written in 1600-1, when Elizabeth I was still on the throne. There was an earlier play, around in the 1590s, now known as the *ur-Hamlet*, of which there's no trace – it was possibly by Shakespeare, but more probably by the unfortunate Thomas Kyd, whose credit survives only through the interesting *Spanish Tragedy*. A vogue for revenge dramas at the turn of the century would have encouraged Shakespeare to rewrite this play (*The Spanish Tragedy* was itself revised in 1601). Behind the old play, and therefore to some extent behind ours, were two main sources, the twelfth-century story in the *Historiae Danicae* of Saxo Grammaticus, its hero called Amleth (which meant 'simpleton'), and a watered-down sixteenth-century version of it by François de Belleforest; but its themes – fratricide, a son's revenge – are of course as old as the Greeks. It seems that the *ur-Hamlet* added a Ghost for the first time, Shakespeare's revision the crucial element of the hero's hesitation.

The play was immediately popular. It was entered in the Stationers' Register (a means of proving copyright) in 1602. All that is really necessary to know about the early texts of *Hamlet* is that there was a first Quarto[12] in 1603, probably put together in large part by the actor who had played three roles in the original production of 1601 – Marcellus, Voltemand and Lucianus – now possibly no longer with Shakespeare's company and working from memory. His account of his own parts, and to some extent of the scenes he is in, is consistent with later, more reliable versions (though he does not remember the names of his colleagues onstage in the first scene, calling them only 1 and 2). The further he gets from home ground, the wilder the text gets, containing such kitsch glories as

> To be, or not to be, ay there's the point;
> To die, to sleep, is that all?

This First Quarto is more or less disregarded by scholars. The Second Quarto is 1604, and is probably drawn from Shakespeare's own manuscript. The First Folio, although not published until seven years after his death, in 1623, may nevertheless have been revised by Shakespeare himself. There are a number of cuts in it, which are made with close regard to the metre; they look like practitioner's choices – the play is very long and the vast majority of them are in the second half, from the scene in the Queen's bedroom onwards. They also show a great writer's cavalier approach to some of his best stuff: Hamlet's soliloquy 'How All Occasions Do Inform Against Me' is removed entirely.

The textual variants are of great (and for some, lifelong) interest: in quoting the play I have been entirely unscholarly, using what my ear has become accustomed to over the years – it is my accumulated version, I suppose. Likewise, most productions combine what they like best from the Second Quarto and the Folio and any number of later versions, with occasional mischievous forays into the First ('Bad') Quarto. It's a matter really of what you like best. More out of mischief than anything else, I secured licence from John Barton in 1980 at Stratford to put the following from the Bad Quarto into Hamlet's advice to the Players, on the reasonable

---

12   The word Folio only means a sheet folded once, into two pages; a Quarto is a sheet folded twice into four pages.

supposition that no-one would have heard it before, at least in that building:

> And then you have some again that keeps one suit of jests, as a man is known by one suit of apparel; and gentlemen quote his jests down in their tables before they come to the play; as thus, 'Cannot you stay till I eat my porridge?' and 'You owe me a quarter's wages' and 'My coat wants a cullison' and 'Your beer is sour', and blabbering with his lips, and thus keeping in his cinquepace of jests, when, God knows, the warm clown cannot make a jest unless by chance, as the blind man catcheth a hare.

The audience, lulled with familiar words, didn't half sit up. The odd thing is, this 'corrupt' stuff sounds very like Shakespeare.

2
THE ACTION

THE ACTION: DAY ONE

Act 1 Scene 1–Act 1 Scene 5

1.1. Just after the midnight bell: a soldier called Francisco stands on guard. He is challenged by another, Barnardo, coming on duty. Barnardo is accompanied by the two 'rivals' of his watch, Marcellus and Horatio, who describe themselves as 'friends to this ground And liegemen to the Dane'. So this is a changing of palace sentinels: despite the Italianate names, it seems we are in Denmark, and it is 'bitter cold'. Marcellus's status is never really clarified: it will appear later on that he may be senior to Barnardo, but not decisively so. Horatio, it will also turn out, is a friend of the Crown Prince (though they have not met for some time); he is an intellectual from Wittenberg University.[1] Like his royal friend, Horatio feels more at home there than he does here in Denmark, on the battlements, about to have his stoicism sorely tested.

Francisco knocks off as usual, after a brief exchange with Barnardo. His watch has been quiet, although he does admit that he is 'sick at heart'. This may be because he is a natural complainer, or because his job lends itself to mournful reflection – or perhaps tonight he has been apprehensive. Hesitantly, the remaining three men now come to the point. Marcellus has brought Horatio with him to verify, or not, his and Barnardo's experience of the previous two nights, when they have seen a spectrally armoured figure in the likeness of the recently dead King (so far unnamed), going by their watch 'with martial stalk'. Why Horatio particularly, with whom they have a tenuous though friendly enough relation-

---

1 This university, 'the Athens of Germany', was quite new, having been founded within the memory of these people's parents; but it was already the one most favoured by Danes living abroad, and a synonym for renaissance humanism.

ship? Because if, as a scholar, Horatio were to see the apparition as readily as they, this could tell them something about its meaning; and Horatio, a link with the dead King's son, might be able to take the crucial decision, what to do next. In the soldiers' acknowledgment of what they have seen is a kind of shame. Even though, in a superstitious age, they admit the existence of ghosts, a tendency to see them on duty is not a strength in a working soldier.

The Ghost, so to describe him, appears with great suddenness, a breath before Barnardo confirms his visitation of the previous night; the soldiers' attention is momentarily distracted, and there he is:[2]

> BARNARDO: Last night of all,
>   When yond same star that's westward from the pole
>   Had made his course t'illume that part of heaven
>   Where now it burns, Marcellus and myself,
>   The bell then beating one –
> MARCELLUS: Peace, break thee off. Look where it comes again.

Does he have his own volition, choosing when and whether to be seen – or is he a victim of time, forced unwillingly to walk by the chiming of the midnight bell? He seems homeless, roaming, seeking something. He is unwilling to speak, but, in a reversal of royal procedure, 'would be spoke to';[3] Horatio attempts this, but misjudges his opportunity:

> HORATIO: What art thou that usurps't this time of night. . .

---

2   We are two minutes into the play. In strict time, it is midnight; but by allowing Barnardo to record that last night the Ghost appeared 'the bell then beating one' Shakespeare is up to his tricks, unobtrusively accelerating the passage of time towards dawn. This early arrival is also a bold stroke if you consider the unsettled circumstances of the first performances. For the Elizabethans there was none of the orderly hush and sense of ceremony that attends our darkening auditoria. The actors entered from opposite doors onto a stage open to the sky in the middle of a noisy city afternoon – an autumn afternoon in 1601, in the case of the first performance of *Hamlet*; later, in fashionable indoor playhouses like the Blackfriars, they had to pass among various dandies sitting on stools on the stage itself, concerned to show off their outfits to the other spectators and often turning up late to make the impression stronger. Thomas Dekker advises in his *Gull's Hornbook*:

> Let our gallant. . . . presently advance himself up to the Throne of the Stage. . . on the very Rushes where the Comedy is to dance. . . . must our feathered Estridge, like a piece of ordnance, be planted. . . .

Through such the dead King of Denmark walked.

3   A belief persisted, even up to the time of Dr Johnson, that ghosts only utter when addressed. So this awesome figure is powerless until a subject releases him.

It was the wrong verb to use: the Ghost is offended and stalks away
– he is, after all, a who, not a what, not a usurper and a king to
boot; and he has his pride. So his responses are human, and
something real can be expected of him.

Horatio, the sceptic ('Tush, tush, 'twill not appear') is now
severely shaken:

> In what particular thought to work I know not

and the soldiers twit him for his unbelief. The apparition has
awakened his long-buried memories:

> Such was the very armour he had on
> When he the ambitious Norway combated.
> So frown'd he once, when in an angry parle
> He smote the sledded Polacks on the ice.

The three men now do what they might conventionally have done
first, discuss the background. Marcellus and Barnardo pretend to
relax while Horatio explains, with a slight patriotic bias, the
political state of affairs that may have led to this ominous portent.
Old King Fortinbras of Norway has been slain, as everybody
knows, in hand-to-hand combat by the old King of Denmark (to
whom Horatio now gives his name, Hamlet) – quite recently by the
feel of it, perhaps as one of old Hamlet's final heroic acts. It was
Fortinbras who made the challenge, so Hamlet's triumph in this
trial of strength was heroic, not aggressive. With his victory,
Hamlet has gained by bargain a proportion of Norway's land – he
would have forfeited the Danish equivalent had he lost. Young
Fortinbras, who has not succeeded his father (as in Denmark, the
crown has passed to the brother, not the son and namesake), is
raising a guerilla army ('landless resolutes', according to Horatio)
to win back the land by force. The result is, for Denmark,
'posthaste and rummage⁴ in the land': shipwrights working through
the night (and on Sundays), brass cannons being forged, weaponry
hastily purchased from abroad.⁵ The soldiers agree that the
apparition may be linked in some way to all this, and Horatio
makes a scholarly comparison with classical Rome:

---

4   Rummage, a word Shakespeare used nowhere else, specifically refers to the ordering of a
ship's cargo, and generalises Marcellus's reference a few lines earlier to shipwrights.

5   The atmosphere is not unlike the eve of Agincourt in *Henry V*, transposed to a northern
setting, with metaphysical fear filtered in. The ideal sound accompaniment in the theatre is
not ominous music, but distant hammering.

> A little ere the mightiest Julius fell,
> The graves stood tenantless, and the sheeted dead
> Did squeak and gibber in the Roman streets. . . [6]

Before we can hear whether the soldiers understand his learned allusion, the Ghost reappears, as unexpectedly as before. Why? If he is his own master, he perhaps regrets 'stalking away' – and he wants to make contact with the newcomer, whom he presumably knows well enough as a friend of his son's. Once again he seems painfully locked in silence, like someone in a dream trying to cry out for help. Horatio asks him a series of questions: What can he do? Is it something in the public interest? (After each demand he leaves half a line's pause for the Ghost to answer.) Or (desperate now) does the Ghost want to reach a hoard of stolen treasure he has buried somewhere ('For which they say you spirits oft walk in death')? In response to this insulting idea (Horatio's last touch of scepticism), the Ghost does not stalk away but at last 'makes to speak'; then, in a fine melodramatic flourish, the cock crows and he rushes away. In a moment Marcellus will say that he has

> . . . faded on the crowing of the cock

– substituting a poetic image for the prosaic reality of the exit, and so declaring the theatre's complicit terms – you must see one thing, wooden boards under an open sky or bars of lights, but agree to imagine something better. If the audience is persuaded to do this, they will be ready for the scene's narrative hook – the decision to go and see young Hamlet – and also its final appeasements: Horatio's lyrical description of the dawn

> But look, the morn, in russet mantle clad,
> Walks o'er the dew of yon high eastward hill

and Marcellus's belief (probably invented for the purpose) that ghosts cannot walk at the time of Christ's birth. Both speeches are rather 'out of character', as we would put it, but they satisfy an emotional need.

---

6   Or at least in the second Quarto he does. *Hamlet* was first played quite soon after *Julius Caesar,* and the new play carries a couple of plugs for the earlier production, most strikingly in the Play Scene when Polonius claims to have played Caesar himself – which he may well have done, with Hamlet in the 'brute part' of Brutus. By the time of the Folio, Horatio's speech is cut; perhaps *Julius Caesar* had been forgotten.

The play's ratchets have been engaged – mainly by a Ghost.[7] Who is he, and what are his terms? Many Elizabethans would have suspected that he was something diabolical: he must have aroused a voyeuristic enthusiasm, and perhaps for the first time in their theatre, awe as well.[8] We are not that far from them: we love ghosts in fiction and are frightened of them in life, and they are often associated with sudden wrongful death, though less commonly with the Elizabethan horror of spiritual unpreparedness. Few people dismiss them: though we no longer smear salt on children's lips in the church porch and bell, book and candle are a last resort, I know a 'wise woman' who is quite commonly called upon by Anglican churchmen to visit a troubled house.[9]

Still, we look back at Hamlet's Ghost through the dark glass of technology and relative scepticism. How spooky should he be? Many supernatural stories depend on their air of normality,[10] their very lack of atmosphere – even as we become more skilled at creating baroque special effects in our entertainment. On film, the choices are wide. The Ghost of the young Ingmar Bergman's father in *Fanny and Alexander* was wonderfully shocking, sitting in its cream suit at a table, looking sadly over its shoulder: of course such alarming naturalness was the product of the most careful composition and lighting. On the other hand, in his *Hamlet* film, Kozintsev (with the resounding bonus of Shostakovich on the soundtrack) created a massive black-armoured figure striding across the skyline, its cloak flying in the wind, its face encased in a dog-like visor which lifted tantalisingly at the final moment to reveal human eyes. Mixing blatancy with secrecy, the image combined childhood terror with spectacular lyricism.

---

7   The designer Edward Gordon Craig describes Shakespeare's ghosts as 'the centre of his vast dreams'.

8   He is certainly highly original compared to the burlesque Ghost described in the contemporary *A Warning for Fair Women*:

A filthy, whining ghost
Lapt in some foul sheet or a leather pilch
Comes screaming like a pig half-stickt
And cries out Vindicta!
Revenge, revenge!

9   And exorcism survives in the Catholic service of adult baptism.

10   I heard one of a monk sitting on a woman's bed, who, on dematerialising, left a warm imprint where he had been sitting.

In the theatre, however, ghosts, like kings, are created by the people around them, whose terror and respect do much of the work. When this is done really truthfully, children saturated with television will hold deathly still for a stage ghost arriving without music, light, or other manipulation – as he did at the Globe in 1601. Nevertheless, various embarrassments have led stage directors many ways round to work: Meyerhold planned to have the Ghost climb out of a trunk in glasses and galoshes, sneezing with the cold (mainly because the Soviet censors would never have accepted a serious ghost); quite often these days he is invisible; sometimes he is on tape; sometimes the whole opening scene of the play is cut and the Ghost internalised by Hamlet. Most of these are bold experiments in a difficult cause – but in fact an actor committed to being old Hamlet in every human detail is probably both what Shakespeare wanted and the most potent means of haunting a sophisticated audience.

Certain choices are in any case prescribed by the text: he must be in armour, and he is described later as having worn his vizor up so that his face was visible, having had a 'countenance more in sorrow than in anger', and having carried a truncheon. It is all rather irritating and literal, but there's no way round it. The director can help by clearing the ground rather than, as remarkably often happens, asking the Ghost to climb steep steps, be hoisted by unreliable stage machinery, or position himself on traps – all of which can bring a most unghostly anxiety into the eyes. A current fashion for moving the set around while the actor is speaking is particularly damaging to the Ghost.

Wonderfully written as it is,[11] this famous sequence rarely seems to work in the theatre – and not, I think, because of the difficulties of the Ghost: the tension so vivid on the page is much admired but rarely realised. It is hard to know why. The scene has

---

11   Shakespeare has given us a taste of his quality very early, in the exchange between two of the soldiers:

BARNARDO: Have you had quiet guard?
FRANCISCO: Not a mouse stirring.

This will be a story which, however ambitious, will refer back always to everyday experience: this homely detail is like seeing the story-teller's face, and shows us what kind of safe hands we are in. No other dramatist has written like that, certainly not then, or, with the same lack of strain, now. (It is a final reason that Marlowe, whose style is known, cannot have written the plays of Shakespeare.)

great presence – whereas *King Lear* and *Antony and Cleopatra* warm up gently with leisurely conversation prefacing the major entrances, *Hamlet*, like *The Tempest*, takes you straight into the heart. The energy and control of tempo – *staccato* to *legato* and back – the unobserved passage of time, the ambience of weather, high battlements, physical and some spiritual desolation, are handed to us on a plate. The set has to be reasonably open and lit brightly enough for seeing the actors but with enough chiaroscuro not to expose the practical details of the Ghost's arrangements – a simple enough challenge in these days of narrow-focused lamps. Is the problem that two of the witnesses, Marcellus and Barnardo, know what to expect? That would hardly make them less frightened. The political discussion that seems to lower the temperature in fact only moderates it, and a sense of fear can affect an actor's breath even when he is speaking deliberately. The Ghost is frightening, whether he is a driven human being or an indistinct shadow. But time and again the soldiers greet his appearance not 'Distill'd almost to jelly with the act of fear' but either as if he were ringing the doorbell at an inconvenient time, or with a phoney and therefore unsustainable horror. Sometimes the coldness of the night is there but not the mental alertness, or the worry but not the fear, or the terror but not the acute need for each other's company. There must, in the end, be some disheartening problem of belief: I don't know what it is, but it can't be final.

1.2. As the brazen light of the Danish court now flares, the audience, their eyes attuned to uncertainty and darkness, almost have to shade them: Hamlet, in describing himself as 'too much i' the sun', will speak right at the outset of his part for us as well as himself. The purpose of the dazzle is indeed to prevent the onlooker defining things too clearly, since there is much in the world of the new King Claudius that is best left indistinct; and his opening address

> Though yet of Hamlet our dear brother's death
> The memory be green . . .

softens all moral edges with a kind of good-humoured bleed. Claudius shows impressive political command and the taste for soothing antithesis that always gives a statesmanlike impression.[12] We learn from him what was left out by Horatio. The period of court mourning after King Hamlet's recent death has been cut short by the remarriage of his widow to his brother, the new King, who has accepted his double good fortune with due regard for the departed – but also with a sensible practicality likely to appeal to his listeners, who prefer life to death:

> . . . so far hath discretion fought with nature
> That we with wisest sorrow think on him
> Together with remembrance of ourselves.

The King's words are attractively ambiguous. Does the plural mean we the citizens, we the King, or we the royal couple? Somehow it is all one, all a great bonding, and there will be a big party tonight to consolidate the uncritical bonhomie. We don't know yet that the royal we stands for a singular personality so driven that regicide, fratricide and a sort of incest are turned to easy account. At present Claudius's confident urbanity pictures forth the court of a Sun King, relieved of the ascetic egotism of old Hamlet (a quality that the Ghost's speech will later reveal), secure in the new ruler's evident ability, excited by his Kennedy-like charisma and his apparent egalitarianism. Without effort, order and continuity have been restored: who knows, there may soon be a renaissance of the arts.

The business of the court this morning is threefold: the induction of the new regime, a report on foreign affairs (the Fortinbras business) and the granting or otherwise of individual petitions: an orderly progress from the general to the particular. Since it is unlikely to be new news to his hearers, the announcement of the Queen's remarriage is the kind of thinly-disguised message to the audience typical of Shakespeare.[13] Whom should we imagine Claudius addressing? Perhaps the unseen public, which to all

12   We should really call him the King – he is nowhere referred to in the play by his name, which he gets only from the stage direction at this entrance and the heading of his first speech. It is surely drawn from the Roman Emperor Claudius, who married incestuously and was the stepfather of Nero, to whom Hamlet compares himself later in the play.

13   It is reminiscent, for instance, of Henry IV's opening address on the state of the nation in *Henry IV Part 1*. In fact the speech of Henry (another usurper) is more skilfully done: its surging emotional rhythms summarise the past and renew a vow for the future (a pilgrimage to Jerusalem) in order to reassure the court: and when, thirty lines later, the play proper starts, we already know much about England's recent past and the nature of its ruler. In *Hamlet* the technique is cruder, the speaker is shiftier, and his language more equivocal.

intents means us in the theatre: the occasion has the air of a press conference, and implicates us as Hamlet is about to implicate us when he is alone – we are forced into a point of view by both men.

The King moves easily through the queasy justifications for his new regime, blending dynastic responsibility with an appeal to long-suppressed instincts for the good life; and he then proceeds to Fortinbras. Rather than confronting his activities directly, Claudius has hit upon the idea of appealing to his uncle, the 'impotent and bedrid' King of Norway (note the sexual self-confidence), to veto his nephew's plans, of which it seems he 'scarcely hears'. From this manoeuvre falls an implicit comparison between Claudius's style of government and his predecessor's. Old Hamlet's control of foreign affairs rested on feudal ceremonies, chivalrous but unstable, violent confrontations formalised by wagers. The new King goes round to work, with an Elizabethan diplomacy, always preferring to set friend against friend, avoiding showdown. Behind this dexterity a military toughness is reserved: Gertrude is 'the imperial jointress of this warlike state', Claudius himself has 'served against the French', and the King of Norway, whose physical weakness he despises, will in the event be anxious to oblige him promptly. For the present, policy comes first. Claudius's instinct is right; but the play will reveal that he is stronger on initial ideas than on following them through, and it may be that alcohol plays some part in this lack of finishing power. For the moment he is masterly, suggesting that he is just the man to drag Denmark kicking and screaming into the seventeenth century.

He moves on to the hearing of petitions. A surprising number of people want to leave this splendid new court. Laertes asks to go back to Paris, where he has an unexplained life. This may be discouraging for Claudius – his regime needs the support of a loyal coterie and Laertes is the son of Polonius, the Prime Minister; certainly anyone who leaves has to be vetted as a safe political export. But he can hardly be seen to refuse, and his consent is pleasantly given, with praise for the father, and a manly complicity with the son. The incident is there to contrast with what follows: Claudius's refusal to let Hamlet, the old King's son, go back to Wittenberg University.[14] This will be dressed up as an entreaty:

> we beseech you, bend you to remain

but understood as an order: Hamlet is far too charismatic a figure, his loss of succession (though legal – this is an elective monarchy) too inflammatory a rallying point, for Claudius to open the borders to him. As it turns out, Laertes is the one Claudius should have kept, and Hamlet dispatched.

The link between the brightly coloured court and the bleak monochromes of the battlements is this figure of young Hamlet, moving in half-shadow, but already silently magnetising our intuitive scruples about Claudius's regime. We sense something of what lies ahead of him, and already suspect that he will inhabit both outer and inner worlds. He may be literally in an 'inky cloak', a 'nighted colour', a 'customary suit of solemn black', or these may be all metaphors: his mind, though, is brilliant and fast.

Entering the play sidelong,[15] he operates with an alienating mixture of bitterness and courtesy. At the moment Claudius turns to him, only he and his mother the Queen, of the principal figures in the court, have not yet spoken. The meaning and effect of his evasive, enigmatic *double-entendres*:

> A little more than kin, and less than kind. . .
> Not so, my lord; I am too much i' the sun

have formed a rallying point for critics of the play. Harley Granville-Barker, for example, gets rather overexcited: 'King, Queen and Court, the whole gaudy gathering lashed alike by the bitter jest.'

14   The story here is quite difficult to follow, but it affects everything in the play. Hamlet has an 'intent In going back to school in Wittenberg' (school in the American sense of university). So has he been at Wittenberg, then returned to Elsinore on his father's death, been disappointed of the succession and disappointed by the marriage, and now wants to resume an academic life? If so, how has he had time to form the relationship with Ophelia which the play will see destroyed? And how does he not know that Horatio has arrived at the same time? Or, was he away in Wittenberg long ago (the Gravedigger much later drops a hint of Hamlet's being thirty years old), and now, having seen happier times in Denmark and weathered all the recent events, has the idea to sequester himself? It is more accessible theatrically to suggest that Hamlet has recently returned to find a court whose new style revolts him.

15   Lacking the automatic knowledge of Shakespeare's company in how to stage a Court Scene, we have to think about it. It is obviously clever to consider Hamlet's position very carefully, as elementary showmanship, albeit of a restrained kind. Should he be 'discovered'? Make a delayed entrance? Sidle on sideways or boldly down the middle? In all acting, getting on and getting started is the problem; the rest may even be easy. I went to see my friend Roger Rees play Hamlet for the RSC in 1984. The one thing I realised watching him was that a director should never ask a Hamlet to climb down a flight of stairs running off into the wings at ten feet or so above the ground and so steep he has to descend sideways. Anyway, there are many alternatives: the decision must create comfort for actor and audience.

Well, sort of. Claudius is quite sturdy, and whatever the heat of the reproach, Hamlet's mother is swiftly into the breach, her intelligent advice

let thine eye look like a friend on Denmark

only let down at the end by clumsy hurtfulness:

Thou knowest 'tis common; all that lives must die,
Passing through nature to eternity

This is cheap philosophy which provokes Hamlet into announcing his integrity and criticising her hypocrisy, as he sees it, in forgetting his father. He takes eleven lines over this, drawing a distinction between feeling and acting, and there is something in it more than natural: his words are at once true, self-righteous, and obsessive. Mother and son are obviously caught in a circle of wariness and correction, love leading always into rebuke: a voice from outside the familial neurosis is needed. So Claudius intervenes, and his stepfatherly handling of Hamlet is expert, tough but seemingly disinterested, the beastliness of urging him to forget his father softened by philosophical melody:

But you must know, your father lost a father;
That father lost, lost his. . .

The Prince's churlishness in appearing at a big public event so ostentatiously uncooperative justifies a degree of firmness:

But to persever
In obstinate condolement is a course
Of impious stubbornness; 'tis unmanly grief. . .

He makes his command to stay seem like a free invitation to live like a king, and doesn't fail to name Hamlet as successor to the throne. Exhausted by the effort, Claudius allows a hint of brutishness to show through:

No jocund health that Denmark drinks today
But the great cannon to the clouds shall tell
And the King's rouse the heavens shall bruit again
Respeaking earthly thunder

– the first intimation that his court might be oppressive company after a while.[16]

Hamlet is left alone – one of the theatre's great potencies. It is the first of four times, three of them after active, densely-populated scenes: the crowd disappears and this most human figure is small in a huge space. As he speaks, he refers not at all to the state of his country or his longing for Wittenberg, only to his feelings about his family, which he shares with a shocking candour new to the play. His pathological melancholy is created mainly by what he sees as his mother's wantonness and only a little by his new stepfather, who escapes with routine sideswipes: Claudius is a satyr next to Hyperion, as far from his brother as Hamlet is from Hercules. The speech is jarring, unstable, a chaos of feelings unresolved by language, studded with unpredictable imagery. Elegiac at first, nearly sentimental:

> How weary, stale, flat and unprofitable
> Seem to me all the uses of this world.
> Fie on't, ah fie. . .

it swings into the morbidly unforgiving:

> 'Tis an unweeded garden
> That grows to seed; things rank and gross in nature
> Possess it merely. That it should come to this!

Hamlet dwells on his mother's dependency on his father in terms both lyrical and lewd, the one confusing the other:

> Why, she would hang on him
> As if increase of appetite had grown
> By what it fed on

– linking classical myth with an image as touchingly humdrum as Francisco's 'not a mouse stirring':

16   The part played by drink in the play (concentrated in the character of the King) is interesting. The Elizabethan respect for the alcoholic capacity of the Scandinavians is reflected in the depiction of the court as one in which a

> . . . heavy-headed revel east and west
> Makes us traduced and taxed of other nations;
> They clepe us drunkards

– there was indeed a contemporary story of a Danish King who drank thirty-five healths in a day and was 'taken away at last in his chair'. Hamlet stands at a critical distance from all this, like one of the temperate Englishmen his audience might imagine themselves to be. In his bias he always aligns Claudius with the stereotype, gross and buffoonish, a dancer of the 'swaggering upspring'; but the fact is that Claudius is generally highly effective, highly professional, highly potent. Hamlet's scorn tells us as much about Hamlet as about his enemy.

A little month, or ere those shoes were old
With which she followed my poor father's body,
Like Niobe, all tears. . .

Having started with a glancing reference to 'self-slaughter', a subject to which he will return at greater length, he closes with sibilant sexual disgust:

O most wicked speed, to post
With such dexterity to incestuous sheets![17]

– in a way the very articulacy of his attack has re-engaged him with life.

The speech is designed to get Hamlet onto sympathetic terms with his audience,[18] but his unresolved sexuality, his moral fanaticism (in a Victorian-dress production he will look like something out of Ibsen), his sorrow, and his rhapsodically returning, returning to the 'little month' that separated the funeral from the remarriage, make for quite a brew. We are warily attracted to him, and his opening of the theatre's fourth wall confirms that he will be our guide through the play. In thirty-one lines we have moved further than in the previous hundred and twenty-eight.

The sequence that begins with this soliloquy and ends with Hamlet's decision to meet his father on the battlements is a graduation into the play's human tones. Invigorated by Horatio's arrival with Marcellus and Barnardo [19] – we have to ignore the odd fact

17   The interpretation of Claudius's marriage to Gertrude as incestuous is shared only by Hamlet and his father.

18   My own experience is that this soliloquy is the hardest of the four to play. There is another approach: although grief has sharpened Hamlet's sense of falsehood, in another way the shock has sent him to sleep – his torpor is disturbing to watch, and probably no figure of comparable importance makes such a demoralised entrance into a play. I was gratified in 1980 to get a letter from a psychiatrist who often dealt with excessive grieving in bereavement at the point that it approaches clinical depression, and who approved the symptoms he saw: the voice falling away, a tendency to hallucinate, overwhelming fatigue. I didn't know that at the time: though I did know that the Iroquois Indians believe that grief damages the sight, so that you cannot see clearly; the throat, so that you cannot speak; and even the ears, so that you cannot hear rightly.

19   Shakespeare is damnably vague about distinctions of rank, here as elsewhere: Marcellus and Barnardo are 'gentlemen' to Hamlet and Horatio, although Barnardo and Francisco are also regular soldiers on guard. Horatio is a loose cannon throughout the play, moving up and down the hierarchy. Our theatre is sensitive about these things, barking its shins repeatedly on Shakespeare's insouciance: we can live with his approximate geography and a cast list of Italian, Latin and English names, but we do want to know who is socially superior to whom.

that Horatio has been in the Court for two months, was at old Hamlet's funeral, but has not looked up his old friend – Hamlet modulates into a typical wit ('thrift, thrift, Horatio') and delicacy ('He was a man'). Both qualities are new sounds in the play, in steep contrast to Claudius's noise. He shows unfeigned courtesy:

> HAMLET: Horatio – or I do forget myself.
> HORATIO: The same, my lord, and your poor servant ever.
> HAMLET: Sir, my good friend; I'll change that name with you

and generosity:

> HAMLET: But what, in faith, make you from Wittenberg?
> HORATIO: A truant disposition, good my lord.
> HAMLET: I would not hear your enemy say so. . .
>   . . . I know you are no truant.

If our first encounter with him has been shocking, he certainly declares himself now in a graceful style unlike anyone else's. At the same time, there is a hint of emotional terrorism:

> HAMLET: But what is your affair in Elsinore?
>   We'll teach you to drink deep ere you depart.
> HORATIO: My lord, I came to see your father's funeral.
> HAMLET: I pray thee, do not mock me, fellow student;
>   I think it was to see my mother's wedding.

This is unsettling for Horatio, and a little unkind: how can he respond to a friend who provocatively jokes about his tragedy? His task was going to be hard, even starting on the right foot.

At first Horatio bides his time, parrying deferentially and waiting for an opening to break news so sensational that it could expose him to who knows what. The opportunity comes in the most unexpected way. With grievous simplicity, Hamlet suddenly seems to see his father in the room:

> My father – methinks I see my father.

It is in his mind's eye only, but it has an odd reality, is almost a statement of fact. Horatio is completely fooled:

> O, where, my Lord?

But he cannot quite bring himself to take up the cue, dropping instead into:

> I saw him once; he was a goodly King.

At the second shot Horatio does it:

HAMLET: He was a man; take him for all in all,
   I shall not look upon his like again.
HORATIO: My lord, I think I saw him yesternight.

The effect in the theatre is electric. Horatio suddenly finds an easy voice to replace Hamlet's arrested one, becoming lucid and energetic:

Season your admiration for a while
With an attent ear, till I may deliver
Upon the witness of these gentlemen
This marvel to you.

Up until this point, Hamlet has shuttled between sincerity and mockery; now his irony is stripped from him, and he investigates in *staccato*, inquisitorial rhythms, at first sceptically:

HAMLET: Arm'd, say you?
HORATIO: Arm'd, my lord.
HAMLET: From top to toe?
HORATIO: My lord, from head to foot.
HAMLET: Then saw you not his face?
HORATIO: O yes, my lord, he wore his beaver up. . .

but then he is forced by the human details – the pale, sorrowful face, the familiar colour of the beard – to believe. His sudden decision to keep watch on the battlements is like a breaking dam, and out of him pours a longing to speak to his father again, just as he earlier almost willed him into the room with his longing to see him:

If it assume my noble father's person,
I'll speak to it, though hell itself should gape
And bid me hold my peace.

He begs them, at some length, to remain secret both now and after the event – 'I will requite your loves' – because he surely has some instinct for the significance of what lies ahead: and the practical detail of the rendezvous is as exciting as his passionate eagerness:

Upon the platform, 'twixt eleven and twelve,
I'll visit you.

For the second time in the scene he is left alone with us. Whereas in the longer soliloquy we depended on Hamlet for emotional information to fill out our picture, we are now, having seen the Ghost, a small step ahead of him, and his apprehension, his amazement and sheer excitement bind him to us. The short closing speech is a caution to the actor: however contemporary his style, he now has to leave us with a sense of classicism, almost of archaism. For all its immediacy this is an ancient play, and the highly-trained sceptic at its centre is eager to believe in a portentous ghost:

> My father's spirit in arms! All is not well!
> I doubt some foul play; would the night were come!
> Till then, sit still, my soul. . .

Shakespeare has introduced Hamlet in three keys, and the modulations between uncomfortable formality, the opening of his emotional blisters and then a form of sociability shouldn't be rushed. He has turned from a hero of whom nothing much can be expected into a man of apprehensive purpose. Soon his life will be properly hobbled, by his father's message from beyond the grave, so this new energy is really taking him towards his doom: his imprisonment in the court by Claudius will turn out to have been his last moment of freedom.

1.3. The battlements were monochromatic, disorientating, without perspective or limit of distance: the court thoroughly peopled, affirmative, claustrophobic. The play's third scene moves into the natural colours of a home. The time is a few minutes later, and Laertes is preparing to leave indefinitely for France – in fact is 'stay'd for'. Shakespeare signals the change by counterpointing sharply the final line of the dying scene and the first words of the next, expecting them to be spoken as tight on each other as possible – an acoustic prototype of the cinema's jump-cut, and the best way, in fact, anyone has thought of to change a scene in a play:

> HAMLET: Till then, sit still, my soul; foul deeds will rise,
>   Though all the earth o'erwhelm them, to men's eyes.
> LAERTES: My necessaries are embark'd; farewell.

The metrical value of these three lines is the same – ten regular syllables; but the words enforce a subtle change of tempo, from Hamlet's *andante* to the sharper drum of Laertes.[20] Implicitly contrasting

---

20   The Elizabethan actor would have had to make these contrasts physically and vocally; for better or worse, we have costume and setting. That being the case, there is, for the modern designer, some danger of vagueness here. In fact he will probably be working on

himself with Hamlet – energetic practicality against boding sensibility – Laertes now curves steeply into instructing his sister on the
delicacies of her intimate life. Perhaps he assumes a masculine right
to march in on her world; perhaps he approaches with hesitancy
and care. The hesitancy, if it is there, doesn't last long – what he
has to say:

> For Hamlet, and the trifling of his favour
> Think it a fashion and a toy in blood;
> A violet in the youth of primy nature,
> Forward, not permanent, sweet, not lasting. . .

is soon anxiously repetitive. He paints an unexpected picture of
Hamlet as a lover of women, and perhaps a fickle and exploitative
one – this won't have crossed our minds. Laertes's and, shortly, his
father's suspicion is partly a distrust of sexuality (Laertes sounds
quite middle-aged expressing it) and partly a practical acknowledgment of the constraints on a royal:

> He may not, as unvalu'd persons do,
> Carve for himself, for on his choice depends
> The safety and the health of this whole state

– and either way the vulnerable Ophelia must not

> lose your heart, or your chaste treasure open
> To his unmaster'd importunity.

We never find out whether these suspicions are justified or not –
whatever the relationship between Hamlet and Ophelia, it soon
becomes contorted by circumstance, and at this stage it seems to
be a matter of some limp versifying from him (he is a philosopher
and satirist, but even Ophelia never describes him as a poet) and
quite a delicate reciprocation by her. But here is Laertes breathing
moral heli-fire. Later in the scene Polonius will echo him:

> These blazes, daughter,
> Giving more light than heat, extinct in both.
> You must not take for fire . . .

---

an abstract structure, establishing a new location more by light, by fast-moving furniture and
by colour in the clothes than by laborious scene-changes covered by expedient music. But
the change must be precise: the location is not some wilderness in the palace, but the
domestic hearth of Polonius, Laertes and Ophelia. If the production can afford the luxury of
second costumes for the men (Polonius and Laertes have had time to change and it is
Ophelia's first scene) a new palate can be established – ordinary browns, unassuming greys
and blacks, perhaps, to undercut the primary tones of the court.

Like his son, Polonius is convinced that Hamlet will use his position for all manner of *droit de seigneur:* his attentions are

> springes to catch woodcocks.

From the grating repetition it is clear that son and father are cut in the same cloth: Establishment men, who (knowing Establishment habits) distrust the heir to the throne and assume that he is more likely to 'wreck' a commoner than marry her. What the Elsinore residents think of Hamlet is emerging: there is little sympathy for his bereavement (was his father unpopular?), he is perhaps not well-known, having been away, he has in dress and manner publicly reproached the King and Queen: he is conspicuously not falling into the new order of things. Laertes and Polonius are implacable: perhaps they sense in Hamlet the anarchy that will destroy their family.

They may also, in their excessive protection of Ophelia, be rationalising a malodorous sexual possessiveness of their own. Their instinctive choice of words is characteristic of men who fear for the virginity of the single woman in their lives. The slimy imagery of Laertes's

> Perhaps he loves you now;
> And now no soil nor cautel doth besmirch
> The virtue of his will

is quickly rationalised into the political vocabulary you might expect of Polonius's son:

> . . . you must fear,
> His greatness weighed, his will is not his own. . . .
> . . . . for on his choice depends
> The safety and the health of this whole state[21]

– but he is unable to keep this up for long, and is soon back in Tennessee Williams territory:

---

21 It is hard to see why she would not be an eligible choice, unless Hamlet is expected to make a dynastic marriage to a foreigner (Fortinbras's sister?). Polonius makes the same assumption:

> Lord Hamlet is a prince out of thy star;
> This must not be.

On the other hand Gertrude, who should know but is perhaps sentimental, in the end

> hop'd thou shoulds't have been my Hamlet's wife.

Then weigh what loss your honour may sustain
If with too credent ear you list his songs,
Or lose your heart, or your chaste treasure open
To his unmaster'd importunity. . . .
The canker galls the infants of the spring
Too oft before their buttons be disclos'd.

Ophelia's reactions to her brother's lecture are witty and restrained, those of an underrated woman who keeps her counsel – unlike Laertes, who a few moments later, lectured in turn by his father, says nothing at all.

Polonius seems shocked that Laertes hasn't already left:

Yet here, Laertes? Aboard, aboard, for shame!

(wasn't he planning to say goodbye?) and he now holds everyone up, instructing the instructor:

And these few precepts in thy memory
Look thou character.

His famous homily sums up the ambiguity in his character, about which it is almost the first evidence. From one point of view the advice is humanistic and wise, so far as it goes: generations of schoolchildren have been made to memorise its edifying clauses. On the other hand, it is strategic and opportunistic. Accept new friends only after extensive screening:

Do not dull thy palm with entertainment
Of each new-hatch'd, unfledg'd comrade

– but once accepted ('their adoption tried'), *possess* them:

Grapple them to thy soul with hoops of steel.

Sit tactically on the fence in an argument:

Take each man's censure, but reserve thy judgment.

Control your budget:

Neither a borrower nor a lender be. . .

Don't communicate unnecessarily:

. . . Give thy thoughts no tongue

Even the famous last sentiment – 'To thine own self be true' – is simultaneously wise and amoral. Laertes departs non-committally (in fact he will not see his father again), reasserting himself by reminding his sister to

> . . . remember well
> What I have said to you.

This betrays their confidence to their father, who leaps on the cue:

> What is't, Ophelia, he hath said to you?

Poor Ophelia. Overbearing, sanctimonious and savage by turns, Polonius now denounces Hamlet and prohibits her contact with him.

Evidently, some bleak interpretative choices are arising: this happy family may or may not be what it seems. The first two scenes of the play are carried more or less by narrative, and the character decisions within them are provisional, even reversible: but a firm choice about Polonius's world is needed for this scene to be playable at all, and it will form a junction from which much flows. What Polonius is reveals much about Claudius's court and affects the balance of sympathies between Hamlet and himself – and therefore the quality of the play's comedy;[22] and his nature as a father deeply affects Ophelia's decline into madness as well as the character of his son's rebellion. It is possible of course to take a genial view. You could argue that the play is deeply concerned with the collapse of families, and that, although incomplete, Polonius's is harmonious enough to contrast with the fracture in Hamlet's and the unreality of Claudius and Gertrude's: a generous broadening of the play's base. From this angle, there is a reassuringly functional air here, and common keynotes: harmless advice all round, everything practical, mundane, recognisable. But these familiarities are actions that a man might play. Undoubtedly, love is interwoven with constriction and male overheatedness: there is a singular lack of a second parent, as often in Shakespeare, and if ever a family was in need of female mediation it is Polonius's.[23] They would

22   Tony Church, who played Polonius at Stratford for Peter Hall in 1964 and again for John Barton in 1980, represented the typical polarities in the part in his two performances – the first as a machiavellian public man, authoritarian with his family but beneath it sexually prurient; and, in the second, a capable professional and a loving father.

23 A man whose family life, as we might call it, was marked by the loss of a child and the discomforts of a loveless marriage, Shakespeare made pointed choices in his plays. Sometimes, where tragedy requires three players, the families are complete units (the

definitely benefit, all of them, from the practical spunk of Emilia or an older Lady Percy, or the maternal appeasements of the Countess in *All's Well That Ends Well*, whose advice to her own son:

> Love all, trust a few,
> Do wrong to none. Be able for thine enemy
> Rather in power than use, and keep thy friend
> Under thy own life's key

compares rather favourably to Polonius's.

The scene closes with Laertes well established as a counterpoint to Hamlet. He is now taken out of the action, returning much later to catalyse it; there has been just enough of him in the opening for us to understand his extremities later. Shakespeare has also added another piece to the mosaic of Hamlet: we know him now for a wit, angry, sensitive, afflicted, and an ambiguous lover.

The action moves on with another jump-cut:

> POLONIUS: I would not in plain terms from this time forth
>   Have you so slander any moment's leisure
>   As to give words or talk to the lord Hamlet.
>   Look to't, I charge you; come your ways.
> OPHELIA: I shall obey, my lord.
> HAMLET: The air bites shrewdly; it is very cold.

1.4. /1.5. After Polonius, the writing becomes so simple and spare that, sitting in the theatre, you feel the barometer drop:

> HORATIO: It is a nipping and an eager air.
> HAMLET: What hour now?
> HORATIO: I think it lacks of twelve.
> MARCELLUS: No, it is struck.

This is the way men are in the open air, when cold clamps the tongue, their terse small talk covering deep anxiety. The even balance of the opening is broken by a sharper shared line, then the third voice breaks in: it is rhythmically perfect. Horatio gives himself away:

Capulets in *Romeo and Juliet*, the King, Margaret and Prince Henry in *Henry VI*); sometimes they are poignantly childless, like Antigonus and Paulina in *The Winter's Tale*; sometimes they are lopsided, as in *Coriolanus*, where the absence of a father is highly significant to Coriolanus's obsessive relationship with his mother and hers with him. Here, as with Gloucester's and Lear's in *Lear*, Duncan's in *Macbeth* and the King's in *Henry IV*, there is no mother: and soon enough, a male-propelled crisis.

> Indeed? I heard it not. Then it draws near the season
> Wherein the spirit held his wont to walk.

In the earlier scene he was the one who called a spade a spade, and the Ghost a 'thing': now he states what everybody knows already, and his calm is unconvincing – and can he really not have heard the midnight bell?

Once again, there are three of them waiting, a mysteriously better number than either two or four,[24] Barnardo having been, surely for that reason only, dropped. Claudius's 'ordnances shot off', a brazen din of trumpet, cannon and kettledrum, makes them jump out of their skins; and again this creates a diversion on the battlements, stinging Hamlet into a critique of the court's alcoholism. In fact what they are hearing is the King keeping his promise to celebrate Hamlet's 'decision' to stay in Elsinore (even though Hamlet is not in the castle). It is difficult to pick up the connection in the playing, as Polonius's business has intervened, and certainly Hamlet makes no acknowledgment of the gesture, correctly reading that this is a party that would have taken place anyway. The acerbity of

> Thrift, thrift, Horatio; the funeral baked meats
> Did coldly furnish forth the marriage tables

is repeated:

> . . . though I am native here,
> And to the manner born, it is a custom
> More honour'd in the breach than the observance

– by which Hamlet implies that Claudius is continuing the traditions of the old King: a small miscalculation of Shakespeare's, who surely didn't intend him to be critical of his father's drinking habits as well as Claudius's.[25]

Continuing, Hamlet tries to provoke Horatio to see things as they really are and become a candid friend: his tone of voice, as it will always be, is undeceived and uncomforting, inclined to round his thoughts into aphorism. Again, it is quite difficult for Horatio –

---

24 The magic number for trilogies, trinities and jokes.
25 The passage is cut for the Folio; by that time King James had come to the throne with a Danish Queen, and stories of her brother King Christian IV's great drinking bouts, accompanied by salvoes of cannon-fire, were no longer à la mode.

here is the Prince satirising the royal household to him, a commoner. We can also see that there is something puritanical and
dog-in-the-manger about Hamlet. Does it matter that Claudius
parties (particularly in Hamlet's honour) if he runs the country
well? He is at this point only a disliked stepfather, not a murderer.
Hamlet's view of the world is the radical conservative's, with a
strong streak of moral absolutism. A young man at odds with a
corrupt establishment, he doesn't want to make a new world, only
restore an old one; disappointed by the society of sexually aggressive men and opportunistic women, he is a chronic nostalgic, and
he hardly ever speaks of the future. Moving on to a discursion
about 'the vicious mole of nature', the blemish in men's characters
that destroys them either 'in their birth' or 'by the o'ergrowth of
some complexion', he intriguingly brings us into his confidence – is
he talking about Claudius, or, in some way, himself? – and the
concentration he provokes means that, once again, we are looking
the other way when the Ghost arrives.

The shock of it lays Hamlet bare, stripping him of smartness:

> King, father, royal dane, O answer me!
> Let me not burst in ignorance, but tell
> Why thy canonis'd bones, hearsed in death,
> Have burst their cerements, why the sepulchre
> Wherein we saw thee quietly interred
> Hath oped his ponderous and marble jaws
> To cast thee up again. What may this mean. . . .
> Say, why is this? Wherefore? What should we do?

The Ghost only beckons. Tantalised, Hamlet decides on the
reckless action that has been gathering in him – he does not set his
life 'at a pin's fee', and he will follow. His friends are horrified, and
he makes a characteristic joke:

> . . . I'll make a ghost of him that lets me.

From the thick of the orchestra, Hamlet continues to emerge as the
soloist, not least because of his heroic sense of humour: confronted
by the inexplicable, his friends sink back into dutiful stereotype,
but he gains greatly in personality. Horatio, once an intelligent
sceptic, has become a superstitious child:

> What if it tempt you toward the flood, my lord,
> Or to the dreadful summit of the cliff
> That beetles o'er his base into the sea,
> And there assume some other horrible form

Which might deprive your sovereignty of reason,
And draw you into madness? Think of it. . .

– but Hamlet has not a trace of this cowardice:

Be thou a spirit of health or goblin damn'd
Bring with thee airs from heaven or blasts from hell,
Be thy intents wicked or charitable,
Thou com'st in such a questionable shape
That I will speak to thee

– and his abandon is splendid:

for my soul, what can it do to that,
Being a thing immortal as itself?
It waves me forth again. I'll follow it.

Hamlet is our man. As the Ghost waves him to 'a more removed place' on the battlements (their private scene will be a direct continuation), he is calling him into the unknown: quickened alike, we are being beckoned into the play itself.[26]

The Ghost made to speak as the cock crew, and answered Hamlet's cries with a gesture. He is on the brink of speech. How will he sound?

Marvellously simple. The opening line is like a quiet bell – 'Mark me'. As he prepares his astonishing story, he combines imaginative terror:

My hour is almost come
When I to sulphurous and tormenting flames
Must render up myself

with paternal correctiveness:

Pity me not, but lend thy serious hearing
To what I shall unfold

– coming to the point with a half line that has all the weight of a full one:

I am thy father's spirit. . .

---

26 Obviously, Shakespeare is good at everything that surrounds the supernatural: the nervous waiting, the midnight lull, the shock of the apparition. This Ghost is his third, if you count the chorus of victims that visit Richard III as a single episode, and Julius Caesar as the second; and it is by far the most ambitious. After this (apart from the masque-like apparitions of Posthumus's dream in *Cymbeline*), there is only a mute Ghost: Banquo at Macbeth's table. Richard III's visitants introduce themselves and briefly urge him to despair: the ghost of Caesar has three plangent lines. But old Hamlet's Ghost is another, voluble matter.

His account of his death exploits elements of Catholic purgatory, Protestant hell, the mythical river of forgetfulness and nursery horrors in a theatrical improvisation. It is full of opposites. He is not particularly old himself, but his provenance is the ancient sagas, his vocabulary as epic as his deeds. He has the traditional ruler's identification with his country's interests (and an apt choice of metaphor to express it):

> So the whole ear of Denmark
> Is by a forged process of my death
> Rankly abus'd

– but he also stands humiliated before his son as a human father who could not keep the love of his wife. He could tell a tale

> whose lightest word
> Would harrow up thy soul, freeze thy young blood,
> Make thy two eyes like stars start from their spheres

– but he resolves the threat into an everyday image like Francisco's mouse or Gertrude's worn-out shoes: the harmless hedgehog whose quills stand fretfully upright. Blessed with the overview of the dead, he has photographic knowledge of all the events leading up to his murder; but he has little understanding of the present, assuming that Gertrude is troubled by her conscience and that the state may collapse. His siesta under a fruit tree, ear exposed to the poisoner, sounds quaintly medieval (and somewhat at odds with the climate), but the description of his symptoms:

> And with a sudden vigour it doth posset
> And curd, like eager droppings into milk,
> The thin and wholesome blood. So did it mine,
> And a most instant tetter bark'd about,
> Most lazar-like, with vile and loathsome crust,
> All my smooth body

has a livid accuracy. Realistically, of course, all this begs several questions (was this the easiest way for Claudius to dispose of him?); but the picture is consistent with the parallel play that Hamlet will later show the King, all homily and sententious archaism. Hamlet's Mousetrap will use the fictional past to provoke a disclosure: this mysterious figure of the night, set against reality, opens a credibility gap it will take the rest of the play to narrow. We are certainly inclined to believe him, but he does not fully discharge the burden of proof, either for us or for Hamlet.

The relationship between young and old Hamlet is one of the most deeply frightening ones in Shakespeare.[27] Imagine a father returning but refusing love and relief, dispensing only pain. The Ghost harrows Hamlet with sorrow and bludgeons him to the ground with orders: authoritarian, sorrowful, passionate but severe, he will not be pitied, though he pities himself, and he catches Hamlet, as fathers will their sons, in an armlock of tenderness and violence. The pity of it is that he may not have been at all like this in life ('so excellent a king. . . so loving to my mother'), though perhaps he could hardly be otherwise now. Condemned to a circle of love, emulation, fear and love, Hamlet mimics his manner, trying to match and impress him:

> Haste me to know it, that I with wings as swift
> As meditation or the thoughts of love
> May sweep to my revenge.

The father's intimacy towards his son is limited to calling him 'thou noble youth' and, unrealistically, urging him

> Taint not thy mind

– he demands revenge but stops short of demanding blood, leaving Hamlet with an implication for which he must take responsibility. Hamlet, driven mad by a Ghost horribly unlike the father he remembers, helplessly blesses him as a 'poor ghost'. His life will no longer be his own.[28]

---

27   The sequence can be shattering for Hamlet to play, and indeed has been the occasion, direct and indirect, of some early departures from the part by otherwise sturdy performers. On the other hand, the writing falls so closely in with life, and is so harassing, that it can positively claim the actor, who may on some inevitable occasions have started the evening tired, unwilling, out of touch; paradoxically, this scene may turn his motor over, creating energy from nothing.

28   How should the scene be staged? The traditional image – Hamlet reaching impossibly to touch his father – has not come about by chance. It is wonderfully expressed in William Telbin's design for Charles Fechter's Lyceum *Hamlet* of 1864: terrific horizontal energy between the two figures, a single tree, twin ship-masts and a huge night sky full of stars. Any design needs to allow for the horizontal: we must see them both, unlike in the earlier Ghost scene, which can probably work up- and down-stage as interplay is not so important. Going on the principle of haunting reality, Raymond Westwell in 1980 sat on a bench to talk to me and I was at his feet: it took 100-odd performances (for me at least) to go off the idea – intimacy gained at the expense of tension; and it raised the question that if the Ghost can sit and talk, why can't he be touched and embraced by Hamlet – which we tried and abandoned for the same reason. In 1965, on the other hand, David Warner was physically enveloped in the embrace of the monstrous zimmer.

The Ghost fades into the morning light. Unable to find a response that is 'apt', Hamlet casts wildly around for an echo from somewhere:

O all you host of heaven! O earth! What else?
And shall I couple hell?

He offers himself extravagantly to his father's cause, rages at Claudius and Gertrude, alarmingly writes notes in his 'tables', and utters a falconer's cry when called by his friends. Hearing Horatio's prayer for the safety of his body, he answers with his own for his soul:

HORATIO: Heaven secure him.
HAMLET: So be it.

When his friends arrive, a strain of mad comedy enters him , and the rhythms are oddly like music-hall patter:

HORATIO: What news, my lord?
HAMLET: O, wonderful!
HORATIO:Good my lord, tell it.
HAMLET: No, you will reveal it. . . . .
   There's ne'er a villain dwelling in all Denmark
   But he's an arrant knave.
HORATIO: There needs no ghost, my lord, come from the grave,
   To tell us this.

When Hamlet at last overtrumps his well-meaning friend:

HORATIO: There's no offence, my lord.
HAMLET: Yes, by Saint Patrick, but there is, Horatio,
   And much offence too [29]

the rhythms settle, and some explanation seems to be on its way: but, through a mixture of shame and instinctive strategy, he finally decides to tell only that this was 'an honest ghost'. As he brings himself almost under control, demanding that his friends keep their counsel, his tempo accelerates again until his father suddenly calls from under the stage. Moving about like an 'old mole', a 'true-penny', a 'fellow in the cellarage' , the Ghost suggests powerfully to an Elizabethan audience that he is something unholy, not 'honest' at all: and to us, baffled by the splendour of his last words:

Adieu. Adieu. Remember me

29   Saint Patrick was thought of as the keeper of purgatory, having found the entrance to it in County Donegal.

that he was really some kind of undignified trick.[30] Whatever he was, he clearly believes in an oath devoutly taken, and wants his secrets kept.

His timing in calling out at each moment that the men's hands are on the sword, ready to swear, is comic, but there is space too for the steady beat of Hamlet's characteristic wisdom:

> There are more things in heaven and earth, Horatio,
> Than are dreamed of in your philosophy.

The sequence amplifies his range, and tips the play into a wild and sinister comedy that is quite modern. It is difficult to know whether the Ghost is leading the three men a macabre dance, eluding them as they are about to swear over him, or whether his sudden presence beneath them obliges them to escape from him: in other words, whether they want to be where he is, so that the oath is confirmed, or where he is not, so that he cannot compromise it. In fact, it is not even clear whether Horatio and Marcellus hear the Ghost's words at all, and that affects how mad they think Hamlet has become.[31] Some decisions in the theatre will always be arbitrary.

It all has the oddest mixture of awe and playfulness: and the strain of it – disturbance, recovery, deeper destabilising – leads Hamlet to an eccentric decision, typically based on self-observation, to take on an 'antic disposition'. It is not clear how this will help him, beyond shutting the world out. He imagines the many ways his friends might betray his confidence:

> With arms encumber'd thus, or this head-shake,
> Or by pronouncing of some doubtful phrase,
> As 'Well, we know', or 'We could, an if we would'. . .

– then, mastering at last his remorseless father below, the best of him, lucid, philosophic and tender, takes the place of the clown:

---

30   The 'cellarage' beneath the stage had been thought of as Hell since the Morality Plays: the Devil was often thought of as a miner. In 'Of Ghosts and Spirits Walking By Night' (1572) Ludwig Lavater describes how metal-miners sometimes meet ghosts dressed like other 'pioneers' who 'seem to bestir themselves in all kinds of labour', though 'they very seldom hurt the labourers. . . except they provoke them by laughing and railing at them'.

31   Whether he is referring to the extraordinary sound of the Ghost or his friend's erratic behaviour, Horatio may get a sympathetic laugh, speaking for us:

> O day and night, but this is wondrous strange.

Rest, rest, perturbed spirit. So, gentlemen,
With all my love I do commend me to you. . .

The matin the Ghost sensed has arrived. Hamlet ends utterly sane, linking his own destiny to the public interest:

The time is out of joint; O cursed spite,
That ever I was born to set it right.

Cheerless mist overtakes darkness, dawn's mantle bringing no comfort this time to Hamlet, the soldiers, or to Denmark.

At this momentary point of rest, the audience has seen, among other things, the new King and the old King in action. The Ghost is vain, immodest and wronged. Claudius is attractive, efficient and apparently a murderer: also, probably, better for Denmark. A mousetrap has been set for him, for Hamlet, and for the state as well, since Hamlet will destabilise his country far more thoroughly in his mission than Claudius did by his murder. We have seen in Hamlet a man fascinatingly put together – and then, at the point of crystallising, blown apart: we wait to see how he will reassemble himself. Everything up to now has been 'a prologue to his brain'; from here on there will be successive shock and repercussion, one man's creative will against the tide of events. For the moment, we can rest from him, and his actor, briefly, can do the same; but the action must keep going, and so the scene ends not with summary, but with the most practical cue:

HAMLET: Nay, come, let's go together.
POLONIUS: Give him this money, and these notes, Reynaldo.

THE ACTION: DAY TWO

Act 2 Scene 1–Act 2 Scene 2

2.1. It's hard to believe it is the same stage.

Once again, Polonius arrives to break the suspense of the supernatural, asserting fussy reality as he instructs his servant Reynaldo, with a mixture of garrulousness, prurience and absent-mindedness, on a routine surveillance of Laertes in Paris. The apparent normality of this signals Polonius's dual role in the play – at once good companion and compulsive intriguer. To watch him digressing, fussing and forgetting what he was going to say in front of his patient servant is entertaining; on the other hand, he seems quite at ease sending a private detective to track his son's sex life, his friendships and his daily habits.

The tactic Polonius recommends is extremely circuitous. Reynaldo is to visit Laertes and give him 'this money and these notes' (what can the notes be? More fatherly advice? His messages?): but to spend a good deal of time first tracing other Danes in Paris to get their opinion of Laertes's behaviour. This is to be done provocatively: Reynaldo will 'put on him What forgeries you please' – exaggerating his peccadilloes but stopping short of 'dishonouring' him. Reynaldo doesn't see how he can do one without the other, and nor do we. But Polonius hopes that attributing 'slight sullies' will provoke 'him you would sound' to confirm that Laertes has indeed been seen gaming, quarrelling on the tennis court, or entering a brothel. He certainly assumes that Laertes will be behaving quite contrary to his painstaking advice – so he perhaps has a low opinion of his son or, less probably, of himself.

At one point, tied in his own knots, he grinds to a halt:

And then, sir, does he this – he does – what was I about to say? By the mass, I was about to say something. Where did I leave?[1]

– or seems to. Perhaps he is testing that Reynaldo is listening. Polonius concludes by philosophically praising his own unsubtle strategy:

> Thus do we, of wisdom and of reach,
> With windlasses and with essays of bias,
> By indirections find directions out

– while we see in our mind's eye the long-suffering servant trudging round Paris on an impossible mission.

Reynaldo understands everything that Polonius tells him, and at one point even ventures a criticism. He sounds well-equipped for his wily mission: his name has a ring of the foxy Reynard, and he can draw some comedy out of his stoicism in taking in all the details. He is, like Francisco in the opening scene, a bystander who gives us brief but important information about the world in which the principals move. We pick up from his manner the smell of the Prime Minister's household, and, distantly, that of Claudius's court.

---

1   To this Reynaldo answers simply in the Folio:

At closes in the consequence.

However, in the earlier Second Quarto he continues

. . . at 'friend, or so' , at 'gentleman'

Editors sometimes describe the Quarto version as 'an actor's elaboration'. It has also crossed many minds that the actor of Reynaldo is improvising because his colleague has forgotten his lines, and, since pure accident often produces good things in the theatre, the effect was kept in for the Quarto. The idea is fanciful and attractive. Reynaldo is prompting Polonius with what he has just said, rather than giving him a clue to the next line: on the other hand, that's what Polonius in his panic has asked him to do, and what he says is exactly accurate to the text, whereas very often in Shakespeare when speech that we have already heard is reported, it is noticeably paraphrased. There is a more convincing example of this sort of thing in *Richard II*, when the Duke of York learns of his sister's death and immediately afterwards addresses the Queen:

Come, sister – cousin, I would say – pray, pardon me.

The line (like every other line in that play) is in metre and therefore seems consciously written; but it is quite easy to improvise in blank verse if you are used to it – it closely resembles normal speech – and these things do happen. Either way, York's mistake produces a wonderful frisson of emotional transference, true both to Shakespeare's gifts and to theatrical accident – misnaming another character on the stage is, for some reason, one of the most common mistakes actors make. Amen. Some things are entertaining, and don't have to be proved.

Meanwhile, the ambiguities of the family persist. Polonius's taking of a sledgehammer to crack a nut might suggest the charming curiosity of an indulgent father, unable to leave well alone and feeling that in return for subsidy he should have a little control over his son. But equally it is devious and voyeuristic, the reflex of a politician haunted by the fear of not knowing everything. This neurotic compulsion will soon lead him to spy on his daughter's interview with Hamlet, with disastrous consequences for her, and then take him to the Queen's bedroom, where he will meet his death, rocketing his children into madness and violence. However, at least this is a moment of more or less ordinary life – when, immediately on Reynaldo's exit, Ophelia arrives seriously 'affrighted' by an extraordinary encounter with Hamlet, the loose tempos are abandoned for the play's dark headlong rhythm, and Hamlet's shadow falls dramatically across the stage.

Ophelia reports that Hamlet has broken in on her as she was minding her own business in her bedroom.[2] The meaning of his appearance is difficult for us to gauge, as we don't understand the clothes – he sounds like a deranged portrait by Nicholas Hilliard, the lyrical Elizabethan miniaturist:[3]

Lord Hamlet, with his doublet all unbrac'd,
No hat upon his head, his stockings foul'd,
Ungarter'd and down-gyved to his ankle,
Pale as his shirt, his knees knocking each other. . .

It is difficult to know what is grotesquely comic and what seriously unsettling in such a picture. It must carry some sexual weight: the encounter is in her closet, and though we may be surprised that she minds that he has no hat on, we can understand the other elements of nakedness – his jacket is open (no shirt?), he has stockings stained with garbage, and they are down, revealing his bare legs.[4]

---

2 Apart from this 'sewing in my closet' and the lute, to which she will turn in her madness, we are given nothing else on how Ophelia spends her time – intense imagination at work in a framework of boredom may be part of her misfortunes. Like so many girls in classic literature, she is waiting for something to happen, and Hamlet is what happens to her.

3 Hilliard's treatise 'The Art of Lymning', the first English text-book on painting, was published at just about the same time as *Hamlet*.

4 Malvolio's appearance in *Twelfth Night*, cross-gartered in yellow stockings, combines comedy and dangerous impropriety in the same way: removed again from the dress convention, we tend to get the fun of it only. Visual paraphrase has become almost automatic with audiences in Shakespeare. A stubbornly Elizabethan production can be

Despite the difficulties of his dress, what Hamlet has actually done is vivid:

> He took me by the wrist and held me hard.
> Then goes he to the length of all his arm,
> And with his other hand thus o'er his brow
> He falls to such perusal of my face
> As he would draw it. . .

He is back in the play after only a few minutes, in full antic bloom. We wonder what to feel about this. It is not Ophelia we would expect Hamlet to turn his first attentions to, and although his madness was to be assumed, the performance he has given is arrestingly sincere: he has scrutinised her, nodded three times as if it has confirmed something for him, sighed profoundly and left the room, never taking his eyes off her. The encounter has a complicated effect on Ophelia's sensibility: mixing reproach, sexuality and eccentricity, Hamlet has tempted her towards the super-sane world of the mad.

Eager for cheap drama, Polonius misinterprets all this: he has the professional politician's stupidity about human behaviour. Having heard of Hamlet's appearance only, he declares that he is 'mad for thy love' – the reaction is so trigger-happy that it often provokes a laugh in performance. Although he has ordered his daughter not to have

> words or talk with the lord Hamlet

he now asks whether she has given him 'hard words' and admits what he mistakes for his mistake:

> I am sorry that with better heed and judgement
> I had not quoted him. . . .
> By heaven, it is as proper to our age
> To cast beyond ourselves in our opinions
> As it is common in the younger sort
> To lack discretion.

The apology is graceful and self-aware enough: but the mistakes of the man are destructive. Polonius has too much of the wrong kind of love: having given his daughter bad advice, he has now misread

---

accurate to the text (Hamlet will also have to have a beard) but will leave the audience with a fair amount of work to do in turning archaisms into something they can feel: transposing the plays to a modern period, we make the choices and ask the audience to accept them – some do and some, feeling interfered with, don't.

the result and suggests the wrong cure, going to tell the King all about it – presumably to the chagrin of Ophelia, who has some feeling for Hamlet and perhaps doesn't look forward to discussing her private life with the monarch.

In the playing, this episode presents a fair challenge to Ophelia, who, like the Ghost, has the job of painting an accurate narrative picture at a time of strong emotion. We need to see what she describes like a piece of film, but it is quite difficult for her not to distort it with her own sharp feeling – which we also have to feel. It is not so much a matter of choosing between two acting modes, cold or hot, as of turning one knob down and another one up: and really the emotion is expressed by the action of recounting it. The problem is quite a common one in Shakespeare – the actor as both character and chorus – and modern players, concerned with their emotional integrity, can get unhappy about it.[5] In fact, with rare exceptions like Othello falling into a trance of jealousy – 'Is't possible? Confess! Handkerchief! O devil!' – strength of emotion invariably leads to articulacy in Shakespeare, rather than, as with so many of us, to incoherence. The revelation in the case of Ophelia is that she has an ominous gift for responding to the uncanny and reliving it.

2.2. The long scene that completes the play's second day is a writer's *tour de force* – nearly four hundred lines of unstrained development like a symphonic second movement, cunningly casting the leading figure (until the very end) in a responsive, not initiatory, role. Following his odd appearance to Ophelia, instead of forming and executing a plan, Hamlet will extemporise and receive visitors, expending characteristic energy, wit and passion on everything except what he should. Even his eventual idea of presenting the King with his own crime in the form of a play is a metaphor for Hamlet's own nature: the best of his actions are shadows. Nevertheless, by the end, we will be in an irreversible relationship with him. Under the scene's apparent realism and its supple natural language is a morality pattern – The Temptations of

5   When I played the Ghost the nights that disappointed me were those when I didn't convey the picture of the man sleeping in his orchard as the poisoner approached because of my overpowering feelings about it. Similarly, when I did Richard II, Aumerle would regularly report to me whether he had actually *seen* the dish of wood that Richard would exchange his figur'd goblets for, or just been aware of a very upset King.

a Hero: in a relay of several episodes, he survives one subtle test after another, and the rite of passage turns him from a 'wretch' who sadly reads a book into a possible revenge hero. The tempters are an ominous buffoon, two dubious friends who would trap him with nostalgia, and finally, a group of esoteric craftsmen, doctors of the heart, from whom, in wild coincidence, he draws purpose.

Greeting Rosencrantz and Guildenstern, Claudius is at the top of his considerable form. According to him, he and the Queen have been longing to see them anyway, and now they really need their assistance – they are helpless in the face of Hamlet's baffling 'transformation'. The two young men know Hamlet better than they: if they could see their way to staying in the lap of luxury at the court for a time, they would have the chance of curing Hamlet and keeping the King and Queen in the picture. There is not a syllable the visitors could take exception to: in making them important, wiser than himself, and offering them *carte blanche*, Claudius has in fact got them completely entrapped – unable to honour their friendship with Hamlet, answerable for everything they do and with no opportunity to refuse – all in the twinkling of an eye. The longish speech feels like one irresistible sentence: there is no full stop at the end of a line – the natural point of interruption – and barely a comma either. All he forgets is their reward, and the Queen, though lacking Claudius's guile, astutely reassures them of that, reiterating that they are Hamlet's very best friends. The two of them are unable to come up with much in reply, establishing themselves only as unoriginal; and she makes a stately joke by inverting their names (it is really a covert theatre device to help us distinguish one from the other):

KING: Thanks, Rosencrantz and gentle Guildenstern.
QUEEN: Thanks, Guildenstern and gentle Rosencrantz.

Polonius arrives and plays a little game with the King: he has the clue to Hamlet's 'lunacy' (the word is brutal after Claudius's euphemisms), but won't let on till the King has attended to state business: the return of the two ambassadors from Norway with good news of their interview with Fortinbras's uncle. The Queen seems not to have heard Polonius's hint about understanding Hamlet (she may have been excluded) because, left alone with her, Claudius repeats it carefully. She is blunt in reply – the problem is simply

His father's death and our o'er-hasty marriage.

Her candour shows some conscience, a chink in her contentment that Hamlet will brutally exploit later on. Claudius toughens up in turn – he will 'sift' Hamlet as carefully as if he were sieving flour. The little exchange, one of very few moments together for them, has a tit-for-tat rhythm that could suggest a growing tension between parent and step-parent.

Voltemand's account of the meeting in Norway is professionally shaped, and the news is in almost every way satisfactory: the feeble King has been shocked to hear of Fortinbras's intentions, has blocked them, and then, relieved at his nephew's acquiescence, has subsidised him to mount a campaign against Poland instead. He asks only that Fortinbras be allowed safe passage through Denmark. This is a sting in the tail that Claudius and Polonius might feel – do they really want the aggressive Norwegian in the country? – but since they are inclined to underestimate Fortinbras and to patronise his uncle, they miss it. Claudius's reply sounds oddly inverted; he is happy, but then he wants to form a reply and then think about it:

> It likes us well;
> And at our more consider'd time we'll read,
> Answer, and think upon this business.

We see a weakness: at this satisfactory moment, he seems to have lost his touch a little, his mind moving ahead either to Hamlet or simply to his next line, which attracts him with a comforting warmth:

> . . . at night we'll feast together.

Polonius grandly opens a new chapter:

> My liege and madam, to expostulate
> What majesty should be, what duty is,
> Why day is day, night night, and time is time,
> Were nothing but to waste night, day and time.

His ceremonious preparation for reading the letter that Hamlet has sent Ophelia is a comic turn as much as a plot advancement, and Gertrude and Claudius are willing stooges. Claudius likes Polonius well enough to wait, understanding his foxy vagueness to be a professional skill; the Queen – whom Polonius seems, with male clubbishness, to exclude – is less patient:

QUEEN: More matter with less art.
POLONIUS: Madam, I swear I use no art at all.

Just as Hamlet's 'antic disposition' plays on madness as a spectator sport, the handling of Polonius here is that of a theatre practitioner exploiting a comic angle without too much regard for logic. Narratively, there is a long trail of inconsistency. In the first of their earlier scenes together, Polonius instructed Ophelia not to have words or talk with Hamlet: in the second she insisted that 'as you did instruct' (he didn't) she has returned his letters. (She has kept his 'remembrances' – she has them in the Nunnery Scene later.) Polonius has rushed her off to the King to tell him about the incident in the closet, but now seems to have lost her en route, instead coming in alone to read a letter which 'in obedience hath my daughter shown me' – even though she has insisted that she has returned them all to the sender. He makes no reference either to the episode of the unbrac'd doublet (in any case they all seem to know by now that Hamlet tends to walk 'three or four hours together Here in the lobby') or to the fact that Ophelia is not with him. He suggests that he and the King should eavesdrop on Hamlet and Ophelia: when that opportunity arises, in the next scene, Claudius will explain the plan all over again to Gertrude, even though she has already heard it here and by her silence accepted it. This is dubious craft, because you notice it in performance: many times, Shakespeare was a gifted tart, scraping a theatrical buck.

Polonius's new version of events is that Hamlet has written this undistinguished rhyme to Ophelia (he is an expert on poetry as well, finding 'beautified' a 'vile phrase'), and this, to him, is conclusive evidence of the strength of his feelings; Polonius has warned Ophelia to keep away from Hamlet; and, far from the casual wrecker he was once believed to be, Hamlet has gone mad as a result. The object of Polonius's plan to 'loose' his daughter to Hamlet 'here in the lobby' is to prove the madman's madness by removing its cause (Ophelia's absence), though quite how that will work in practice is not clear. As usual, Polonius's elaborate spying is that of a man as interested in the gathering of information as in the information itself.

His style, as he unhurriedly holds the floor, is based on preamble and parenthesis – his prolix preparations form a simple statement followed by elaborate qualifications – and sometimes the nub of the matter is rather brutally expressed, from the point of view of the worried parents:

> . . . Your noble son is mad.

He will not be rushed:

QUEEN: Came this from Hamlet to her?
POLONIUS: Good madam, stay awhile, I will be faithful

– at other times there is pure waffle, verbal water-treading:

> That he is mad, 'tis true; 'tis true, 'tis pity,
> And pity 'tis, 'tis true. A foolish figure. . . .
> . . . And now remains
> That we find out the cause of this effect,
> Or rather say, the cause of this defect,
> For this effect defective comes by cause.
> Thus it remains, and the remainder thus.

This is the vanity of a politician, who, confident of attention, talks nonsense for no special reason, not failing to remind his listeners of his indispensability:

POLONIUS: What do you think of me?
KING: As of a man faithful and honourable.
POLONIUS: I would fain prove so. But what might you think. . .
    If I had played the desk or table-book
    Or given my heart a winking mute and dumb
    Or look'd upon this love with idle sight. . .

He is quick on the draw the moment the King seeks a second opinion:

KING: Do you think 'tis this?
QUEEN: It may be, very like.
POLONIUS: Hath there been such a time – I would fain know that –
    That I have positively said ''Tis so'
    When it prov'd otherwise?
KING: Not that I know.[6]

---

6   In theatrical terms, all this does leave the King and Queen with a problem. They have respectively six and four lines of brief interjection in the eighty-two lines of the sequence. What are they to do? Exhausted with the possibilities of playing 'come on, get-on-with-it' towards Polonius, and wanting always to express their own relationship, they may set up a line of communication that excludes him: they are only half-listening, being obsessed with each other. They may even do some cuddling. But the decision to make a court in which the King and Queen canoodle and everyone ignores it, including the Prime Minister, is quite a far-reaching one; and if they are distracted it underestimates the significance of the mad Hamlet's being at large, a fact big enough for them to have summoned Rosencrantz and Guildenstern, and then to 'long to hear' Polonius's revelations. So they probably just must listen and wait.

Hamlet comes in, reading 'sadly'. It is a famous surprise, Hamlet as he is, not as he wishes to be. How does the 'madman' look? Not so eccentric as to beg the question of why nobody comments on his appearance. How will he sound? Up to this point, he has spoken in blank verse: now that his real engagement has begun, he works mainly in prose. By speaking in our own manner, he will insinuate himself into our sympathies: however profound, he stays in touch.[7]

Hamlet is not the initiator of this brief and funny encounter: Polonius continues as the inquisitive driving force.[8] Their scene together has the rattle of vaudeville:

POLONIUS: How does my good lord Hamlet?
HAMLET: Well, God-a-mercy.
POLONIUS: Do you know me, my lord?
HAMLET: Excellent well. You are a fishmonger.

For the first time in the play Shakespeare uses audience asides, allowing Polonius some of the benefits of stand-up comedy. Hamlet alternates between *double-entendres* – a fishmonger also meant a whoremaster, just as the nunnery he recommends to Ophelia later also meant a brothel – and pungent free-association: by setting Polonius's daughter alongside the maggots in a dead dog, he insults by implication if not direct meaning. It is a morbid, wilful eccentricity whose style keeps changing. His attitude to Polonius is of complete scorn, expressed rather adolescently while he is there – 'old men have grey beards. . . ' – and then with blunt rudeness after he has gone:

These tedious old fools.

---

7 Hamlet moves, at the end of this long initial sequence, into the theatrical verse of the Players' texts, remains in verse for two consecutive soliloquies, then goes back into prose, returning to verse for his tribute to Horatio just before the Play. He is then in prose until the very end of the Play Scene. Altogether, three quarters of the part is in prose. The preponderance is unusual in a tragic hero – quite different from Macbeth, Othello, Lear and Cleopatra (though not unlike Rosalind in comedy) – and it is more than a technicality. Though it's dangerous to generalise about why Shakespeare uses one rather than the other – prose structure can be just as elaborate as blank verse, which in turn has the natural rhythm of speech – clearly there can be an accessibility in prose. In Hamlet this is fortified by a characteristic range of imagery: his metaphors, as Caroline Spurgeon has identified, are more often drawn from gardening, sport, the law, carpentry and engineering than from metaphysics.

8   The links in the scene's relay are worth noting: Claudius and Gertrude run the first two episodes before discreetly handing over to Polonius for the third and fourth; and he is in turn taken over by Hamlet for the next three.

However, Polonius is certainly not a fool: he has an instinctive understanding of madness:

> How pregnant sometimes his replies are – a happiness that often madness hits on, which reason and sanity could not be so prosperously delivered of

– even, if like everyone in the play, he only half-believes in it in Hamlet. Within his own mistaken terms, Polonius can be very perceptive, and Hamlet is by turns infantile:

> POLONIUS: What do you read, my lord?
> HAMLET: Words, words, words.

and brilliant:

> POLONIUS: Will you walk out of the air, my lord?
> HAMLET: Into my grave?

Having achieved little, Polonius leaves him to his university friends: he apparently never reports back to the King what has happened. Perhaps it would be too embarrassing.

Hamlet has given nothing of himself away: an unexpected king of comedy, he is also an intellectual strategist using his gifts as political defence. With the arrival of Rosencrantz and Guildenstern, he moves up a gear. Pleasantly taken aback, he greets them without reserve, and they slip into undergraduate routines – the talk has the self-regarding smack of the intellectual locker-room:

> HAMLET: . . . Good lads, how do ye both?
> ROSENCRANTZ: As the indifferent children of the earth.
> GUILDENSTERN: Happy in that we are not over happy;
>   On Fortune's cap we are not the very button.
> HAMLET: Nor the soles of her shoe?
> ROSENCRANTZ: Neither, my lord.
> HAMLET: Then you live about her waist, or in the middle of her favours?
> GUILDENSTERN: Faith, her privates, we.
> HAMLET: In the secret parts of Fortune? O most true, she is a strumpet.

– it could be *Love's Labour's Lost.* The two visitors just stand there, verbally rallying, saying nothing about why they have arrived – surely they ought to have had a story ready – so that Hamlet's enthusiasm darkens quickly:

> HAMLET: . . . What have you, my good friends, deserved at the hands
>   of fortune that she sends you to prison hither?

Such sardonic provocations are as difficult for them as for Horatio:

GUILDENSTERN: Prison, my lord?
HAMLET: Denmark's a prison.
ROSENCRANTZ: Then is the world one.
HAMLET: A goodly one; in which there are many confines, wards and
    dungeons; Denmark being one of the worst.
ROSENCRANTZ: We think not so, my lord.

They are happier with aphorism and posture, and the rally seizes
up.[9] Faced soon enough with the inevitable question – whether
they have been sent for or whether this is 'a free visitation' – the
two spies do no better than at first:

GUILDENSTERN: What should we say, my lord?

Unable to come up with anything, they stand there waiting to be
found out. The lack of guile is attractive: friendship matters, even
in a trap. It certainly matters to Hamlet, who seems to mind not so
much their being set on him as their honesty in admitting it:

> . . . let me conjure you, by the rights of our fellowship, by the
> consonancy of our youth, by the obligation of our ever-preserved love,
> and by what more dear a better proposer can charge you withal, be
> even and direct with me whether you were sent for or no. . . if you love
> me, hold not off.

Their truthfulness – 'My lord, we were sent for' – breaks a deadlock, and provides an emotional trigger – part relief, part disappointment – for Hamlet's great statement 'What a piece of work is
a man. . . ' that stands at the middle of the scene and in a sense at
the centre of the play. It doesn't answer the implied question:
Hamlet knows very well why he has 'lost all his mirth', but he will

---

9 Even without the unspoken burden of deceit, there is a typical unease in the relationship
between Hamlet and his friends (which will end with him sending them to their deaths). He
shares with Prince Hal in *Henry IV* an unavoidable social distance, which he, unlike Hal,
seems quite happy not to bridge. Rosencrantz's opening conceit is of the poor student – he is
one of 'the indifferent children of the earth. . . on Fortune's cap . . . not the very button'; but
soon Hamlet bluntly pulls rank:

> I will not sort you with the rest of my servants; for to speak to you like a honest man, I
> am most dreadfully attended. . .

Our Prince of Wales would do this sort of thing better: even in jest, a royal should surely
never refer to the social chasm. Hamlet is uncomfortable company: he keeps his distance
when it suits him, and will then use his intellectual gifts to provoke a reaction:

> O God, I could be bounded in a nutshell, and count myself the king of infinite space,
> were it not that I have bad dreams.

When he leaves both intellect and status aside and suddenly acknowledges his love for
Horatio just before the Play, it is touching, rather arbitrary, untypical.

not declare his real secret, only the symptoms it has provoked. Historically, the speech resounded with a keenly-felt conflict between Renaissance idealism and the debasing discord of the age; for us its attraction is its sudden lack of guile, its heartfelt lucidity in acknowledging man as simultaneously close to the gods and the worms – it opens up a new range for the play, in which humans will travel from bestiality to divinity and back. Hamlet's disappointment in his friends has provoked him to comprehensive self-awareness.

Rosencrantz seizes on the opportunity of Hamlet's unanswerable 'Man delights not me' to announce the approach of a company of Players. Hamlet immediately imagines them in action: an authoritative King, opportunities for an heroic knight, love interest, a happy ending for 'the humorous [moody] man', an easy house for the comics, and good unlicensed speeches for the leading lady. It could be a happier version of *Hamlet*: Old King Hamlet, Laertes, Ophelia, Hamlet himself, the Gravedigger, with Rosalind thrown in for good measure. The Players are indeed Shakespeare's point of self-reference, actors such as the actors at that moment performing his play, Burbage and the Lord Chamberlain's Men, his company. Since he had no hesitation in bringing the day's news into the script (compare the Porter's scene in *Macbeth*, with its references to the Gunpowder Plot, grain-hoarding and contemporary tailoring), Denmark is forgotten for sixty lines, and we are deep in the intrigues of late Elizabethan theatre. Hamlet's and Rosencrantz's talk of the 'little eyases that cry out on the top of question' refers to the War of the Theatres, when the Children of the Chapel, a company of boy actors performing satirical, 'railing' plays which often caricatured current trends, became fashionable in London. This 'eyrie of children' had played at the Blackfriars Theatre in the previous winter of 1600-1, and from their 'carry(ing) away . . . Hercules and his load too' it sounds as if they were threatening the business and reputation of the Lord Chamberlain's Men at the Globe, whose emblem was Hercules carrying the world on his shoulders. Always under pressure in the city – if it was not this new fashion, it was plague, or the legislation of 1600 limiting the number of active London playhouses to two – the company had regularly to 'trot from town to town on the hard hoof', returning to the life of 'strowlers'.[10]

10   Off they would go, according to Ben Jonson, ' their shoes 'full of gravel. . . after a blind jade and a hamper' to 'stalk upon boards and barrel heads, to an old cracked trumpet'. On

Perhaps understandably, Shakespeare indulges his subject – there is a great deal here as difficult to understand now as it was easy then, and probably best cut.[11] Hamlet is grumpily satirical about the children: this is the side of him, churlishly resistant to change, that should have a weekly column in the Tory press:

> HAMLET: Do the boys carry it away?. . . It is not very strange; for my uncle is King of Denmark, and those that would make mouths at him [make fun of him] while my father lived, give twenty, forty, fifty, a hundred ducats a piece for his picture in little. 'Sblood, there is something in this more than natural, if philosophy could find it out.

In the process, he abruptly restores the play to its Danish frame.

As the Players approach, Hamlet winds up with Rosencrantz and Guildenstern by dropping them a brilliant hint, inexplicably betraying himself to Claudius:

> . . . my uncle-father and aunt-mother are deceived. . . I am but mad north-north-west; when the wind is southerly, I know a hawk from a handsaw

– and finally, the actors arrive, prefaced by Polonius, who announces (unless he is an expert on the theatre as well) what sounds like their advance publicity:

> . . . the best actors in the world, either for tragedy, comedy, history, pastoral, pastoral-comical, historical-pastoral. . . . . these are the only men.

Silly with Polonius (one of his very few truly 'antic' passages) Ham-

---

arrival in each new town they had to perform in front of the Mayor first so that they could be screened. Apart from the doubtful propriety of his material, the actor on the road had a reputation for being 'a slow payer, seldom a purchaser, never a Puritan' [J. Cocke, *The Strolling Player*, 1605] and, in places, he inspired a scornful pity:

> Players, by reason they shall have a hard winter, and must travel on the hoof, will lie sucking there for pence and twopences, like young pigs at a sow newly farrowed. . .
> *The Raven's Almanac*, 1609

For all that, they had good costumes, since it was the way for noblemen to bequeath their best clothes to their servants, who, obviously unable to wear them themselves, would sell them to the Players for a few pennies. But they were poor: provincial fees lagged far behind metropolitan ones. It is this defiantly bedraggled flavour, not merry somersaulting and tabor-dances, that the Players should bring into *Hamlet*.

11   The lines about the children have in fact never been very secure. They were in the original play, then cut from the Second Quarto – they would still have been very topical, but their tone is scornful, and by now the new King James had given the children a royal licence. Oddly enough, they are back in the Folio, by which time they are well out of date.

let is very excited by their arrival – they awaken a typical nostalgia, though his jokes are the clumsy ones of an amateur:

> O old friend, why, thy face is valanced since I saw thee last. Com'st thou to beard me in Denmark? What, my young lady and mistress! By'r lady, your ladyship is nearer to heaven than when I saw you last. . .

The speech that he immediately wants them to perform comes from a favourite play which he rather snobbishly describes as 'caviare to the general', backing up his judgment with the dour praise of 'one whose judgments in such matters cried in the top of mine' (a university critic, working the weary metaphor?):

> I remember one said there were no sallets in the lines to make the matter savoury, nor no matter in the phrase that might indict the author of affectation, but called it an honest method, as wholesome as sweet, and by very much more handsome than fine.

Aeneas's account to Dido Queen of Carthage of Pyrrhus's slaughter of King Priam (in revenge for the death of his father Achilles) has stuck in Hamlet's mind.[12] It is, significantly, about a vengeful hero who, although his 'sable arms' were 'black as his purpose', unaccountably hesitated before slaughtering Priam. The tone of violent adventure is turned rather effectively into pathos (with the help of Polonius's interruption at the turning point – 'This is too long') as Hecuba comes upon Pyrrhus mangling her husband; her generalised grief, lacking the Shakespearian touches, say of Constance in *King John*, is still given the Player's best shot:[13]

> Look whe'er he has not turned his colour and has tears in's eyes. Prithee, no more.[14]

As a professional, he throws his mood off immediately – it was just

---

12 It has the ring of strong early Shakespeare, and needs to be played with the passion of the best of *Henry VI* or *Titus Andronicus*, only a few years back in the audience's memory. It is quite easy not to listen to the speech, lulled by its musicality into missing the story, which carries a crucial theme. (For a long time I had the idea that at one point Pyrrhus's ear is cut off, perhaps by the falling towers of Troy).

13 The Player knows the speech immediately, and seems to pick up Hamlet's cue – 'So proceed you' – cleanly. Elizabethan actors had to hold as many parts in their heads as opera singers do now.

14 The effect of a Player being so moved by a revenge that could be Hamlet's and being admired by the player of Hamlet who then, in a soliloquy of great virtuosity itself, expresses shame at not being moved enough to act, brings on an odd theatrical vertigo: Shakespeare's experiment initiates something that Pirandello rather overworked three centuries later.

another, better piece of acting – but his tears were real all right. Polonius can't get over it: able at first to interrupt rudely, he is now dumbfounded by the Player's emotion. Men like him hate the theatre: it can be awfully unsettling. The Players are specialists and tricksters, as well as shamans, priests, the nub of the matter: they have brought in an air more fantastic and artificial than life but yet truer to life, and a lot healthier than the air of Elsinore.

Waiting for the hero to experience his own story with proper intensity, we see that an actor at two removes from us can, at the throw of a switch, express a truth that Hamlet has been avoiding. Hamlet's respect for the actors is (or becomes) real; he hands the profession a precious slogan

They are the abstracts and brief chronicles of the time

– recognising at the same time the flimsiness of reputation in a world at once morally authoritative and genetically bitchy:

After your death you were better have a bad epitaph than their ill report while you live.

Beneath all the apparent frittering of time an idea has developed: he calls for a performance of *The Murder of Gonzago* for the next day with a speech of 'some dozen or sixteen lines' of his own (hopefully more persuasive than his poem to Ophelia) added into it. For this, and other things, Hamlet surely owes us an explanation. The stage again depopulates:

Ay, so, God buy' ye

and the lens zooms in:

Now I am alone.

For the first time since the Ghost's departure on the battlements, we have Hamlet to ourselves. What follows, in a rush of self-discovery, is analytical and appalled. Where he was going to sweep to his revenge

with wings as swift
As meditation or the thoughts of love

he sees himself

fall a-cursing, like a very drab,
A scullion.

He recapitulates the Player's symptoms in fascinated detail –

creating common ground with us, as we have watched them too.
He turns over the confidential central question:

> what would he do,
> Had he the motive and the cue for passion
> That I have?

It hangs in the air, implying a self-knowledge that allays our
bewilderment at having watched his stern promise thinning into
perversity. In ruthless close-up now, he demands:

> Am I a coward?
> Who calls me villain? Breaks my pate across?
> Plucks off my beard and blows it in my face?. . .
> . . . Who does me this?
> Ha?

-- questions so direct that he must surely have got an answer to
some of them at the Globe; even in these restrained days, the
responses sit at the front of our mouths. This sudden contact is the
most daring and intimate (with the possible exception of Leontes in
The Winter's Tale) Shakespeare ever attempted. Lear addresses the
storm and its victims, Othello his soul, Coriolanus has the briefest of
monologues, even Macbeth does not come down among us in the
way of Hamlet. His language, although it is now verse, has the jolt
of thought, the explosiveness and bathos of unconsidered speech:

> Remorseless, treacherous, lecherous, kindless villain!
> O vengeance!
> Why, what an ass am I. . .

-- the effect is so real it is nearly comic. In trying to make himself as
authentic as the actor, Hamlet finds himself only a garrulous
whore. All the same, his progress is such that when he now
denounces Claudius he takes us easily with him even though we
know as well as he does that the case against the King is still wide
open, that

> The spirit that I have seen
> May be the devil. . .

Abandoning neurosis, he redeems himself with a cunning plan that
quickens the pulse. The excitement is realised musically: after the
cautious two- and three-syllable patterns of

> I have heard
> That guilty creatures sitting at a play

Have by the very cunning of the scene
Been struck so to the soul that presently
They have proclaim'd their malefactions;
For murder, though it have no tongue, wIll speak
With most miraculous organ

there are, in the last eleven lines of the speech, only three words of more than two syllables, and many monosyllables, driving towards the famous couplet

The play's the thing
Wherein I'll catch the conscience of the King.

This second confession – experimental, turbulent, showy, brain and heart working together – brilliantly galvanises Hamlet and hurls the play forward. His response to life – 'What a piece of work is a man' – has already raised unbidden questions and made a contract with us. His heroic charm has predisposed us in his favour: frustrated by his lethargy, seduced by his self-admonishment, caught up in the exultation of his winning idea, we are complicit by now in his very heartbeat.

In nightly practice, the scene gives the principal actor the chance to work himself in and begin to shape the evening. The passage with Polonius is easy and relaxed – not at all the taut disciplines of 'high' comedy, but highly intelligent without intellectual effort – and in working it the actor gets a sense of his audience, a presence at his elbow that he will need more acutely later. In the Rosencrantz and Guildenstern scene he is the one who knows least: we are ahead of him, and his vulnerability advances our sympathy. The energy brought on to the stage by the Players makes a wave that he and we can ride, and his enthusiastic improvisation with them tells us something we didn't know: that he loves the theatre (even if he overestimates its power), remembers whole speeches by heart, and is prepared to make himself look silly trying them out in front of professionals. He then has a great soliloquy. The actor's heart is beating faster, and he knows a good deal about the performance's chances on the night. He may also, with luck, be allowed an interval.

THE ACTION: DAY THREE

Act 3 Scene 1–Act 4 Scene 4

3.1. Between the booking of *The Murder of Gonzago* and its performance, while the Players learn their extra lines, is set drama's most celebrated speech and an important scene between Hamlet and Ophelia, prefaced by Rosencrantz and Guildenstern reporting back to the King and Queen on their meeting with Hamlet. Just as Polonius has found method in Hamlet's madness, it has occurred to Claudius's swift mind that he only 'puts on this confusion' – for some disruptive purpose presumably, though Claudius would link it to his own secret only at the most subliminal level. The Queen assumes on the same limited evidence that her son is really disturbed, and there may be some implied conflict here with her husband. He now has to listen to her solicitously questioning Rosencrantz and Guildenstern

> Did he receive you well?

and demanding to know what therapy they have tried:

> Did you assay him
> To any pastime?

The two men are honest enough – and since they have discovered nothing to speak of, they do not have to betray their friend: they can only report his 'crafty madness' and his unwillingness to admit its cause. On the other hand, they need to cover their backs by reassuring the King that they have been diligent: so Rosencrantz tells one lie – that Hamlet has been

> Niggard of question, but of our demands
> Most free in his reply.

In fact the reverse is true: Hamlet has peppered them with questions and the few that they have asked him have been easily deflected. The news that he has entertained a troupe of Players and asked them for a show tonight (Rosencrantz does not go into the impromptu performance and the Player's tears) seems to be welcome to Claudius; though why a man of his temper thinks that a show put on by a possible madman that they will all have to attend is a good idea is hard to see.[1]

As often, Claudius's dissimulation is so thorough that his text offers no chink through which to see any contradictory feelings he might have; it may be that in sending the two of them off:

> Good gentlemen, give him a further edge,
> And drive his purpose on to these delights

he is anxious to be shot of them and on to the Ophelia plan. Courteous as he is to Rosencrantz and Guildenstern, he has less faith than Gertrude in their abilities: from where he is standing, they are a fairly unimpressive pair.

The King now tells the Queen something she already knows: that he and Polonius mean to spy on Hamlet's meeting with Ophelia. Why he sends her away and she acquiesces isn't clear: perhaps this is man's work, and he doesn't want her humanising their efforts to flush her son out. The actress has to decide what attitude to take to this exclusion as she turns to Ophelia, hoping that her 'good beauties' and 'virtues' will be curative. Ophelia accepts the compliment, modestly or otherwise:

> Madam, I wish it may.

Polonius sets Ophelia up with a book; after all, Hamlet was reading when he met him the previous day, so this is obviously a good means of dissimulation. She is also burdened by the 'remembrances' she is going to return to Hamlet. Polonius then, improbably, laments the hypocrisy of it all (the things you have to do in politics. . .):

> 'Tis too much prov'd, that with devotion's visage
> And pious action we do sugar o'er
> The devil himself.

Ophelia is hardly diabolical; the real reason for the speech is to cue Claudius to do an even more surprising thing – he turns to the

---

1   Polonius avers that Hamlet has specially requested the King and Queen to come; strictly speaking, he hasn't, though of course it's implied.

audience and announces his guilt, not specifically of the murder, but of a 'deed' amounting to 'a heavy burden.' It is hard to know why Shakespeare has done this. It would seem dramatically very much better to extend the tense open question of Claudius's crime, and with it the reliability of the Ghost, until the Prayer Scene after the Play, when he could thrillingly confess for the first time. At this earlier point he is not under pressure, least of all from the sententious Polonius: he is confident and unthreatened. The speech is therefore very difficult for the actor to motivate: in 1994 I was all for cutting it, feeling that the psychology was not worthy of Shakespeare, and that Sophocles would have made a better fist of the story-telling. In the end I'm glad we didn't. Something about Hamlet fills Claudius with a worry he can't name, and out of it comes this self-hating aside: compared to Hamlet's baffling integrity, he is no better in his own eyes than a harlot with a painted face. Beneath his every line ticks his nagging knowledge of himself: at any moment, touched by the right word, his politic skin might blister. Now that we know he is to face a very big test, it is best that we also learn of this precariousness in him.

Productions of Hamlet sometimes place To Be Or Not To Be and the Nunnery Scene with Ophelia not here but at the point of Hamlet's entrance in the previous scene, transposing the 'Fishmonger' sequence from that point to this. The thin authority is the First, 'Bad' Quarto, which is so unreliable throughout that there seems no particular reason to trust it on this point when the two later texts are consistent. The real reason for the change is a kind of reader's bewilderment: after his experiences on the battlements should we not next see Hamlet debating the great question of life and death and rejecting the ties of sexual love, rather than fooling around with Polonius, Rosencrantz and Guildenstern and the Players? But which is more typical of this writer? I know where my money is – Shakespeare is the first absurdist playwright, who later has Hamlet chatting with a clown who is digging a grave for his lover, who he doesn't even know is dead: who once held up the action after the apparent death of Juliet for fifty quibbling lines between Peter and a group of musicians who suddenly had no gig to play: and who goes on in *Antony and Cleopatra* to bring in a funny asp-seller to help with the Queen's suicide. He rarely does anything on the nose; and the theatrical surprise of To Be Or Not To Be following on from The Play's The Thing – Hamlet disconcerted by a mortal *coup de foudre* at his moment of greatest purpose – is typically bold.

The speech that provokes this experimentation is very famous. If you mention the author to anyone who's heard his name only distantly, they will probably say or think 'To Be Or Not to Be'; no doubt somebody is doing it somewhere at this moment.[2] It has become an identification tag, together with Yorick's skull, in cartoon, headline and soundbite, a sort of universal shorthand. In *Hamlet* it is not so much a narrative necessity as a haunting refrain, ostensibly leading from and to nothing; no wonder the memory of the compiler of the First Quarto played him false in placing it. Actors approaching the speech worry about it – how to get on for it, how to take the audience by surprise, how not to forget the lines because everyone knows them – and then realise it is far from the most important part of the job.[3]

According to Albert Camus, suicide is the only philosophical question of any interest; and Hamlet's eye-to-eye encounter with it, expressed with all his intellectual lucidity, is perhaps the nearest drama can come to pure philosophy. Like many great insights, it is essentially banal, a trite (or profound) phrasing of a profound (or trite) question. It is odd that the qualities we are most moved by in Hamlet – courage, wit, human optimism – are almost completely lacking in his most famous utterance: like the reflection on Yorick's skull, it is utterly negative apart from the grace of its phrasing. Perhaps that is the shocking point. The Christian inhibition against self-slaughter which Hamlet recognised in his first soliloquy has gone now, replaced by fear, and his typical strengths have deserted him: he proposes that it might be better to end your life than to

---

2   *Essere o non essere; questo e il dilemma. Byt' ili nye byt'; vot fchyom vapros. Iru to imasen; shitsumon-wa desu.* There must be a T-shirt. Most people can get a few lines on, though

Whether 'tis nobler in the mind to suffer
The slings and arrows of outrageous fortune
Or to take arms against a sea of troubles
And by opposing end them

tends to lodge itself in the memory with a false meaning – 'nobler-in-the-mind to suffer', rather than 'nobler in-the-mind-to-suffer'. In fact, 'in the mind ' is counterpointed with 'to take arms': the alternative doesn't mean anything much.

3   Perhaps in retaliation for my comments about his first entrance, Roger Rees tells me that he remembers me once coming on for this speech at a run, as if diving into a cold pool: my feet arrived first, then my trunk and finally my head. He had never seen such a union of reluctance and eagerness.

endure it, but for the cowardly fact that the dreams after death would be bad, and the unknown is terrifying. Helpless to resolve this problem, we sit, courage drained, resolution

sicklied o'er with the pale cast of thought,

unable to do anything at all.

How is this negation made tolerable, even definitive? Invited to empathise with the despair behind the lines, we might find its determinacy tainted by a young man's self-pity – it seems to reach out of the play and negate everything, including the activity of sitting watching *Hamlet*. But there is a particular technique at work, withdrawing the speaker from the speech. There is no personal pronoun at all in its thirty-five lines, so it is in a sense drained of Hamlet himself: although the cap fits, it also stands free of him as pure human analysis. In the earlier admission of despair, O That This Too Too Solid Flesh Would Melt, self-regard was kept at bay by humour, as when Hamlet compared himself to Hercules: To Be Or Not To Be is bleaker, drained of wit, energy and even personality, replacing them with a remorselessly clear vision, expressed in limpid, easy, but formal rhythms. The form is everything – it is Bach, not Stravinsky – the emotions are suppressed and the utterance perfect of its kind.

Suddenly, Hamlet sees Ophelia. Intrigued by his visit to her closet, we need to know more about their relationship, but we will be little wiser by the end of the scene: the meaning of the encounter is opaque, largely because it is not easy to judge how much Hamlet is acting the part both of an eccentric and of an evasively manoeuvring lover. Every line can be taken either straight or on a curve, and this is a very nutty matter indeed for the director and actors, since they are deciding an important area of Hamlet's sexuality and much of what drives Ophelia mad.

Having stood about[4] in this unspecified place (in truth it is just the stage), waiting for Hamlet to finish his monologue and notice her, Ophelia now offers back to him 'rich gifts' that have 'wax[ed] poor' because of his neglect of her – an unreasonable position, as it is she who, under her father's instruction, has kept away from him.

---

4 Shakespeare is borrowing from the twelfth-century narrative source by Saxo Grammaticus an incident in which a woman is placed in Amleth's way by his uncle Fengo to seduce him and expose his madness as dissimulation. Amleth more or less rapes her: the frisson of that situation survives in Shakespeare without the sexual crime.

Polonius hasn't asked for the business of the gifts, only that she should read, so the mild sexual provocation is her initiative. Her role is at once conventional and, since only she knows they are being observed, very equivocal.

After the uneasy opening – an exchange thick with the tension of lovers uncertain of their circumstances – Hamlet breaks through the formality (Ophelia always calls him 'my lord'), disorientating her with jagged, interrogative prose:

> HAMLET: Ha, ha! Are you honest?
> OPHELIA: My lord?
> HAMLET: Are you fair?
> OPHELIA: What means your lordship?

– and the scene begins to move, unpredictably and on his terms only. Difficult to identify at first, these become startling. However nobly rueful a tone the actor wants to take towards a woman he can no longer love, the bitterness that he turns first against himself, and then, with violent misogyny, against her, is inescapable:

> wise men know well enough what monsters you make of them . . . I have heard of your paintings too, well enough; God hath given you one face and you make yourselves another; you jig, you amble and you lisp, you nickname God's creatures, and make your wantonness your ignorance. . .

Though there may be residual gentleness along the way, the sexual game-playing ('I did love you once. . . I loved you not'), the mock self-laceration, the ambiguous kindness ('get thee to a nunnery') and the mingling of friendship with verbal assault,[5] are typical male devices to oppress and baffle: from the moment he takes the initiative, Ophelia has a total of eight helpless and repetitive lines out of the fifty-odd, while Hamlet does several circuits of sexual unkindness. She has done little to deserve this. As a means of justifying his savagery, productions commonly insert a moment when Hamlet realises he is being watched, so that 'Where's your father?' becomes a trick question, and Ophelia's untruth – 'At home, my lord' – provokes his disappointed rage. Certainly his violent rejection here, and the humiliation he then inflicts on her in

---

5   Physical too sometimes – in my case and in others'. Though logical for the actor, it's probably wrong for the play – surely even Polonius would come out of hiding if he saw his daughter being hit.

the Play Scene, are spectacularly difficult to justify unless he feels she has betrayed him in this way – even then, he might have understood her predicament better. It is true that Hamlet has been crippled by his mother's sexual choice, and her distressing image keeps superimposing itself on the innocent Ophelia; but after the distinction of the soliloquy, his cruelty, however articulate, is deeply alienating. Within one scene, he has reached a philosophical climax and a moral low point.

He has also, once again, walked Ophelia along the edge. On the verge of breakdown, she is able to account for his lacerations only by thinking him mad, and she clings tightly to definitions to keep control:

> O, what a noble mind is here o'erthrown!
> The courtier's, soldier's, scholar's, eye, tongue, sword. . .

Her lyrical description, bespeaking not so much love as disappointed admiration, idealises the rat we have just seen. She then breaks into quite a new style for her, metaphorical and imaginative: the vivid description of his

> sovereign reason
> Like sweet bells jangled out of tune and harsh,
> That unmatch'd form and feature of blown youth
> Blasted with ecstasy. . .

has a dangerous magnetism for her – soon enough she will be where she imagines he is.

Claudius, on full alert, has seen that it is neither a lover nor a lunatic that he is dealing with, but a man with

> something in his soul,
> O'er which his melancholy sits on brood

– he is threatening enough to be deported, rather than, as at the beginning of the play, domesticated. For the first time he speaks of sending Hamlet to England

> For the demand of our neglected tribute.[6]

---

6   At the time of the play, Denmark had tried to revive the traditional demand of tribute from England. The sources shadow the play again here. In Saxo Grammaticus, Amleth is sent to England as part of the same stratagem as Claudius's; but he discovers its real meaning, and marries the King of England's daughter. Later on he marries the daughter of the Scottish King as well.

Even with his confidential Polonius he dissembles, pretending an avuncular concern for Hamlet's health:

> Haply the seas and countries different,
> With variable objects, shall expel
> This something settled matter in his heart. . . .

and Polonius, indifferent to his daughter's ordeal:

> How now, Ophelia;
> You need not tell us what lord Hamlet said;
> We heard it all

musingly concurs – though he still believes, perhaps pruriently, that the problem has something to do with love. As the two of them leave, oblivious to the girl, the King's conclusion:

> Madness in great ones must not unwatched go

has, again, a hypocritical feel – he has just said that Hamlet's words were not like madness. Even the most genial interpreter of Polonius, meanwhile, is hard put to find much care for Ophelia now; he has comprehensively shopped and abandoned her. The two men bustle away, leaving her alone or trailing behind, friendless and in real danger.

3.2. The Play Scene stands exactly at the centre of *Hamlet*, a junction and point of no return. It begins, between the fierce emotions of the Nunnery and the high tension of *The Murder of Gonzago*, temperately, with Hamlet advising the Players on their job. His rather messianic garrulousness shows his need for them to be at their best if he is to achieve what he hopes for. His tone is presumptuous but brilliant: he identifies for good the meaning of acting, and we have been using the job description ever since. Whether in naturalism or epic tragedy, poetic realism, tragical-comical-historical-pastoral, the touchstone is essentially the same:

> Suit the action to the word, the word to the action, with this special
> observance, that you o'erstep not the modesty of nature; for anything
> so overdone is from the purpose of playing, whose end, both at the first
> and now, was and is, to hold as 'twere the mirror up to nature. . . . [7]

Consequently he has sharp words for the ham actors who 'tear a

---

[7]   Though with Christopher Marlowe still in the repertory, and ghosts in leather pilches, it is quite a radical assertion, Shakespeare pointing a way forward to Stanislavski.

passion to tatters' and for the comedians who elaborate their parts and 'laugh, to set on some quantity of barren spectators to laugh too'.[8] For this he draws the mildest of rebukes from the First Player: no 'my lord' this time, just

> I hope we have reformed that indifferently with us, sir.

The actors, delayed by the royal opinion, make ready, and, in a criss-cross of movements, Polonius arrives with Rosencrantz and Guildenstern to confirm at the eleventh hour the crucial point that the King and Queen will attend, in fact are on their way. Rosencrantz and Guildenstern stand there without purpose – except perhaps the dramatic one of contrasting their doubtful friendship with what follows – and are also sent to bustle the poor actors: and Hamlet, mercurial as ever, suddenly calls for a true friend.

He needs to tell Horatio the purpose of the Play; but he is so emotionally charged, so hemmed in with intrigue, that an overriding need falls from him for the human touch he has done without until now. He knows that he is about to encounter something crucial to his life. As with Rosencrantz and Guildenstern earlier, he refers (to us, uncomfortably) to the difference of status between himself and his friend:

> Why should the poor be flatter'd?
> No, let the candied tongue lick absurd pomp
> And crook the pregnant hinges of the knee
> Where thrift may follow fawning. Dost thou hear?. . .

– it is all rather drawn-out and sententious; but soon he finds a simple contrast between his temperament and his friend's, idealising in Horatio the stability whose loss has, for example, cost him Ophelia:

> Give me that man
> That is not passion's slave, and I will wear him
> In my heart's core, ay, in my heart of hearts,
> As I do thee.

---

8   The advice to the clowns would seem to be of a general nature, since it is unlikely that Hamlet imagines that kind of interlude for Claudius. In the real Elizabethan theatre it was in fact quite common to end plays with dancing and clowning – the Epilogue to *Henry IV Part 2* is spoken by a dancer. This dispersal of grave matters is a bit reminiscent of the Japanese pattern whereby Kyogen ('wild words') are inserted in the Noh plays, and of the practice of ancient Greek theatre festivals, where three tragedies were followed by a satyr play (*Cyclops*, *The Trackers of Oxyrhynchus*).

The practical point to convey – they will be interrupted any moment – is that during the Play Horatio must

> Even with the very comment of thy soul
> Observe mine uncle

– confirming, in his dry and undeceived way, what Hamlet may excitedly misinterpret. In this rather one-sided friendship, Horatio is burdened with a large responsibility he didn't ask for.

As the court, with their signature of 'Trumpets and Kettle-drums', fill the stage and the Play begins, Hamlet and Claudius confront each other in code. Claudius and Gertrude see enacted, first in mime (the Dumb Show), and then in old-fashioned rhyming verse, a story so close to their own experience that they cannot mistake its meaning: a King and Queen profess deep love, the Queen declares that her faith to the King will last forever beyond death and condemns second marriages in general, the King sleeps 'on a bank of flowers', and poison is poured into his ears by an intruder. This 'fellow' then woos and wins the widow and the scene closes. In the spoken Play that follows the mime the same story is told up to the point of the poisoning, when the action is stopped. In *The Murder of Gonzago* we are watching a story taken from the Italian, in which a duke is murdered by his nephew, who then marries his widow Baptista, the action taking place in Vienna. In *Hamlet,* we are watching in a stylised form events not vouch-safed us, particularly the alleged murder of old Hamlet; and we observe Claudius with the same need for confirmation as young Hamlet does. At the point at which Claudius interrupts and leaves, calling for lights, Hamlet will be almost out of control with excitement: believing Claudius a 'stricken deer', he will now 'take the Ghost's word for a thousand pound'. At that moment, what has he achieved, and is it any different from what he thinks he has achieved?

From the point of view of the suspect, this is what happens. The Dumb Show begins. The King and Queen make loving action, and the King sleeps – for Claudius, a first small memory. A fellow comes and poisons him, in a very specific manner.[9] To Gertrude

9   It might seem arcane to us – to the Elizabethans, a degree less so. In Christopher Marlowe's *Edward II* (1593) Lightborn, a professional murderer, lists some methods of poisoning, of which this is one; and the Roman author Pliny (23-79 A. D.) refers in his *Natural History* to the pouring of oil of henbane in the ears, not to kill but to make the victim mad. This is one of many moments when the antique nature of *Hamlet* may clash with a

and the court, this is in the realm of the theatrical; Claudius turns to ice. His private interest in outlandish means of murder (later he will prepare a chalice for Hamlet that will kill after a single drink) is being broadcast. It is a mockery. Who has chosen this play? Is it part of these actors' repertoire, in which case it is a ghastly, innocent coincidence? Or – the worst possibility – has it been selected, and possibly written, by Hamlet? What was it Polonius said at that moment when Claudius was thinking about eavesdropping on Hamlet and Ophelia? That there were players in the court, and that Hamlet

> . . . *beseech'd* me to *entreat* your majesties
> To hear and see the matter.

Claudius could settle this bothersome question with a glance at Hamlet's face; but that is the one eye he shouldn't catch. As the 'fellow' then seduces the widow who 'seems loath and unwilling awhile, but in the end accepts his love', Claudius becomes certain that Hamlet is watching him and Gertrude closely; he must give the performance of his life (and the actor playing him must remain impassive, even if that means deceiving the audience too). He needs time to think – and after the Dumb Show, while Hamlet flicks innuendoes at Ophelia, he has it. [10]

A Prologue comes on. Claudius quickens again. Will he make things better or worse, give some clue how far it is all to go?

> For us, and for our tragedy
> Here stooping to your clemency
> We beg your hearing patiently.

The usual stuff. At the edge of his vision, more misogyny from Hamlet:

modern production's desire to be relevant to its time: one of the play's main challenges is to strike a balance between its archaism and its searing up-to-dateness. Claudius is both this quaint poisoner and an accomplished modern politician.

It's possible to get some vertigo here. *The Murder of Gonzago* is not a received text, but written by Shakespeare for the purpose; however, it refers to a known murder, when, in 1538, the Duke of Urbino was poisoned by (confusingly) one Luigi Gonzaga by means of a drug in the ear. The 'dozen or sixteen lines' by Hamlet/Shakespeare never show up in the Play – either they lie beyond the point of interruption, or Shakespeare has forgotten the idea.

10   We have become used to the Dumb Show being cut in production, as if Shakespeare meant nothing in particular by it, so that the first sign Claudius gets that there is a poisoning involved comes at the moment just before he rises, self-control suddenly lost, at the climax of the spoken Play. The real intricacy of the scene and the subtlety of Claudius's role in it is much simplified if this is done.

OPHELIA: 'Tis brief, my lord.
HAMLET: As woman's love.

The King and Queen come on and speak.

KING: Full thirty times hath Phoebus' cart gone round
    Neptune's salt wash and Tellus' orbed ground,
    And thirty dozen moons with borrow'd sheen
    About the world have times twelve thirties been
    Since love our hearts and Hymen did our hands
    Unite commutual in most sacred bands.
QUEEN: So many journeys may the sun and moon
    Make us again count o'er ere love be done. . .

In one sense, this is trite stuff, like 'the posy of a ring'. But behind the jingling verse there is an antique idealisation which touches Claudius: this is the paradise he has destroyed. He watches like a child: although some things don't tally – the Player King, unlike old Hamlet, is already 'sick of late', and the murderer is his nephew[11] – he recognises the archetypes for his brother and the woman sitting beside him. It is now obvious what Hamlet is up to: this naive form, carrying its big truths lightly, shows him the most painful image of his transgression.

To Gertrude, it means little enough, since the murder is strange to her.[12] But she is next. The Player Queen says:

In second husband let me be accurst
None wed the second but who killed the first.

It is like a bucket of dirty water thrown at her. Hamlet interrupts to rub home the point – 'Wormwood, wormwood!' – and a chink opens for Claudius. Hamlet is presenting a Queen who either kills her husband or receives his killer's stolen goods – it is an outrage, and a godsent alibi. The court is alienated in a second, and the King has something to be indignant about, a sense of affront masking his real fright. Three lines later the Player Queen says it again:

A second time I kill my husband dead
When second husband kisses me in bed.

11   But Hamlet's sudden casting of himself in the role of the regicide obviously carries its own threat.

12   In fact, there is nothing in the text to say that Gertrude is not complicitous – but because she never confesses and lacks guile, we assume she is innocent.

Claudius should really stop the play now and retreat with dignity, surrounded by his scandalised court. But sympathy may be accumulating for Gertrude and himself: and there could be something to be gained from seeing how far up the leg Hamlet can shoot himself. From the point of view of Claudius's conscience, this turns out to be a mistake. He hears the Player King sound a tocsin:

> What to ourselves in passion we propose
> The passion ending, doth the purpose lose.
> The violence of either grief or joy
> Their own enactures with themselves destroy. . .
> This world is not for aye, nor 'tis not strange
> That even our loves should with our fortunes change;
> For 'tis a question left us yet to prove,
> Whether love lead fortune or else fortune love.

The old Play has developed new power; the impermanence of love, on which Claudius has traded, and which Gertrude has demonstrated, is Claudius's own great fear: what can turn once can turn again.[13] The Player Queen goes on protesting her faith; Hamlet keeps underlining the irony – 'if she should break it now!'. Claudius is as ashamed as he is angry.

Hamlet teases the King and Queen, asking Gertrude her opinion and re-naming the play The Mousetrap (a good laugh in London this last half-century), but doesn't really get a rise from them. The murderer, Lucianus, comes on but Hamlet holds him up by bickering obscenely with Ophelia: Claudius pays out more rope to him (and punishes himself further) by doing nothing, and watches the poison go into the sleeping King's ears. Hamlet yells the message still more offensively:

> He poisons him i' the garden for his estate. . . you shall see anon how the murderer gets the love of Gonzago's wife.

and the King takes action. The text runs:

OPHELIA: The King rises.

---

13 He carries these lines in himself until he re-states them later in language very similar, when describing the decline of love to Laertes:

> . . . I know, love is begun by time,
> And that I see in passages of proof,
> Time qualifies the spark and fire of it.
> There lives within the very flame of love
> A kind of wick or snuff that will abate it. . .

HAMLET: What? Frighted with false fire?
QUEEN: How fares my lord?
POLONIUS: Give o'er the play.
KING: Give me some light: away!
ALL: Lights! Lights! Lights!

We all of us in the theatre wish our trade were a weapon of conscience. If only it were. We generally find (except perhaps in Shakespeare) that its most intent messages can be shrugged off by the people who should attend to them most. Yet we have come to believe that *The Murder of Gonzago* has acted like aversion therapy on Claudius, and productions often have him now run uncontrollably out of the scene, able to endure no more. But in fact, Hamlet's hopes for an unmistakable spasm from him have been so intense (as well as so fearful) that they have infected the audience as well: his and their judgments may be distorted by the desire for proof. Claudius, after all, is a man with the *sang froid* to poison his brother in the middle of the afternoon, take his wife, manoeuvre himself into the succession, and run the state with a high degree of expertise. Calling out for lights may sound like a *cri de coeur*, as if metaphorical darkness was closing in on him (and indeed it is for 'me', not 'us'), but it is also a practical instruction, to deprive the players of theirs and illuminate those moving ahead through dark corridors. Hamlet may choose to believe he is distraught and incompetent; in fact he is righteously infuriated, a good King drawing the line.[14]

---

14 Mikhail Nazvanov (for Kozintsev) ironically applauded Hamlet before he went; Brewster Mason (1965) slapped David Warner's face; I tipped the Players a bag of money to remind them what they were. As a point of interest, when Queen Elizabeth I visited Huntingdonshire on her royal progress in 1564, some Cambridge scholars acted a play for her lampooning the Catholic faith – a dog carried a communion wafer in his mouth, and a bishop chewed on a live lamb. The Queen rose in a fury and demanded lights to follow her, depriving the actors of their visibility. They must have been fearful and startled, having assumed that they were on safe ground attacking a rival faith; but Elizabeth was a shrewder politician than that, holding a difficult *via media*, and so is Claudius. Like those students, Hamlet misreads his victim.

The actors have to agree about all this, and the director may have to be firm. Hamlet is completely dependent for once on what Claudius gives him, which, as in the play itself, may not be what he wants. There is potential for tension in the playing of these two parts, despitethe general desire of actors working together to co-operate. It is really spillage from two strong personalities with different agendas in the play. Mercutio and Romeo can get up each other's noses for similar reasons (youthful friendship under strain) and so can Toby Belch and Andrew Aguecheek (one has a funny name and does all the work, the other has a funny name and gets all the laughs).

Now, gauchely clowning, hysterically convinced of his not-yet-closed case, Hamlet calls for music instead of acting on his 'discovery':

> Come, the recorders!
> For if the King like not the comedy,
> Why then belike he likes it not, perdy.

Cooling down, we watch his exultation in the latter half of the scene with the same thoughtfulness as does his friend Horatio, who cautiously awards him only 'half a share' in a 'a cry of players'; he himself noted the King 'very well', but that is all. The unspoken thought is that Hamlet has botched a potential coup, his first big initiative in the play.[15] Throughout, he has behaved with a characteristic mixture of brilliance and incompetence. Even at the outset, he spoiled his own scathing wit at Gertrude –

> O heavens, die two months ago, and not forgotten yet? Then there's hope a great man's memory may outlive his life half a year. . .

– by talking obsessively dirty to Ophelia ('Lady, shall I lie in your lap?'). Then, his moralising about second marriage was a typical mistake – indeed he always uses his sexual revolt against his mother as an alibi for avoiding the difficult task of avenging his father. By rubbing Gertrude's nose in it all so persistently, he has left his flank vulnerable to Claudius. And at the crucial moment, mistaking shadow for substance, he has willed his own version of events into being, and shown his enemy an exit along the high ground.

Guildenstern shows new authority when he arrives to bring Hamlet to heel – no puns on 'choler' and 'distemper', no more verbal dancing:

> Good my lord, put your discourse into some frame. . . this courtesy is not of the right breed.

If Hamlet will shut up and listen, Guildenstern will give him the message: his mother is very upset and wants to see him before he goes to bed. Rosencrantz is less skilful, clumsily appealing to Hamlet's affection to get an answer which all three know would go straight to the King:

---

15   One of only three, if you add the murder of Polonius and the dispatch of Rosencrantz and Guildenstern to their deaths.

Good my lord, what is your cause of distemper?

– and his blunt weakness gives Hamlet the chance to steady himself. He disposes easily of the question and then hits the top of his form with the recorders (which he has called for either to play some wild tune himself or to listen to), shaming the two of them with a fine improvisation:

> Why, look you now how unworthy a thing you make of me. You would play upon me, you would seem to know my stops, you would pluck out the heart of my mystery, you would sound me from my lowest note to the top of my compass; and there is much music, excellent voice in this little organ, yet cannot you make it speak. 'Sblood, do you think I am easier to be played on than a pipe? [16]

With Polonius he becomes silly again:

> HAMLET: Do you see yonder cloud that's almost in shape of a camel?
> POLONIUS: By the mass and 'tis like a camel indeed.
> HAMLET: Methinks it is like a weasel. . .

In happier times the fooling would be good; but the intent arrival of Rosencrantz, Guildenstern and Polonius give us a sense of events on the move behind Hamlet's back (what is Claudius doing?). Polonius now has no time for Hamlet at all: to him these are 'the pranks [that] have been too broad to bear with'. The court is closing ranks.

We may be becoming impatient as well: his self-esteem high and his credit low, Hamlet is losing crucial moments. He closes the scene with melodramatic rhetoric, now believing himself capable of great things: [17]

> 'Tis now the very witching time of night
> When churchyards yawn and hell itself breathes out
> Contagion to this world. Now could I drink hot blood. . .

---

16 The Players, who obediently bring him the recorders, may be packing up their equipment during all this, preparatory to dropping silently out of the play. They have had the licence of entertainers, just doing their job, but this is a date they must be glad, one way and another, to get away from.

17 It is quite common in practice for him to move into this new purposeful phase by making some identification with the Players – wearing a multi-coloured Player's cloak (me), the Player King's crown (Dillane), a Player's mask (Ralph Fiennes). Such unanimity among actors does suggest something true: that, face to face finally with 'proof' and therefore the need for action, Hamlet retreats, making himself an actor whose deeds are only gestures.

typically finding a role model, Nero this time rather than Pyrrhus, to bolster himself – but inside the pyrotechnics may be insecurity and fear. He has given himself away to Claudius at the moment he hoped Claudius would give himself away to him; his Mousetrap now awaits only his own foot on the trap.

3.3. From here on Hamlet, alone in the cast, is marked to die. Claudius reappears – accelerating, distempered, self-justifying and practical. Like Achilles in *Troilus and Cressida*, his

> . . . mind is troubled like a fountain stirr'd,
> And I myself see not the bottom of it.

Before the Play, worried but unthreatened, he had planned to send Hamlet to England as an ambassador demanding tribute. Now, alarmed by his nephew's knowledge of him, he will send Rosencrantz and Guildenstern as well to keep an eye on him. As he briefs them on the importance of national security, panic threatens to break the surface:

> The terms of our estate may not endure
> Hazard so dangerous as doth hourly grow
> Out of his lunacies

– and Rosencrantz and Guildenstern can smell the fear. There are subtly different meanings lurking inside their dutiful replies. For once, Guildenstern initiates:

> We will ourselves provide.
> Most holy and religious fear it is
> To keep those many many bodies safe
> That live and feed upon your Majesty.

He speaks for the subject, the use of 'holy' and 'religious' emphasising the sacredness of the King's trust. The man and the office should be one; but now there is the possibility that the subject needs protection from the King. Rosencrantz moves in to correct this drift, emphasising the King's indispensability:

> The single and peculiar life is bound
> With all the strength and armour of the mind
> To keep itself from noyance; but much more
> That spirit upon whose weal depends and rests
> The lives of many. . .

He takes Claudius's fears at face value: the monarch must be protected from external danger. However he too has caught the whiff of cravenness in the King, and he goes on to re-state Guildenstern's sentiment, more politely and at greater length: the collapse of kingship, like that of a great wheel, affects 'ten thousand lesser things' and leads to 'boisterous ruin'. The two speeches are anxiously long-winded: they have a braking effect on the action and are often pruned in performance. But they are there for both character and thematic reasons: for the first time, ideas of social instability – a distinction, as in *Macbeth,* between the King's robe and the dwarfish thief within it – are being insinuated through someone other than Hamlet. Rosencrantz and Guildenstern have seen the Play too, and Hamlet has just exposed their invidious position so brilliantly (Guildenstern, significantly, took the brunt in the matter of the recorders) that there may be some small rebellion within them.

Working at full stretch, Claudius rushes apprehensively towards solitude. On his way to the Queen's bedroom, Polonius, the supportive minister, gives him the credit for something he has in fact not done:

> And as you said, and wisely was it said,
> 'Tis meet that some more audience than a mother
> Since nature makes them partial, should o'erhear
> The speech of vantage

– drawing a warmer sentiment than usual from the King:

> Thanks, dear my lord.

Left alone, trying to pray, he finally leaves no doubt:

> O my offence is rank, it smells to heaven;
> It hath the primal eldest curse upon't –
> A brother's murder. . .

and the scene pauses to reassemble itself.

It is characteristic of Shakespeare to use a political trigger to fire an emotional revelation: terror of detection has provoked real remorse in Claudius. But he carries into his confessional the mental habits of the politician, arguing sophistically this way and that:

> What then? What rests?
> Try what repentance can; what can it not?

Yet what can it, when one cannot repent?[18]

and objectifies his sense of damnation with aggrieved paradox:

> O wretched state! O bosom black as death!
> O limed soul, that struggling to be free
> Art more engaged!

This is a sound very different from Hamlet's, the other intellectual in the play and the only other character allowed sustained monologue.[19] Where Hamlet speaks as he thinks, then meditates, turns over and over, Claudius remonstrates, asking ten questions in twenty-six lines, and chalks up five exclamatory vocatives; however, this noisy self-justification, typical of a man used to public address, doesn't water down the flavour of his private anguish. His dilemma is less sympathetic than Hamlet's of course, his self-reproach less candid, his despair less accessible; but there is a typical sensuality in his language, and some profane splendour in his thought:

---

18   First cousin to the silken antitheses of his earlier confident self:

Have we as 'twere with a defeated joy,
With one auspicious and one dropping eye
With mirth in funeral and with dirge in marriage. . .

19   Generally speaking there are two approaches to Shakespearian soliloquy, both depending on character and neither of them absolute. One is to treat it as thought overheard, rather like a voice-over in film: the audience is privileged to spy but is not acknowledged. The other, generally more helpful, is to think of it as a form of dialogue with the spectators, in which, with absolute candour, the speaker advances his understanding of himself and his complicity with them. There are times when this is done with unique audacity by Shakespeare, particularly towards the end of his career: the audience is intimately challenged when Leontes in *The Winter's Tale*, wracked by sexual jealousy, dares us to think him exceptional:

And many a man there is even at this present,
Now, while I speak this, holds his wife by the arm,
That little thinks she has been sluic'd in's absence
And his pond fish'd by his next neighbour, by
Sir Smile, his neighbour. . .

At the other extreme, Prince Hal is not a sharer. At the beginning of *Henry IV Part 1*, we get a glimpse of his attitude to his royal destiny immediately after our first sight of him in the company of Falstaff, an alcoholic thief and scoundrel:

I know you all, and will awhile uphold
The unyok'd humour of your idleness. . .

He addresses not us, but, ruminatively, his companions, and we eavesdrop, feeling excluded by this chilly young man, whom – and this is his strength through to the end of *Henry V* – we will never quite know.

> What if this cursed hand
> Were thicker than itself with brother's blood;
> Is there not rain enough in the sweet heavens
> To wash it white as snow?

He fails to wrestle logic into a bearable shape; and his clearsightedness is quite heroic as he faces the crunch – he cannot give up his crime, so he cannot be forgiven:

> May one be pardon'd, and retain the offence?
> In the corrupted currents of this world
> Offence's gilded hand may shove by justice;
> And oft 'tis seen, the wicked prize itself
> Buys out the law; but 'tis not so above. . .

Nevertheless, he bows his stubborn knees, and Hamlet, coming upon him, sees an obvious opportunity. The play is in the balance: the two men who vitalise it are alone together for the first time, their two consciences exposed. There is in a sense no location for the scene, just a stage on which the play's main point is made, one character locked in debate with the audience, the other oblivious. Predictably, Hamlet's language is more ours, lucid and even humorous:

> A villain kills my father, and for that
> I, his sole son, do this same villain send
> To heaven.
> Why this is hire and salary, not revenge.

The rhythms are spontaneous, not versified, an inevitable pause built into the four silent beats of the short line. As he approaches the critical moment, fear grips him and he blooms into rhetoric:

> He took my father grossly, full of bread,
> With all his crimes broad blown, as flush as May,
> And how his audit stands who knows save heaven

This could be the Ghost speaking, 'unhousel'd, disappointed, unanel'd'.[20] Claudius, Hamlet realises, is going to die shriven, or at least in a penitent posture. The audience holds its breath, Hamlet his; nobody knows the outcome, the spectators, the two men, all

---

20   Hamlet tends to appropriate the language of everyone else in the play, speaking in all their tongues: with the theatrical flourish of the Players, the bluntness of the Gravediggers, in the out-Osricking of Osric. In a sense he is, wonderfully, the whole play in one person, speaking with Shakespeare's own range, while the other characters are held in a singular voice; but he may also be too much of a mimic to be an avenger.

held for a moment on the same edge. The answer to the play's crucial question – can he, will he do it? – is answered by a great line of blank verse:

No.

The audience breathes out with Hamlet, and he justifies himself out of the room, painting his usual picture of Claudius as lecher, drunkard, swearer and gambler – he must die with no more reckoning made than old Hamlet. The audience is disappointed and relieved. By now we are in rhythm with Hamlet and want his fulfilment; we are also glad that he cannot use his sword on a man looking the other way. By the end of the play, this satisfaction will have gone: he becomes able to destroy Rosencrantz and Guildenstern, men as innocent as Claudius is guilty, their backs turned as surely as was old Hamlet's when he slept. But by that time he is even more deeply – and confusingly – in our hearts: profoundly implicated in what he expects of himself, in his failings and fortitude, we have become him. Out of such moral tangles the play's enormous range is constructed.

The scene ends with a joke – Claudius has been unable to pray anyway:

My words fly up, my thoughts remain below;
Words without thoughts never to heaven go.[21]

He is at large again, his every breath dangerous: and Hamlet has scrupled himself into chancery. We sense his father's reproof, which will soon come.

---

21   The last couplet allows an actor who's shrewd at assessing himself to correct his performance. If he's veered to self-pity in the main speech, he can toughen these lines up; if he's been too emphatic they can be simple and direct; if too armoured, he is now vulnerable.
    Claudius's speech is really quite difficult, more so than Hamlet's: the balance between interesting an unsympathetic audience in his dilemma and playing a vulnerable man alone in a room, making terms with his creator, is really hard to catch. However, much depends on it for the actor. While some Shakespearian protagonists – Macbeth, Hamlet, Isabella, Prospero – make a habit of keeping us in the picture, some men of action – Henry V, Claudius – speak to us directly only once. Like Henry's meditation before St Crispin's Day 'Upon the King. . .' Claudius's prayer is a glimpse of the public man's private face. The emotions are tied very tightly to the argument, and a too easy release of grief or terror into the lines makes them self-indulgent and tiresome. Only as the speech gathers for its climax can you loosen the reins and let the horse go, feeling the motion of bones and muscle beneath you: but they have to tighten again for the unexpected simplicity of the final phrase:

All may be well.

3.4. Polonius's obsession with eavesdropping has led him to an appointment in the Queen's bedroom – his final snoop. Long after the King and everyone else has lost interest in discovering the cause of Hamlet's distemper – as opposed to dealing with its effects – Polonius is still using it as an excuse to hide behind curtains and observe encounters between men and women. The Play has duly offended him, and increased his determination: and if there is any turmoil in Claudius as a result of it, Polonius either hasn't noticed or is loyally ignoring it. Also, he knows that this will be his last chance of investigating Hamlet before he is sent away.

What the Queen privately thinks of Polonius barging into her bedroom, telling her what to say and listening to her intimate talk with Hamlet, isn't explicit, any more than is her attitude earlier to the same set-up with Ophelia. Although Hamlet's behaviour has

> struck her into amazement and admiration

she may or may not welcome the chance to confront it. She appears painfully complaisant in the interview, which is the King's and Polonius's idea: unlike Ophelia, she presumably has the power to refuse to be used as a stool-pigeon, but perhaps she will do anything for Claudius, even truly betray her son. She deals with Polonius curtly and complicitly:

> I warrant you, fear me not

and prepares herself for the momentous meeting, its spring wound up by Hamlet's ominous call as he approaches:

> Mother, mother, mother.

Their crackling opening exchange:

> QUEEN: Hamlet, thou hast thy father much offended.
> HAMLET: Mother, you have my father much offended

promises much; till now Hamlet has only spoken so freely in soliloquy, and his tone is utterly uncompromising – she is 'you' now, never 'thou'. Gertrude is really not up to the job – it would be hard to imagine a more tactless opening than to refer to Claudius as Hamlet's father; and within a few lines she is flattened by his tremendous correction:

> You are the Queen, your husband's brother's wife;
> And, would it were not so, you are my mother.

She gives up and calls out for male help:

Nay, then, I'll set those to you that can speak.

Hamlet is so tough in restraining her that she thinks she is in physical danger, and calls out more desperately – maybe to Polonius behind his curtain, maybe to Claudius in his quarters, maybe to the security corps. Polonius is alarmed in a way he wasn't on behalf of Ophelia in these circumstances, and calls out too. Hamlet, hearing the voice and blinded by a vision of the lecherous king hanging around waiting for him to go, murders the wrong man. It is as if he doesn't really care ('Nay, I know not; is it the King?'): after his hesitation over Claudius, he finds he can use his sword easily if he closes his eyes and doesn't have a chance to think. Having acted too little, he now, hunting not a man but 'a rat', acts too fast, and his cherished mission is reduced to its messy ingredients: a tangle of curtains, mistaken identity, something beastly and comic.

Polonius's obsequies are ridiculous: he gets three lines of vale-diction and is then forgotten till the end of the scene. The lines sound terse, but tenderness can be squeezed out of them if the actor wants:

Thou wretched, rash, intruding fool, farewell.
I took thee for thy better. Take thy fortune;
Thou find'st to be too busy is some danger.

Perfunctory or not, this is a point of no return for Hamlet, and the play darkens. We shall miss Polonius as its comedy becomes ever more morbid.

The death in her bedroom knocks the stuffing out of Gertrude, but the effect on Hamlet is of a more subtle and slow-acting kind. For the moment he returns swiftly to his theme, holding up a mirror to Gertrude's 'act'. Their ensuing battle is a great family reckoning conducted over a corpse. Gertrude gets the benefit of Hamlet's most ulcerous rhetoric, moral outrage turned vicious by months of containment: it is a fury that presages Shakespeare's later figures of rage, Timon, Thersites and Lear. His denunciation of her 'deed' – replacing a rose with a blister,[22] a good ear of corn with a mildewed one, divorcing the eye from the heart, sensation

---

22   A typical image in the play – for Ophelia, Hamlet has been 'the expectancy and rose of the fair state'.

from beauty, lechery melting virtue like candle wax – is justified, like Lear's curse on Goneril, Thersites's on warmongers and whoremongers, and Timon's on everyone, only by its splenetic articulacy. It is violently unreasonable: Hamlet has forgotten the Ghost's order not to 'contrive' against his mother, and he now takes for granted that she is mortally guilty:

> A bloody deed? Almost as bad, good mother,
> As kill a king and marry with his brother.

However, that sin is no greater in his eyes than making

> marriage vows
> As false as dicers' oaths.

His rage at her having transferred her favours from a heavenly husband to a king of shreds and patches is so infantile that of course Freud was on to it and productions of the scene now often culminate either in some open sexuality or childish regression in her arms[23]. In fact Hamlet's emotions are commonplace, as long as he is a genuinely young man or has a youngness in him[24] – he articulates every small jealousy known to a reconstructed family. Gertrude, no analyst, immediately smells the animal nature of the attack and responds sensually – she feels the spots of decay in her soul, his words hurt her ears like knives. A really frightening climax

---

23 Sigmund's wings have flapped over several parts of this play, but really *Hamlet*'s promising case-studies are links in a rapid narrative chain, meaningless when isolated. Faced by his mother's actions, Hamlet's brain characteristically teems – his emotions are extreme but not abnormal, being sustained by a genuine, if misplaced, moral drive. Anything physical that develops from them is the product of the extreme tension of events. But, alas, an Oedipal stain has been on the scene ever since Tyrone Guthrie got together with Ernest Jones, a disciple of Freud's and author of an essay called *Hamlet and Oedipus*, over his 1938 production with Alec Guinness. The Oedipus complex is as inappropriate to this play as it is to *Oedipus*: Oedipus sleeps with his mother and kills his father circumstantially, proving only his political sense and a violent temperament.

In fact, the father of psychoanalysis, though a fan, made something of an ass of himself over Shakespeare, casting around all the time for a better candidate for authorship of the plays. After alighting briefly on the notion that Shakespeare's name was a corruption of Jacques Pierre, so that he wasn't an Englishman at all, he settled on the son-in-law of Thomas Burleigh, the Earl of Oxford (a long runner in this game) after reading the case made in a book by a Gateshead schoolteacher with the unfortunate name of Thomas Looney. Obsessed with psychobiography, Sigmund found more direct parallels with Othello, Lear and his three daughters and Hamlet in Oxford's personal life than he could in that of the actor from Stratford, and that was that.

24 Directors casting Hamlet and Gertrude should keep this scene as a touchstone: it is where a Hamlet could badly show his age and Gertrude be too young for him.

is forestalled by the astonishing appearance of the Ghost, and the whole unfortunate family is before us.

The Ghost is dressed differently, 'in his night gowne',[25] no longer an awesome figure stalking spaciously, but close and domestic. In a way, he has been conjured up by Hamlet himself, who has yearningly invoked him with the 'picture' he has shown his mother;[26] typically turning to mythology in his vehemence, he conjured the god from his likeness –

See what a grace was seated on this brow,
Hyperion's curls, the front of Jove himself. . . [27]

– but in the end, it is his father as a human being that is precious. 'He was a man' he told Horatio; now, his picture can 'give the world assurance of a man'. The Ghost is wished into being to complete an idealised group, and he is even, poignantly, dressed for the present moment, a father remembered from childhood at bedtime.

But in the audience's imagination, the Ghost has been imminent since Hamlet failed to take Claudius at prayer. From somewhere, he has watched his son in his antic disposition, in his theatrical experiments, in his mockery of Polonius, in his squandering of opportunity: the young man's knife, so loudly sharpened, is dull. He must be reproved for his 'blunted purpose' and the dead husband must protect the woman that he loved with 'dignity' even if he did not satisfy her.

Gertrude does not see him, this Ghost that everyone else sees (would Claudius, if he were here?) – manifestly, since she would have to be the master of a self-control she does not possess to do so and still feign

---

25   I am taking advantage here of the First Quarto, which is the only text that refers to the Ghost's costume. The one thing this corrupt version can sometimes do is take us straight to what actually happened onstage at the Globe, and this modulation of the Ghost into human terms was obviously what was intended.

26   Macbeth, with a spooky recklessness, does the same thing with the ghost of Banquo, daring the devil at the banquet:

I drink to the general joy of the whole table
And to our dear friend Banquo, whom we miss;
Would he were here!

in *Hamlet*, the invocation is not ominous, but leads to a sort of resolution.

27   David Garrick used two full-size portraits, and so did Stephen Dillane; Gielgud and most others a medallion on a chain around the neck.

how is't with you
That you do bend your eye on vacancy. . . [28]

This is partly a subtlety of Shakespeare's – Gertrude has simply wiped old Hamlet out, forgetful of his body and spirit, and for that reason is blind to him now – and partly a stage expediency: he does not plan a lengthy discussion of the Ghost after he has left, but he does want Gertrude to be convinced of Hamlet's derangement. Once again, the father is in sorrow as much as anger. 'Remember me' he called as he left the battlements; 'Do not forget' he demands now. On the battlements he treated Hamlet with 'courteous action'; now it is with 'piteous action'. In what he says, his dual role as independent visitant and as Hamlet's subconscious creation come together: the two lines of reproof to Hamlet and the four of protectiveness to Gertrude are at once good fatherly advice and the sound of Hamlet's own conscience:

Do not forget; this visitation
Is but to whet thy almost blunted purpose.
But look, amazement on thy mother sits;
O step between her and her fighting soul.
Conceit in weakest bodies strongest works.
Speak to her, Hamlet.

From now on, disarmed, Hamlet does so: from the Ghost's departure 'out at the portal', the air between son and mother fills with grief and openness and the possibility of reunion. Gertrude becomes 'mother' or even 'good lady'. Although there are still bursts of reproach, there is fatigue in them, and they alternate with gentler tones:

Confess yourself to heaven;
Repent what's past; avoid what is to come;
And do not spread the compost on the weeds
To make them ranker. Forgive me this my virtue. . .

Hamlet briefly repents of Polonius's death; twice he bids her goodnight and then returns to beg her to keep away from Claudius:

---

28 It happens that in both versions of this scene I have been in there has been brinkmanship; in 1980 at Stratford Gertrude almost – almost! – saw the Ghost: I grabbed her head and forced her to look 'On him, on him. . . why, look you there!' – and then rejected the knowledge, just as she rejects all her other instinctive knowledge in the play. Playing the Ghost in 1994 I tried blindly to reach Gertrude, to within a few inches of her hand, until she recoiled as if at an electric shock. Excluded like Victor Frankenstein's monster and not understanding it, the Ghost gave up and left the play for good.

but in his tormented imaginings, he no longer thinks of her as the hungry initiator, but only someone who may passively

> Let the bloat King tempt you again to bed,
> Pinch wanton on your cheek, call you his mouse. . .

By appearing in the heart of his family, the Ghost has had the mediating effect of a father, causing Hamlet to treat his mother like a human being and Gertrude to respect her gifted, adult son.

The scene now unspools rather loosely, risking a loss of pace but allowing time for its gradual reconciliation. The first necessity for that is passionate honesty, and Hamlet, determined to disabuse his mother, gives her his main secret:

> Ecstasy!
> My pulse as yours doth temperately keep time,
> And makes as healthful music.

So does his verse, which falls into the rhythm of a steady heart-beat, with a grave, articulate splendour. But its steady surface nurses a paradox: a man who has insisted he is mad now sets himself the task of proving his sanity. Really, Hamlet is in a bleak twilight where the terms lose their meaning – for someone in such complete tribulation, madness is neither here nor there – and he and his invented identity have become one. He shuttles between the body he has mistakenly killed and his wayward mother,[29] the twin poles of his misfortunes, regretting and re-regretting the death, returning obsessively to her sexuality; it is like his hell, but at the same time his safety, for as soon as he leaves the security of his mother's room – and in this sense at last there is something Oedipal in it all – the dead body will become a crime to be answered for in a most unforgiving court.

For all his musicality, something is out of true in Hamlet. His hints at subverting Rosencrantz and Guildenstern (whom he thinks of unfairly as 'adders fang'd') on their journey to England are crafty and paranoid:

> . . . I will delve one yard below their mines
> And blow them at the moon: O, 'tis most sweet
> When in one line two crafts directly meet.[30]

29 He bids her goodnight five times, only finally with Polonius's body in tow.

30 Actually, this is based on information he doesn't have yet, the journey to England.

Losing proportion, he mythologises himself: the terse balance of

> The time is out of joint: O cursed spite,
> That ever I was born to set it right

now becomes, grandiosely:

> Heaven hath pleas'd it so.
> To punish me with this, and this with me,
> That I must be their scourge and minister.

The tone may be lucid, but the thought – the plural 'their' hinting at the randomness of heathen gods – is hubristic; Hamlet's self-awareness has become confused by the rhetoric of theatre.

For the principal player, the Closet Scene is the latest episode in a remorseless sequence and a big stress point, coming at a time when he may be tired and still some way from a break. Much in the performance crystallises here, and a careful balance needs to be kept between black comedy and heroic emotion. A kind of existential flipness is opening out in Hamlet:

> I'll lug the guts into the neighbour room

and it is tempting to make comic capital out of it. The danger is that it can turn into facetiousness. Just as he dares his friends to laugh in the face of death (the funeral baked meats and the marriage tables) Hamlet is now drawing the audience into his own moral vertigo by means of sinister burlesque. Calculated bathos is attractive to actors – in the classics it's a way to modernise; but be careful, be sparing.

From Gertrude's point of view, the Closet is the main point of the part. It is her only sustained scene, and she describes an arc from outrage through physical fright to horror at the murder to a giddy place where her assumptions about Hamlet's condition are all thrown up in the air. He holds her up a glass that she will no longer be able to look away from, and her brief responses in the later stages become ever simpler and more touching:

> O Hamlet, thou hast cleft my heart in twain. . .
> What shall I do?. . . Alack,
> I had forgot: 'tis so concluded on.

Shakespeare cut these lines between the Quarto and the Folio – perhaps for this reason, or perhaps because the scene had become very long. In the process, the famous tag ''Tis the sport to have the engineeer Hoist with his own petard' went down the drain.

Like Ophelia, she has to fight for the chance to speak; but she is quietly being prepared for a major change of sensibility in the second half of the play, when everything about her may be different: her speech, her sense of others, perhaps her clothes.

For the audience too, the scene is a great purge in which the play's primal emotions are at last let go at considerable length, like a wound that suddenly just keeps flowing. The talk is often scabrously intimate, but it is all in the service of expiatory emotion, not alienation or reductiveness. The final effect is brutal catharsis, and a new bond between mother and son now excludes the King – although in fact Hamlet and Gertrude exchange no further word until their two brief contacts in the Duel Scene. We can see that the devastated mother now longs for a consolidation of her son's love; but no sooner is he gone than she has to deal with Claudius, demanding an explanation.

4.1. Despite the scene division, the meeting of the Queen and King (at first accompanied by Rosencrantz and Guildenstern) is a direct continuation of the Closet. As between movements in music, there is only a pause, to prevent the departing Hamlet meeting the arriving Claudius, so that Claudius witnesses only Gertrude's 'sighs', her 'profound heaves'. It is unusual – one might have expected a brief bridging soliloquy from Gertrude – but perhaps her wordlessness is as eloquent. The Elizabethan stage dealt easily with this traffic jam (opposite entrances), and in any case tolerated imprecision of place, whereas we who worry about location ask why Rosencrantz and Guildenstern enter the Queen's private quarters. Perhaps we can justify it with the thought that Claudius now views everything to do with Hamlet as a police matter, not a family crisis.

With the two inadequate spies dispatched, Claudius and Gertrude are briefly alone – but again under the pressure of events. Claudius needs to know the outcome of Gertrude's interview with Hamlet, and may be puzzled at Polonius's absence; Gertrude has a fast decision to make about how to represent Hamlet to her husband[31] and the news of Polonius to break, which she does first. Her account of his death is true as far as it goes; what she leaves

---

31   She declares in the Bad Quarto:

But then he throws and tosses me about
As one forgetting that I was his mother. . .

out is what she learned afterwards – that her son, mad in craft only, can speak lucidly about her circumstances and his. So she tells Claudius that Hamlet is

> Mad as the sea and wind, when both contend
> Which is the mightier.

The contrast between her language and the King's shows the fissure opening between them. Claudius's reply:

> It had been so with us, had we been there

seems to say everything about him – relief at his narrow escape, apparently no sorrow for Polonius, just its surrogate, righteous anger with Hamlet. He immediately moves on to how he is to contain the catastrophe:

> Alas, how shall this bloody deed be answered?

It will take all his 'majesty and skill'. The only human note he strikes:

> so much was our love
> We would not understand what was most fit. . .

is ambiguous – he bears Hamlet no real love, and if this is his love for Gertrude, he is implying that it has softened his political judgment. Her description of her son's state meanwhile, as later at Ophelia's funeral, has a poetic quality declaring her new involvement with him: she even romanticises the action of dragging a corpse around, attributing a grief to him we haven't really seen:

> his very madness, like some ore
> Among a mineral of metals base,
> Shows itself pure; 'a weeps for what is done.

Claudius will have none of it: to him Hamlet, who previously only 'put[s] on this distemper', is now 'this mad young man'. Rosencrantz and Guildenstern, called back and put onto the case, do not even get a chance to speak: the priority is to get moving, to surround the King with his 'wisest friends' and stave off public criticism, which must instead 'hit the woundless air'.

Thirty-odd lines is all the royal lovers have; but it is enough to show where they are going. Obviously, their loyalties are diverging: but I think it is a mistake to play too deep a split, as if they were now simply a mother caring for her son and a ruthless politician trying to destroy him. Gertrude has not stopped wanting Claudius

– he is still 'mine own lord' – and she mourns her son's victim; Claudius loves Gertrude but has no time to indulge himself or properly to mourn Polonius, which in fact he might care to. The texture of the scene lies in between the hectic lines, the division between the two implied by Gertrude's deepening silence: but it is provisional, and could be reversed. They might be physically close, or separate, or something of both: they could leave the scene together or apart. It depends what you want to emphasise.

4.2. Everything about Polonius's death is demeaning, huggermugger. A man whose charm was tainted by voyeurism, distrust and mean little ploys has been destroyed in a humiliating tangle and stuffed into a corner by Hamlet – the sense is no longer of a royal palace but of some understairs in a dark Elizabethan house. After a life of *amour-propre*, of status if not exactly dignity, he will eventually be buried with no ceremony at all: now that the play has reached a stage of real action, one *reductio ad absurdum* of human life will follow after another.

Hamlet presides over the nocturnal hide-and-seek leading to his arrest with an uncanny philosophical calm, like a solemn jester in a feast of fools:[32]

What noise? Who calls on Hamlet? O, here they come.

He deliberates the urgent questioning of Rosencrantz and Guildenstern (they have orders to 'speak him fair') with intellectual pause:

ROSENCRANTZ: What have you done, my lord, with the dead body?
HAMLET: Compounded it with dust, whereto 'tis kin.
ROSENCRANTZ: Tell us where 'tis, that we may take it thence,
   And bear it to the chapel.
HAMLET: Do not believe it.

Then he devastates Rosencrantz (as he earlier did Guildenstern with the recorders) with the brilliant conceit of the 'sponge. . . that soaks up the king's countenance, his rewards, his authorities': he lives in the King's cheek, and when his information is squeezed, there is nothing substantial left of him. It is the sort of joke that makes final enemies. Rosencrantz claims not to understand, but he

---

32 Some physical image for his strange mood is invited: Mark Rylance washed his bloody clothes in a bucket; Stephen Dillane took off all his except a prop crown (even braver in the rehearsal room than on the stage – I remember Rosencrantz's and Guildenstern's faces well); Innokenti Smoktunovsky lay calmly on a bronze statue, feigning sleep.

understands very well, and the two men – only agents in all this, behaving as decently as they can – must hate Hamlet now for his injustice, as he hates them for what he calls their betrayal.

4.3. The tremendous sense of energy and movement following the digressiveness of the Closet continues as Claudius rushes forward. He is surrounded by his 'wisest friends', and he chases out of the air the ambiguities that Hamlet has loaded into his obscurely threatening

> The body is with the King, but the King is not with the body. The King is a thing. . .

Claudius replaces this with the real world of facts:

> I have sent to seek him, and to find the body.

He is reorganising the journey to England as a decoy for Hamlet's assassination. His nephew is now a disease 'desperate grown', an unextenuated danger. Armed with a new pretext, the murder of the Prime Minister, he has a tough justification ready: Hamlet is too attractive to the 'distracted multitude', so easily swayed by appearances and only too willing to blame the poor responsible agent of justice and to 'forgive the offence'. It must look as if the decision for exile has been reached after 'deliberate pause', though in reality the situation is in need of 'desperate appliance'. The attractive option of capital punishment – 'the strong law' – is a vote-loser. This is the unmistakable voice of a politician confidential with other politicians, a leader flattering his court – for whom too a void has been left by Polonius's death – with his confidences. The contempt for the public, the strategic timing, the question of presentation: you can see them every day in Westminster.

Hinted at in his earlier scene with Gertrude, concern for public opinion is oppressing Claudius; and it comes as a surprise in a play with so little reference to the Third Estate. Present as crowds in the Roman plays and proportionally represented in the Histories, it is absent from the stage in *Hamlet* apart from a group of Players, two Gravediggers and Laertes's small army. But from this point forward, Claudius is increasingly troubled by it – he discusses it again, with Gertrude, as he contemplates the madness of Ophelia and Laertes's rebellion; and Hamlet's popularity plays a large part of his argument as he entraps Laertes. He senses that even in his absence Hamlet is gaining public initiatives he can only respond to, not control.

This battle for endorsement between Hamlet and the King becomes, in a magical sense, a battle for the audience too. The more brilliant and subversive Hamlet is, the more attractive he is to the customers; the more Claudius's agonised skill is on show, the more perversely admirable he is. In dramatising political arguments, Shakespeare implicates his audience by setting up tournaments between the actors. No sooner has Hamlet pulled his fine trick on Rosencrantz and Guildenstern and started a crazy chase – 'Hide, fox, and all after' – Claudius appears and rebukes the audience's enjoyment:

> He's lov'd of the distracted *multitude*
> Who like not in their *judgment* but their *eyes*. . .

When he arrives, Hamlet is the more entertaining:

CLAUDIUS: Now, Hamlet, where's Polonius?
HAMLET: At supper.
CLAUDIUS: At supper? Where?
HAMLET: Not where he eats, but where he is eaten. A certain
    convocation of politic worms are e'en at him.

Claudius seems slow and obtuse next to such morbid inventive-ness: like all the sane people in the play, he is bemused by Hamlet's eccentrically racing mind:

HAMLET: A man may fish with the worm that hath eat of a king, and eat
    of the fish that hath fed of that worm.
KING: What dost thou mean by this?
HAMLET: Nothing, but to show you how a king may go a progress
    through the guts of a beggar.

On the other hand, Claudius has for once a certain right on his side and Hamlet at his mercy: he is to be shipped to England as a mur-derer, and the letters arranging for his death are on their way to the English King. So, from a position of strength, he can let Hamlet pirouette. He does need one piece of information – the where-abouts of the body – and after three insistences he gets the blunt reality:

> You shall nose him as you go up the stairs into the lobby.

Who finally wins this showdown between two men with little to choose morally between them (both have killed one man)? It is a spectator sport, and the answer to some extent depends on your age. Hamlet is a young man's hero and a young woman's desire – he has the nerve to stand up to his step-parent, indeed the whole establishment, and say brilliantly what we in his place can only do rudely and badtemperedly: this is a righteous brat, cathartically knocking the King for six. On the other hand, if you've made the mistakes of the middle-aged, and been at the receiving end of the intolerant moral idealism of the young, Claudius may be your man.

Claudius makes a correct speech that neither of them believes for an instant, explaining the benefits of banishment to Hamlet:

> Hamlet, this deed, for thine especial safety,
> Which we do tender, as we dearly grieve
> For that which thou hast done, must send thee hence
> With fiery quickness. . . .

and then seems to make an odd mistake:

HAMLET: For England?
KING: Ay, Hamlet.
HAMLET: Good.
KING: So is it, if thou knew'st our purposes.

Perhaps he no longer cares that Hamlet can guess how sinister his purposes are:

HAMLET: I see a cherub that sees them.

With a final flick ('Farewell, dear mother') that makes inter-changeable sexual puppets of Claudius and Gertrude, and perhaps planting a kiss, Hamlet is off, and that is the last they will see of each other chin to chin until Hamlet turns to Claudius with a poisoned sword.

Claudius's closing soliloquy includes an arcane reference – the English 'cicatrice' is 'raw and red' only if we are now not in the Renaissance but back in the tenth century, when Denmark extracted danegeld from King Ethelred the Unready as an insurance against further attacks. It climaxes in a *cri de coeur:*

> Do it, England!
> For like the hectic in my blood he rages,
> And thou must cure me.

Rationally, Claudius no longer has anything to fear: he is surely now shot of the man. But Hamlet's is the face he will meet in his worst dreams till confirmation comes back from England. He doesn't yet know that sorrows never come single-spied, that Ophelia's madness and Laertes's rebellion are lying in wait for him.

4.4. Suddenly, a key change and the world outside Elsinore invades the play for the first time. Even if a theatre designer cannot achieve the cold shore of the Skaggerak, a thousand men tramping through mud and Hamlet confronted by the unpitying sea, it's to be hoped he can open the stage out to the back and sides and pour white light onto it from lamps unused till now (but useful soon for the Graveyard as well). The staging of the scene presents another problem in these days of reduced casts. Hamlet's dispatch to England under guard calls for a body of attendants; twelve lines later we need an army for Fortinbras. The quick change whereby one can become the other is a shocker, clattering away behind the King's monologue about England; yet separately, you can hardly afford more than half a dozen people for each purpose.

At the crest of the scene stands a new character, dominating it though he says little: indeed Fortinbras has hovered over earlier parts of the play without appearing at all. There is a connection between him and the rattled tyrant we have just seen leave the stage: the two are enemies under restraint, and Fortinbras's first words form a diplomatic message to the King of Denmark. Claudius has packed Rosencrantz and Guildenstern off after Hamlet with the prolixity of the insecure:

> Follow him at foot, tempt him with speed aboard;
> Delay it not; I'll have him hence tonight;
> Away, for everything is seal'd and done
> That else leans on the affair; pray you, make haste. . .

– but on the Danish borders Fortinbras is circumspect and courteous, presenting his respects with the ring of quiet control:

> Go, captain, from me greet the Danish King. . .
> If that his majesty will aught with us
> We shall express our duty in his eye
> And let him know so. . .
> Go softly on.

In personal authority, Claudius is simply not to the manner born compared with the younger man.

This appearance of one of Shakespeare's important small parts in order to star in one of the hero's most searching soliloquies is a favourite among *Hamlet*-fanciers. This is only partly because it is likely to precede an interval, either the second of two or a long-delayed single one (in which case, audience and company will have been working for anything between one-and-a-half and two-and-a-half hours, depending on the cuts, and the strain on muscle and gland is undeniable). Amazingly enough, there is evidence that Shakespeare underrated his own work here. Both in the Bad Quarto and the supposedly definitive Folio, the scene is a mere eight lines long: Fortinbras dispatches his Captain to greet Claudius, the army passes by, and Hamlet, Rosencrantz and Guildenstern never come on at all. This leaves out everything that is of interest to us, which was perhaps written for some revival, published in the Second Quarto, and then cut again. Thank goodness it has survived; but a dizzying distance opens up between ourselves and Shakespeare. What was the point of the shorter version? Processional and factual presumably, to show that Fortinbras has arrived: within twenty seconds or so the play moves from Claudius's dispatch of Hamlet to Ophelia's Mad Scene. This makes Elsinore more important than Hamlet, but at the cost of removing what for many people now is a central image. A self-confident and untrammeled man of action, Fortinbras stands in fierce opposition not only to Claudius but to Hamlet as well, at the point of his most morally complex and ambiguous circumstance.

There is a fascinating small encounter between Hamlet and Fortinbras's Captain, an independently-minded man who allows his guard to drop for a moment to a stranger (he addresses Hamlet only as 'sir', as Hamlet does him, so presumably he does not recognise the Prince). He lets out a characteristic soldier's complaint about the campaign:

> CAPTAIN: Truly to speak, and with no addition,
>   We go to gain a little patch of ground
>   That hath in it no profit but the name;
>   To pay five ducats, five, I would not farm it. . .
> HAMLET: Two thousand souls and twenty thousand ducats
>   Will not debate the question of this straw.

Fortinbras's invasion of Poland is utterly pointless; every greedy border war since 1600 stands condemned in four brilliant lines.

Astonished, Hamlet turns to us: much has happened since he last did so. How All Occasions Do Inform Against Me is the least-known and perhaps the best of Hamlet's monologues. The anarchy of Rogue And Peasant Slave has been chiselled down to a fine blade of self-reproach. The contrast between man who has 'capability and god-like reason' and man-as-beast, the 'market of whose time' is 'but to sleep and feed', is much more refined than in the disgusted turbulence of O That This Too Too Solid Flesh Would Melt, where a beast was simply one 'that wants discourse of reason'. The speech is less enigmatic and more personal than To Be Or Not to Be. The monosyllabic, self-inflicted hammer blows at its centre:

> I do not know
> Why yet I live to say 'This thing's to do',
> Sith I have cause, and will, and strength, and means
> To do't

form a climax in the part, absolutely concentrating the man's problem. There is a new lucidity in Hamlet, undeceived, no longer intellectually evasive, that anticipates the simplicity of the end of the play, by which time he will at last give a straight answer to almost any straight question. However, bad dreams are not shaken off so easily. In the second part of the speech lurks a self-negating irony, since Fortinbras is being simultaneously admired for his brutal decisiveness and criticised for risking twenty thousand lives for an 'eggshell', a plot too small to bury them in. Finally, Hamlet wills himself out of rationality and into the imagined avenger's role, which also embraces the fascism of Fortinbras, the player hero. He asserts forward movement:

> O from this time forth
> My thoughts be bloody, or be nothing worth!

at the very moment he is carried away from us, lacking opportunity, knowing less than we do of his destination: purposeful and determined, he has his back to us, receding.

The great middle arc of the play's third day has been the most taxing for Hamlet, the action moving in rhythm with his own precipitate, unstable organisation of events. He has been through a tunnel in which success lies side by side with defeat; where violent impulses have been checked by deep introspections; where the supernatural has modulated the real world, and where all emotional and rational certainties have been rocked. He has unexpectedly achieved a rapprochement with Gertrude which will save both their souls but hasten their deaths; at the same moment a murder committed by accident has put him outside his own moral framework for good and all. It has been the hour when the part has shaken the actor like a rat, throwing him from one crisis to the next with scarcely time to draw breath; and at the end of it he is washed up on the chilly plateau of his bleakest soliloquy, looking out from the bleak borders of the country in the bleak hours of dawn.

In watching him, we have travelled far as well. Each scene has had an apparent but also a hidden shape, each has contained a surprising reversal, and each has set sympathy and judgment at odds in relation to Hamlet. It is typical of our dealings with this character, as with Lear and Othello, that empathy often collides with moral shock: the articulation of To Be Or Not To Be has been followed by lousy behaviour to Ophelia; the Play Scene he thought was a triumph, but led to nothing except, by one step, his own extinction; the Prayer Scene aroused some sympathy for Claudius and acknowledged Hamlet's weakness; and the Closet was akin to the Nunnery in its signal disrespect for female choice. Hamlet surprised us in the second day by allowing himself to be a passive agent of events; now he has achieved a frenetic sense of purpose, and our apprehension of him has become complicated. We have encountered an unnerving second hero in Fortinbras: the play is becoming heavy with the absence of the third, Laertes. An 'imposthume' is gathering, inwardly ready to break, in the play as well as in Poland. Time for another break.

THE ACTION: DAY FOUR

Act 4 Scene 5 – Act 4 Scene 7

4.5. Denmark without Hamlet. He has so effectively burned up the play's oxygen that the vacuum might seem uninhabitable, but Shakespeare now provides two inspired scenes of virtuosity, adventure and political cunning, calling on Ophelia, Laertes, Gertrude and Claudius to carry them. The temptation to edit these down and accelerate towards the return of the interesting protagonist is understandable, since it may be getting on for half past ten when we first see Ophelia mad and eleven before Hamlet returns: but you lose a lot.

The virtuosity lies mainly in Ophelia's madness, a vision so compelling that it rates with Yorick's skull and To Be Or Not To Be in the iconography of the play. It has been played this way and that: we assume that an earlier age favoured the lyrically wet and floral, now we often see a raucous sexuality and Turette's Syndrome. Either way (or preferably neither), just as the Closet Scene entices Gertrudes, the Mad Scene is the only reason any actress wants to play Ophelia.

However, the virtuoso scene in Shakespeare is always a *trompe l'oeil* – politics invariably lurk behind it, aimed into the play and, sometimes, boldly lobbed outwards from it. As Lear's wits begin to turn in his great scene on the heath, he delivers a social critique which flew provocatively out to Shakespeare's audience, many of whom were very poor; and in 1994 Robert Stephens opened at the Barbican on the day that John Major condemned London's street beggars as unacceptable eyesores, scoring a bullseye with:

Poor naked wretches, wheresoe'er you are
That bide the pelting of this pitiless storm,

How shall your houseless heads and unfed sides,
Your loop'd and window'd raggedness, defend you
From seasons such as these?. . . . Take physic, pomp,
Expose thyself to feel what wretches feel. . . [1]

The device of a holy fool, stripped of normal restraint by suffering and speaking the uncomfortable truth, operates in Ophelia as well, although its effect is confined within the limits of the play: her madness has a narrative meaning, and its subject is Claudius's court. Her appearance is carefully set up: Horatio, who now seems to be someone that royalty listens to, warns Gertrude of the subversive effect of her 'half-sense':

> . . . she may strew
Dangerous conjectures in ill-breeding minds

– and the Gentleman (a figure who seems to have taken over some of Polonius's influence) elaborates the warning:

> Her speech is nothing;
Yet the unshaped use of it doth move
The hearers to collection. They aim at it . . .

So Ophelia is better confined inside the palace than out of it and available to the public.

Gertrude is frightened to see her – her son killed the girl's father in her bedroom, and she has had enough of madness – but realises she must. Everything to Gertrude is ominous now: undeceived, she speaks, for the first time, to the audience. Her candour is disarming, and oddly rephrases Hamlet's earlier hopes that Claudius would suddenly break out at the Play:

> So full of artless jealousy is guilt
It spills itself in fearing to be spilt.

She is then confronted, as if she had been overheard, by the ambiguous Ophelia, asking her where her state of grace has gone:

> Where is the beauteous majesty of Denmark?

This is not just a means of getting Ophelia onstage, but a line to hit

---

1 Conservatives sometimes smell a kindred spirit in Shakespeare and they will try to hijack him. But he blows up in their hands: he is an instinctive egalitarian working under political censorship, and many of his great moments carry a subversive code – they are there throughout *Henry V*, for instance. The Prince of Wales may nowadays urge children towards Shakespeare; but if they overshoot a bit they could end up in the arms of Marx.

Gertrude between the eyes – it asks, simultaneously, Where is beauty? Where is true regality? Where is old Hamlet? Where is his son? If this is madness there is withering method in it, and now she pulls on the same string with a song:

> How should I your true love know
> From another one?

The old King was Gertrude's true love: was there no difference between him and 'another one' – Claudius? Ophelia goes on to picture the dead man as a pilgrim piously going to a holy shrine:[2] she knows him

> By his cockle hat and staff
> And his sandal shoon

– and to sing about a death which is both her father's and Gertrude's better husband's:

> He is dead and gone, lady,
> He is dead and gone.
> At his head a grass-green turf
> At his heels a stone.

Gertrude has seen something like this: in *The Murder of Gonzago*, the King lay down upon a bank of flowers and soon lay dead on it.

So Gertrude is the 'lady' of the song, and its references rattle in her brain: and this is not a girl singing vaguely to the dress circle, but a pitiless vision identifying its own losses with the Queen's. Appropriately, the King now takes the brunt – whether he arrives by chance or forewarning is not clear, but for him it is a vexing new crisis. Ophelia disarms him with a reference to the odd folk-tale that Christ once turned a baker's daughter into an owl for giving him too small a loaf of bread: and then she goes straight for him with the very distinction between being and seeming with which Hamlet taunted Gertrude at the outset, and with which Claudius, his harlot's cheek beautied with plastering art, has punished himself:

> Lord, we know what we are, but know not what we may be.

This nothing's more than matter: Claudius can only deflect it with 'Conceit upon her father' (which it isn't). He means this as an

---

2 Specifically of St James of Compostela in Spain, whose pilgrims wore a cockle shell on their hats.

aside, but the afflicted girl's hearing is preternaturally acute, and she catches him:

> Pray you, let's have no words of this.

Then she is at him again, smelling him as a sexual being (under the story of the baker's daughter lurks the tradition that they were whores) and singing a song about the loss of maidenheads:

> Tomorrow is Saint Valentine's Day. . .

– four insistent verses of it, punctuated by Claudius's vain attempt to bring her back to her innocent self:

> Pretty Ophelia. . . .

Her refrain of male sexual duplicity is obvious, and implicates both Hamlet and, in some way, Claudius. Preparing to take her out of the scene, Shakespeare suddenly gives her back her grace with the most simple and affecting line she has, devastating after the knowingness that preceded it:

> I cannot choose but weep to think they would lay him in the cold
> ground.

She issues an ominous warning:

> My brother shall know of it

calls everyone 'ladies' (a distant echo of Hamlet addressing Claudius as his mother) and leaves, so far as we know for good.

Thirty lines later, a messenger is warning that Laertes is at the doors. If he arrived sooner, Ophelia's second-sighting of him and his being there on cue would be hard to accept: but time is elasticated by Claudius's review of his circumstances, which interweaves personal anxiety with political alarm:

> O Gertrude, Gertrude! . . .
> Next, your son gone, and he most violent author
> Of his own just remove; the people muddied,
> Thick and unwholesome in their thoughts and whispers
> For good Polonius' death; and we have done but greenly
> In hugger-mugger to inter him. . .

The protest is characteristically evasive, with the self-pity of the overstressed manager, and it rewrites material elements. He insists that Ophelia's madness is all to do with the death of Polonius, omitting the matter of Hamlet's banishment; in his view the people are discontented only because of his mistake in burying Polonius secretly; and in declaring that Ophelia has become one of the 'mere beasts', he naturally ignores the meaning of what she has had to say. Somewhere, he is conscious of losing his grip, and, at the same rate, of losing Gertrude, and he appeals to her:

> O my dear Gertrude, this,
> Like to a murdering-piece, in many places
> Gives me superfluous death.

She says not a word.

The messenger reproduces the clamour at the doors for Claudius – 'Laertes. . . King! Laertes. . . King! Laertes King!' – Gertrude, surprisingly, condemns the revolutionaries as 'Danish dogs!' (where is she from?) and then Claudius, abandoned by his Swiss mercenaries, has a sword at his throat:

LAERTES: O thou vile King,
    Give me my father

and Laertes's boorish rhetoric – himself a bastard, his mother a harlot, his father a cuckold – in his ears. He sees that Laertes is under-informed – it is Hamlet he should be after – and unstable; this gives him the strength to abandon the whining tone he has allowed himself with his wife and to match a bully who needs bullying in his best style:

> What is the cause, Laertes,
> That thy rebellion looks so giant-like?

When Gertrude panics, Claudius, daring damnation more than Laertes, makes the breathtaking claim that as King he is safely hedged by 'divinity' – he who has poisoned a King.

It is always the extreme situation that brings out the best of Claudius's nerve: the mundane matters, like safe passage for Fortinbras and foreseeing public reaction, he tends to butterfinger. His man-management here is as impressive as his courage: knowing that euphemisms are likely to inflame a swordsman, he calls a spade a spade:

LAERTES: Where is my father?
KING: Dead.
QUEEN: But not by him.
KING: Let him demand his fill.

Laertes, though dangerous, is exclamatory and blind, really no match for him: and when Claudius has the chance to express an authentic emotion:

> . . . I am guiltless of your father's death
> And am most sensibly in grief for it. . .

he has nearly won him. Ophelia's unexpected return is probably not welcome, but in fact it plays into his hands: she deflates her brother's violence but deepens his sense of wrong, so that he becomes a force that Claudius can easily aim at Hamlet.

In performance, the actor playing Laertes has the worst of all this, being asked an impossible split-second reaction to his sister's madness, before she can say or do anything:

> O heat, dry up my brains! Tears seven times salt
> Burn out the sense and virtue of mine eye. . .

– it is actually incredible, a horrible burden which becomes heavier as he blandly generalises:

> Nature is fine in love, and where 'tis fine
> It sends some precious instance of itself
> After the thing it loves. . . .
> A document in madness: thoughts and remembrance fitted.[3]

However, Laertes does say something important to his colleague playing Ophelia:

> Thought and affliction, passion, hell itself
> She turns to favour and to prettiness

– so she must, within reason, suit her action to his word, which some Ophelias, bent on frenzy, may not want to do. Mania is a small part of her madness only: faced with too much of it, Laertes's lines become silly and Claudius and Gertrude might react with fear or disgust, not pity.

Ophelia continues her excoriation of the world around her in a most disarming disguise: that of a harmless idiot handing out flowers.[4] Her 'document in madness' is rich in folklore and the

---

3   It is like Edgar in *Lear* on seeing his blinded father:

> And worse I may be yet; the worst is not,
> So long as we can say 'This is the worst'.

Yes: it stinks.

4   The Bad Quarto gives her the line 'I a bin gathering of flowers'.

natural world, as fresh as a wild English garden; it is also heavily coded. Her line:

It is the false steward that stole his master's daughter. . .

(which, unlike much of what she says, has no folkloric origin) carries implicit meaning for Claudius and Gertrude. She gives out rosemary, which is for remembrance, including of the dead;[5] fennel, which is for flatterers; columbines, which are for infidelity; rue, which is for regret and repentance – since Claudius's regret is not the same as hers, he must wear his rue 'with a difference' – and the daisy, for dissembling. Her references seem criss-crossed and disarranged, but they are not accidental.

In this second appearance, her images of death become bleaker – 'they bore him bare-faced on the bier. . . and on his grave rained many a tear' – and they are disconcertingly crossed with jolliness – 'Hey non nonny, nonny, hey nonny. . . you must sing "A-down, a-down".' She forms the beautiful conceit that at the moment of her father's death the faithful violets instantly died, and insists on a brave untruth:

They say he made a good end.

There is nothing at all deranged about the simple lament with which she resolves everything:

And will 'a not come again?
Will 'a not come again?
No, no he is dead,
Go to thy death-bed,
He never will come again. . .

– its finality is hers. She leaves her brother winded, an easy prey to Claudius's intelligence, and goes out of the play with an undeceived vision of the world around her – the last thing we expected of this submissive, timid girl – and no further means of living in it.

4.6. The short scene between Horatio (whose irresistible rise has brought him a 'servant' who asks permission to bring visitors in)

---

5 'I let rosemary run all over my garden walls, not only becase my bees love it but because it is the herb sacred to remembrance and to friendship, whence a sprig of it hath a dumb language.' – Sir Thomas More (1478-1535).

and the sailors who deliver Hamlet's letters is of course a mechanism. It brings Hamlet back into the edge of the picture, and allows Claudius and Laertes to cover some ground before the following scene – we will not have to listen to Claudius explaining events that we already know. The link has a haphazard, semi-improvised air, but there is a deal of information to be precisely conveyed.

The Bad Quarto is particularly wild at this moment: the scene is entirely replaced by one in which Horatio tells the Queen of Hamlet's return and the exchange of letters on the boat, so the Queen then has knowledge of what the King has done. It is hard to see how this could be a failure of memory by the actor reconstructing the script, since it is by so much a different idea: perhaps Shakespeare changed his mind after the early performances. In this new version the sailors simply have, among the other letters, one from Hamlet to Gertrude that never gets read; though it is quite unprovable, it may be that this is meant to expose Claudius to her.[6] One way or another, it seems likely that the intention was to make her aware in the final stages of the King's murderous activities, and that this was the practice in performance.

To the sailor delivering the letters, Hamlet was the 'ambassador', which technically he was – the sailor would not necessarily have known him. Horatio learns from his letter that although Hamlet has had an exceptional adventure, being taken prisoner by pirates on the high seas, even that is not the best of it – 'I have words to speak in thine ear that will make thee dumb'. He is mysterious about Rosencrantz and Guildenstern: 'of them I have much to tell thee.' Horatio is to accompany the sailors with Hamlet's letters to, or near to, the King and Queen: and he hopes that they will then bring him to meet up with Hamlet himself – who must be incognito in Denmark, since the sailors are here too. The hero's imminence nudges a pressure into the action as the final movement begins, and the adventuresome language of the letter – 'in the grapple I boarded them' – is intriguingly unlike him. Why is he also warning the King of his return? Because he is, characteristically, more interested in showing him that he has found out his stratagem than he is in trapping him; and he can hardly wait to tell Horatio what a fearless tactician he has been.

---

6   By this implicit logic, the Queen would get the letter after the Messenger's appearance in the scene after this, in time to read it before her Willow speech and the burial of Ophelia.

4.7. The long duologue in which Claudius wins Laertes round, inciting him to the rigged duel against Hamlet, is one of Shakespeare's great temptation scenes. The fact that it is unfamiliar compared to its equivalent in *Macbeth*, or to Richard III with Anne or Queen Elizabeth, or to Angelo with Isabella, is only because, a victim of the inordinate playing length of *Hamlet*, it is frequently cut to its bare essentials: the stark laying of the plot and the grace-note of Gertrude's description of Ophelia's death. Claudius's discourse on love's decline, the talk about horsemanship, the Norman visitor and 'the scrimers of the nation' magnetically attract the blue pencil: the loss is much. Just as Polonius used to loosen the tempo of the play when needed, now a daringly sustained naturalistic duologue between two men towards a tactical end is oddly relaxing for the audience. The intimacy of the two of them weighing up, venturing, withdrawing, defying, deferring, demurring and finally coming together in an unholy alliance brings us, in its realistic tones, close to modern theatre and indeed television or film: it is certainly a relief from the strain of believing in ghosts, plays within plays and heroical mayhem. It follows that the staging needs to be simple and tightly focused, and the actors' tone quite easy (though precise), not unduly weighted. It is probably best if they are mainly seated, avoiding the pointless drifting about that is designed only to change the picture. The argument itself can do the movement.

The sight of Claudius, going here and about to catch his fish, proves once again that the devil can call upon the best arguments; the richness is that in this perverse activity he reveals his own vulnerabilities. Laertes is defeated by his own nature, his sufferings and a consummate tempter; and when at the close Claudius finally opens his hand:

> KING: . . . so that with ease,
>   Or with a little shuffling, you may choose
>   A sword unbated, and in a pass of practice
>   Requite him for your father.
> LAERTES: I will do't. . . .

there should be both narrative fizzle and a plangent sense of Laertes's fall from grace. Courageous if not imaginative, and sorely vexed, he pauses, then hands over the keys of his soul to a conspirator who cares nothing about him at all: in a tragic half-line, this honest man is reduced to a mechanic of evil.

Lest it should become too discursive, the temptation is cut into by two momentous interruptions, one introducing the pressure of time and the other altering the emotional temperature. First, the letters from the supposedly dead Hamlet inform Claudius that he is on his way home, disabused; and then Gertrude brings news of Ophelia's death. So even as he concludes each stage of his entrapment, Claudius is forced to change tack, improvise, and recapture his initiative. Even at the end of the scene, as Laertes rushes away in grief, he may yet lose his volatile victim.

At the start the King has the unusual advantage, for him, of injured innocence. Not only did he have nothing to do with Polonius's death, but the death-thrust was pretty clearly intended for himself: so he too is wronged, and can make common cause. Still, Laertes has a big grievance: why did Claudius not pursue the potential murderer with more determination? Faced with this, the King's best move is a switch to the confessional:

> The Queen his mother
> Lives almost by his looks; and for myself,
> My virtue or my plague, be it either which,
> She's so conjunctive to my life and soul
> That as the star moves not but in his sphere,
> I could not but by her.

He did it for the Queen. There is a small element of truth in this, but it is very selective, of course. The effect on the younger man of the King's personal confidence is surely strong. Claudius consolidates with an elaborate political image, reflecting his new obsession with Hamlet's popularity:

> The other motive
> Why to a public count I might not go
> Is the great love the general gender bear him
> Who dipping all his faults in their affections,
> Would, like the spring that turneth wood to stone,[7]
> Convert his guilts to graces; so that my arrows,
> Too slightly timber'd for so loud a wind,
> Would have reverted to my bow again,
> And not where I had aim'd them.

So he has managed to link Gertrude's love for Hamlet with that of

---

7   An English phenomenon. One of the springs that has this effect – depositing limestone on the wood – was at King's Newnham in Warwickshire.

the public, drawing out a picture of himself as the one wise man misunderstood, a decent fellow giving up gracefully.[8]

It is a fair volley; but Laertes is still playing strongly from the base line, simply restating in human terms the consequences of all this confusion and injustice:

> And so have I a noble father lost;
> A sister driven into desperate terms. . . .
>   But my revenge will come.

Claudius's reassurance that indeed it will confidently implies something up his sleeve:

>   You must not think
> That we are made of stuff so flat and dull
> That we can let our beard be shook with danger
> And think it pastime. You shortly shall hear more.

He means, of course, when news of Hamlet's death arrives from England: instinctively he does not spell it out.

So the battle for Laertes's soul is evenly pitched when a messenger arrives with the reverse of good news: the letters, which should have been from the King of England, are in fact from Hamlet, alive, strangely courteous, and communicating through sailors.[9]

Hamlet's style is playful, mocking, slightly ominous:

> High and mighty, you shall know I am set naked on your kingdom.

It leaves Claudius blank:

> What should this mean? Are all the rest come back?
> Or is it some abuse, and no such thing?

– and then, lost for a stratagem, improvising wildly:

>   If it be so, Laertes,
> As how should it be so? How otherwise?
> Will you be rul'd by me?

He hardly knows what he is going to say next: he has Laertes hot for revenge, Hamlet on his way home, liable to cut so convincing a

---

8 Interestingly enough he never refers to Hamlet's 'madness' – perhaps it would weaken his argument, making him seem to Laertes like a negligent health visitor who has not seen danger arising.

9 Horatio's sailors have given Hamlet's letters to this messenger via someone confusingly called Claudio. It may be that Horatio has devised this circuitous route so that Claudius will not be aware of his involvement and sense a conspiracy.

figure as the victim of royal duplicity that he may make terms with Laertes against him. He moves delicately towards his major idea, which he has either conceived at the speed of light or is developing in the very act of speaking. He assures Laertes of its security:

> . . . even his mother shall uncharge the practice,
> And call it accident

and goes on subtly to flatter him with 'reputation': Laertes has been

> . . . talk'd of since your travels much,
> And that in Hamlet's hearing, for a quality
> Wherein they say you shine. . .

Claudius's movements are becoming quite baroque. The 'quality' turns out, quite a little later, to be his swordsmanship; but before revealing that, Claudius extols the virtues of Laertes's greatest fan – a Norman called Lamord[10] – whose main skill is not so much with the sword as on his horse. Lamord rides as well

> As had he been encorps'd and demi-natur'd
> With the brave beast.

In fact he is so famous that Laertes recognises the description immediately and is wide open for the tremendous compliment that, in fencing, Lamord feels

> 'twould be a sight indeed
> If one could match you.

It is like being commended for your tennis by a great cricketer; and the praise, according to the cunning King, has aroused Hamlet to venomous envy (an ungenerous version of the competitiveness we know to be in him). When, between Laertes's departure from the play and this moment, all these events could have taken place, is hard to know: perhaps Claudius has invented it all.

As he comes to the point:

KING: Now, out of this . . .
LAERTES: What out of this, my lord?

the King drops in a taunt thick with emotional blackmail:

---

10   Editors have made much of the implication of death in the name – rather unnecessarily, since its bearer seems to be a gallant chevalier.

Laertes, was your father dear to you?
Or are you like the painting of a sorrow,
A face without a heart?

Laertes nearly explodes and Claudius immediately makes another
emotional confession; this time he doesn't mention the Queen's
name, but he clearly includes her, as well as Laertes's love for his
father, in its tissue:

. . . I know love is begun by time,
And that I see, in passages of proof,
Time qualifies the spark and fire of it.
There lives within the very flame of love
A kind of wick or snuff that will abate it. . . .

Paradoxically, his fast footwork has revealed his complicated
humanity.
     Laertes is ready for anything, preferably

To cut his throat i' the church.

The violence is shocking, understandable and sad. The two, like
over-excited children, plot worse and worse revenges, and their
dammed-up ideas multiply macabrely: an untipped sword, a
poisoned unction, a lethal drink to back it up.[11] It is a dismal vision,
the two of them competing for more and better means to kill a
man.
     The corruption of Laertes is the first statement of a recurring
theme – personal heroism declining into banal violence – that
generates the chaotic end of the tragedy. It is repeated in the Graveyard Scene that follows and then in the first half of the final scene,
when spiritual truths will be painfully won (particularly by Hamlet)
and then thrown away, or bartered for humiliating conflicts. In this
first case the effect is softened by Laertes's heroic reaction to his
sister's death and the sheer beauty of Gertrude's description of it.
This is of course a set piece that must not feel like a set piece, but
be informed by any number of decisions the actress may take – the
degree of sorrow she feels for the girl, the difficulty she has
breaking the news to the brother, her own new apprehension of

11   Why does Laertes carry deadly poison about with him? Does he share Claudius's arcane
hobby, or has his fury brought him from Paris armed with everything he might need for
revenge? A mountebank has interested him in a poison that works through the merest scratch
– unknown to the scientific world but believed by the Elizabethans to be wolfsbane.

pain, even perhaps her knowledge of Claudius's guilt. Meanwhile the hoary old question – why didn't she save her instead of watching her drown? – is best left in the Green Room, since we know by now that Shakespeare will sacrifice anything for a good speech. A modern playwright wouldn't get away with it.

Whenever Shakespeare speaks of flowers, whether it is through Perdita in Bohemia, Caliban on Prospero's island, or Ophelia and Gertrude in Denmark, we are of course in Warwickshire. Gertrude's speech is abundant with the imagery of the English countryside, one rich name after another in half-a-dozen lines: willow, brook, hoar leaves, stream, crow-flowers, nettles, daisies, boughs, weeds.[12] The euphemism of Ophelia dying among flowers, as she latterly lived, obscures the real agony of death by water. But lovely as it is, the speech is lacking in the intimate human detail instinctive to Shakespeare – the worn-out shoes of Gertrude herself, for example – and even at the moment of death, when

> Her clothes spread wide
> And mermaid-like awhile they bore her up. . .
> . . . But long it could not be. . .

the effect is a little formal and incantatory, and the player must decide whether that indicates obstructed feeling or only an inability to express it.

Laertes leaves with a fine expression of rage punctured by grief:

> Adieu, my lord;
> I have a speech of fire that fain would blaze,
> But that this folly douts it.

Claudius, worried that this inconvenient event will undo his good work, brings us back to squalid earth:

> Let's follow, Gertrude;
> How much I had to do to calm his rage
> Now fear I this will give it start again.

His naked expediency and lack of interest in Ophelia's fate completes the breach between himself and his Queen, who is now

---

12   As a matter of interest, the

> long purples
> That liberal shepherds give a grosser name
> But our cold maids do dead men's fingers call them

were the wild orchis, which was also sometimes known as dog's cods, fool's ballocks and priest's-pintle.

ennobled by a degree of sympathetic eloquence (perhaps more aware, too, of who he is); maybe she does not follow him at all.

THE ACTION: DAY FIVE

Act 5 Scene 1 – Act 5 Scene 2

5.1. Since the fourth day closed with a flurry of reactions to Ophelia's drowning, it is logical enough that the theme should be picked up immediately:

> Is she to be buried in Christian burial that wilfully seeks her own salvation?

What nobody would expect is that these lines, and the disquisition that follows on suicide, canon law and social influence, should be prosily put into the mouths of two men preparing her grave, opening a scene in which the protagonist will finally return to the action.[1] The shock is immediate. On the Elizabethan stage, no sooner would Claudius have spoken than the trap-door – last used when the Ghost rose from or sank into it – would have been thrown open and these two comedians from the death trade would have popped up from it. Such a theatrical audacity, far ahead of its time, is the first in a series of semi-comic juxtapositions that Shakespeare ventured from now to the end of his career, moving on to Cleopatra's asp-seller, the Porter in *Macbeth*, and Imogen mistaking Cloten's decapitated body for Posthumus's in *Cymbeline*.

In any case, at some point in tragedy and history, Shakespeare invariably swings the focus away from the charmed circle of

---

1 Voltaire, rewriting *Hamlet*, contemptuously omitted the *fossoyeurs*, feeling they lowered the general tone. David Garrick, supposedly rescuing Shakespeare for the eighteenth century in England – "'Tis my chief wish, my joy, my only plan, To lose no drop of that immortal man' – did likewise. How could he? For the same reason that he removed the Fool from *Lear*, gave Romeo and Juliet a last conversation in the tomb and Macbeth a dying speech – he was completely confounded by Shakespeare's toughness and breadth. Henry Irving had more sense: he hired Alan Howard's great-great-grandfather as his Gravedigger.

aristocrats, so that the action is seen from the perspective of the working man, who shows a wisdom proportionate to his lack of influence: he did it early on with the Gardeners in *Richard II*, and, more recently, with the English soldiers in *Henry V*. Humorous or not, the effect always makes a pungent comment: it is extreme in *Hamlet*, since the hole over which the hero will shortly come and chat with the Gravedigger is, if he knew it, being prepared for Ophelia. This scene is also a cadenza anticipating the play's finale. Since Hamlet's adventures on the sea and Laertes's acquiescence in Claudius's plot, death is seeping into the action, and here are some of its mechanics.

Ophelia's death has suddenly been transposed from a doomed northern court to an English setting, and subjected to petty analysis. The First Gravedigger's language, and indeed his character – a correctly-minded man who is affronted by any breach of precedent – is from Warwickshire town life, just as Gertrude's recent description of the drowning was drawn from its countryside:

> SECOND GRAVEDIGGER: . . . therefore make her grave straight. The crowner hath sat on her and finds it Christian burial.
> FIRST GRAVEDIGGER: How can that be, unless she drowned herself in her own defence?

The coroner sitting on the dead body is both correct terminology and obvious burlesque: this is not to be a world in which rank will be respected. For these two men, this is an ordinary working morning, enlivened only by the curious circumstance that today's stiff, although a suicide, has been approved for burial in sanctified ground: a most unusual thing, and obviously to do with privilege.

The poignant idea of a girl who either slips or throws herself into the river is based on the death in 1579 of Katherine Hamlet (it was not an uncommon name), who drowned in the Avon near Stratford: the coroner's report was delayed for several months until suspicions of suicide were laid to rest. The First Gravedigger's developing conceit of a person 'not guilty of his own death [who] shortens not his own life' comes both from this and from a 1560 lawsuit in which a man who drowned himself forfeited the continuing lease of his property because he was alive when he committed the sin of killing himself. The Gravedigger makes great capital of this absurdity; and his impossibly elaborate analysis of 'crowner's quest law':

> Here lies the water – good. Here stands the man – good. If the man go
> to this water and drown himself, it is, will he nill he, he goes. Mark you
> that. But if the water come to him and drown him, he drowns not
> himself

is satirically disingenuous, in Shakespeare's best manner – by
pretending foolishness, the Gravedigger has nailed the pettifogging
bureaucrats and small-minded lawyers without offending those of
them in his audience.

As ever, Shakespeare's attitude to his working men is ambiguous: they are figures of fun who deal a truth. As a countryman
himself he has a natural sympathy and often gives them winning
lines – and yet, working in London, often for a court audience, he
feels more or less obliged to make fun of them at the same time.[2]
The Gravedigger makes ridiculous mistakes – 'se offendendo' is a
misreading of 'se defendendo', and 'argal' is a corruption of 'ergo'
– and yet in the end he hits a core of dignity:

> There is no ancient gentlemen but gardeners, ditchers and grave-
> makers. They hold up Adam's profession.

His mate cuts through the quibbles:

> If this had not been a gentlewoman, she should have been buried out
> o' Christian burial

and his complaint is enthusiastically taken up by his opinionated
partner:

> . . . . the more pity that great folk should have countenance in this
> world to drown or hang themselves more than their even-Christian.

On that injustice at least, the two men are united. The social
critique lightly trips us up: in a sense the play is mocking itself.

The Second Gravedigger, who started the scene as if he was in
charge, instructing the First in his duties, now drops back into the
role of apprentice, and junior in a comic partnership: and the two
men continue to relieve the great events of the play of their
claustrophobic significance, both undermining the pathos of
Ophelia and unobtrusively preparing the ground for the return of
Hamlet. The First Gravedigger poses an impossible riddle:

> What is he that builds stronger than either the mason, the shipwright
> or the carpenter?

---

2 Shakespeare soon returned to Stratford to make fun of the country himself, as a land-
owner conniving at enclosures and the criminalisation of the poor.

As the apprentice labours to solve it:

> The gallows-maker, for that frame outlives a thousand tenants

and fails, we realise he is being drawn in a circle back to himself:

> FIRST GRAVEDIGGER: . . . when you are asked this question next, say 'a
> gravemaker'. The houses that he makes lasts till Doomsday.

This circularity makes for a good joke and a neat means of closing the episode, so that Hamlet can arrive and start a new movement: it also implies the ominous inevitability that will underlie the whole subsequent scene.

The Gravediggers' talk has been both sense and nonsense, but it is not intellectually morbid: Hamlet now brings that quality on, as he approaches, 'naked', Claudius's court again, as if inviting his fate. The First Gravedigger dispatches his mate for refreshment (to Yaughan, a very un-Danish innkeeper, probably next door to the Globe), and, in a typically Shakespearian technique of detachment, he sings, only a few minutes after the play's other singer, Ophelia. Appropriately, his song is about young love:

> In youth when I did love, did love,
> Methought it was very sweet
> To contract – O – the time for – a – my behove,
> O methought there was nothing – a – meet.

Skilfully linking him with his new client, this is a corruption of *The Aged Lover Renounceth Love*, a well-known long poem, not a song; and it is confused not because the Gravedigger is stupid, but because he is using it as a worksong, just as disjointed phrases were to be used in the chain gangs or the cotton fields. We remember Ophelia and her flowers overtaken by the muddy ooze: now the Gravedigger's spade slaps into the ground and he uses the words to establish a natural rhythm of work:

> A pickaxe and a spade, a spade,
> For and a shrouding-sheet;
> O, a pit of clay for to be made
> For such a guest is meet.

Hamlet, accompanied by Horatio, observes him.

There is absolutely nothing romantic in the encounter that follows, and a familiar view that Hamlet has returned from England cleansed and full of philosophical calm has to be treated with caution, though there certainly is a new limpidity in his thought, which Horatio, brought to their rendezvous by the sailors, will have noticed. He is mentally flexible and attentive: conventionally believing at first that a man can have 'no feeling of his business' if he sings in making a grave, he immediately accepts Horatio's perception that habit dulls such sensitivities with an elegant acknowledgment:

'Tis e'en so, the hand of little employment hath the daintier sense.

For a moment the two men are intellectually equal, and as close as friends as they ever are. Suddenly, undercutting the stylishness, the Gravedigger pitches a random skull out of his pit. Hamlet is riveted. Twentieth-century curiosity about the mechanics of cremation or surgery can be shame-faced; the Elizabethans were unapologetically interested in material decay, at the same time as they believed in, and were thrilled by, the fabulous nature of ghosts – and Hamlet now represents this fascination. His unblinking stare into the eyes of death is close to the glare of obsession: in its grip he becomes ever more desperately rational, as if, like a philosophical Scheherezade, his inventiveness could somehow forestall the inevitable. He spends three lines imagining the skull to be that of a politician; then nine as that of a courtier, interestingly defining it as male and the destruction of the flesh as the work of a woman – 'my lady Worm's'. He will return to this theme later. The Gravedigger throws up another skull. Hamlet considers it for half-a-dozen lines as a lawyer's (the law gets a hammering generally in this scene), and a further ten, highly technically, as that of a dealer in land: his accumulating verbosity exclaims against the meaninglessness of life. He then decides to 'speak with this fellow'.

After a fair initial joke:

HAMLET: Whose grave's this, sirrah?
GRAVEDIGGER: Mine, sir. . . .
HAMLET: I think it be thine indeed; for thou liest in't

he surprisingly allows the Gravedigger to run quibbling rings round him, retaliating only with the snobbish:

By the Lord, Horatio, these three years I have taken note of it, the age is grown so picked that the toe of the peasant comes so near the heel of the courtier he galls his kibe.[3]

---

3 Hamlet perhaps implicitly dates the decline to his father's death and his uncle's accession: this has now become 'three years', so Shakespeare is elasticating the audience's sense of time once more.

Encouraged by the Gravedigger's fortuitous mention of his birth – on the very same day, improbably, that his father killed old Fortinbras and the Gravedigger commenced work – he takes advantage of the fact that he does not know who he is to make a sly enquiry [4] into how his own behaviour has been received:

> Ay, marry. Why was he sent into England?. . . How came he mad?. . . How strangely?

– and gets it in the eye, incidentally giving rise to a cast-iron joke about the mad English. Beaten, he moves abruptly on to human perishability:

> How long will a man lie i' th' earth ere he rot?

This is certainly not someone full of new spiritual grace, but rather of morbid self-regard; but his intensity is mocked by the Gravedigger's analysis of the durability of human remains, expressed in probably the best joke in the scene:

> A tanner will last you nine year. . . his hide is so tanned with his trade that he will keep out water a great while. . .

In terms of comedy, Hamlet has lost game, set and match: his febrile intellectuality has strayed into a world in which he cannot compete.

Beneath the contest is a deeper irony. The enquiring Prince, never at a loss for a word and normally winning every argument, has busily elaborated his ideas only to meet his match in a humorous unyieldingness as final as death itself. Although he is not disguised, the Gravedigger has not recognised Hamlet, knowledgeable as he seems to be about his age and career, so in a sense he has lost his identity. The linking of Hamlet's birth with the mention of old Fortinbras's name has opened up a vista of Hamlet's life from his infant past to the present, and in a moment he will describe himself being carried on the back of a jester as a child. This latest circularity, the cradle indeed to the grave, implies Hamlet's shortening future.

Suddenly he finds an old friend's skull in his hands. [5] This image has been softened by familiarity: the Prince nestling against the skull is an archetype quite at odds with the real meaning of Yorick's

---

4   Not unlike the Duke's in *Measure for Measure* ('I pray you sir, of what disposition was the Duke?')

5   The Gravedigger, a man who also considers curiously (but not neurotically) has completed a last symbolic act – he has identified a particular skull as Yorick's (which in reality he could not possibly do) in order to confront Hamlet with what he needs.

remains – an object 'abhorred' to Hamlet's imagination, so disgusting in fact that his 'gorge rises at it'. There is no comfort here, just a juxtaposition of desperate ideas – the kissing of lips hanging from a slack jawbone, the utter futility of carrying children on your back when your jokes soon become a dead grin – crowding in on him till he bitterly sends Yorick to counsel womankind against painting over their death's-heads. 'My Lady Worm' is here once more, linking Gertrude and Ophelia too to the scene which, alive and dead, they are about to enter. Accelerating, Hamlet imagines Alexander 'stopping a bunghole' – Horatio is roused to mild protest:

'Twere to consider too curiously to consider so

– but cannot stop him. He describes another circle – a great arc of transience – and invokes the legendary past in a nursery rhyme:

Alexander died, Alexander was buried, Alexander returneth into dust. The dust is earth, of earth we make loam, and why of that loam whereto he was converted might they not stop a beer-barrel?

Imperious Caesar, dead and turn'd to clay, Might stop a hole to keep the wind away. O, that that earth, which kept the world in awe, Should patch a wall t' expel the winter's flaw.

The bones of the play are being blown clean: there should be a deep, unbreakable silence. But life, or a new form of death, breaks in, with the arrival (in verse) of Ophelia's cortege. The stage is filled with mourning figures black as Hamlet's was, against a white wintry light. Perhaps it begins to rain.

Hamlet and Horatio conceal themselves. Hamlet, an expert on suicide, spots immediately from the 'maimed rites' – no sounding bell, no proper coffin, very few mourners – what Horatio might not, that although 'of some estate' (the King and Queen are here) the departed is being penalised: it perhaps

did with desperate hand Fordo its own life.

The Priest in attendance confirms that the death was 'doubtful', and that the female corpse

. . . should in ground unsanctified have lodg'd Till the last trumpet.

He dislikes the whole equivocal business, tolerating it only because
he has no choice. It may not be exactly 'hugger-mugger' like the
disposing of Polonius: but it breaks all the canonical rules.

The discreet ceremony that follows is absolutely cheerless:
through it whistles the wind and a cold poetry. The churchy
formality of the Priest deepens into Laertes's mourning tones, as he
contradicts Ophelia's distracted

> I would give you some violets, but they withered all when my father
> died . . .

by hoping that

> from her fair and unpolluted flesh
> May violets spring.

The Queen's tribute, mixed in with the surprising claim (perhaps
for the occasion) that she

> hop'd thou shouldst have been my Hamlet's wife.
> I thought thy bride-bed to have deck'd, sweet maid,
> And not t'have strew'd thy grave

plays out the elegiac mood so that Laertes can break it with a clash
of rhetoric:

> O treble woe
> Fall ten times treble on that cursed head
> Whose wicked deed thy most ingenious sense
> Depriv'd thee of!

He attacks the 'churlish priest' and names Ophelia for the first
time. Shakespeare is rigorous with Hamlet's reaction, allowing him
only a half-line – 'What, the fair Ophelia!' – in the middle of a flow
of dialogue that obviously shouldn't be interrupted, and Laertes
makes his leap into the grave, forcing Hamlet, likewise full of
bravura self-definition, out of cover:

> This is I,
> Hamlet the Dane![6]

---

6 Apart from the ominous rotation of its arguments, this scene is one in which the
audience is ahead of the characters: the Gravedigger doesn't know who Hamlet is; Hamlet
doesn't know it is Ophelia's grave; the court doesn't know that Hamlet is anywhere near.
This unusual technique creates an atmosphere of permanent foreboding, as we watch the
characters catch up with their fates. Meanwhile, if the Gravedigger is still on the stage, his
actor might, for the sake of some decorum, have to be restrained from expressing his amazement that it is the Prince he has been dealing with after all.

There is a violent bustle over her corpse. Hamlet, so definitively clear-sighted a few moments ago, becomes competitive:

> I lov'd Ophelia; forty thousand brothers,
> Could not, with all their quantity of love,
> Make up my sum. What wilt thou do for her?

We have seen no evidence of his love for the dead girl, and he never mentions her again, though he will apologise for his harsh words to her brother. The fight is ridiculous and ugly: there is no room, there is a dead body as well, presumably thrown down casually, and the exercise of pulling the men out is ungainly and difficult. Claudius holds on a split second before ordering them parted – Laertes has his hands on Hamlet's throat and might do the job for him – but then is obliged to do his duty. Hamlet rails at length at Laertes (he must prove himself the greater rhetorical actor), his ever-available energy wasted and his articulacy debased in satirical rhetoric:

> Be buried quick with her and so will I;
> And if thou prate of mountains, let them throw
> Millions of acres on us, till our ground,
> Singeing his pate against the burning zone,
> Make Ossa like a wart. Nay, an thou'lt mouth,
> I'll rant as well as thou.

Reducing Mount Ossa, where the giants waged war on the gods, to a skin blemish is the work of a corrupted sensibility. In its emotional artificiality this is quite tiresome to listen to, and less impressive than Laertes's absolute silence, which is, in view of his plan, heavy: he is menacingly holding onto his nerve. The only grace is Gertrude's, tender and perceptive to her son:

> . . . thus awhile the fit will work on him;
> Anon, as patient as the female dove
> When that her golden couplets are disclosed
> His silence will sit drooping

if a little indulgent – we have seen little of Hamlet's 'silence'. Elsewhere, everybody is at their worst: Hamlet querulously demands why Laertes should be angry with him (which is rich) and leaves swearing that 'dog [Claudius?]' will have his day'; Claudius, in a stepfather's retaliation, rudely tells Gertrude to set some watch over *her* son and promises Ophelia 'a living monument' (a dead

Hamlet). The trap-door closes on her body, and the scene tumbles matter-of-factly to its close.

The theme of decline is repeating itself. Just as Laertes has been turned from his prime by Claudius, Hamlet's hard-won insights have been obscured by a scrap in a grave and some unappealing self-justification. It is only a few moments since the Gravedigger and he created a sort of clearsighted, musing peace between them: now we are racketing around in the dirt. And, most significantly, there has been a real physical conflict between Laertes and Hamlet which will shortly be ritualised, with very real consequences.

5.2. The long final scene of *Hamlet* starts dangerously slowly as, for sixty-odd lines, Hamlet brings Horatio up to date with his adventures on the way to England. He is firm and businesslike, but cannot resist an opportunity for Wittenbergian disquisitions, for which it is a little late in the day, on the nature of impulse:

> Rashly –
> And praised be rashness for it, let us know,
> Our indiscretion sometimes serves us well
> When our deep plots do pall. . .

and on literary style:

> I once did hold it, as our statists do,
> A baseness to write fair, and laboured much
> How to forget that learning. . .

These elaborations, showing the hero to be still in part an undergraduate, can of course be cut: they are quite trying at this juncture, after the implied climax of the fight in the grave.

The hapless Rosencrantz and Guildenstern are traduced and dead, and Hamlet's epitaph is not generous:

> Why, man, they did make love to this employment;
> They are not near my conscience; their defeat
> Does by their own insinuation grow.[7]

In fact they have not insinuated at all: they were summoned by the King and forced to spy on Hamlet, which they did very badly.

---

7 Playing the part over a period of two years, I changed my mind about the question of conscience towards Rosencrantz and Guildenstern, sometimes playing these lines with some self-doubt. I wonder now if this was sentimental: on the whole I think not.

There is a lack of scruple in Hamlet here: perhaps Horatio, who has escaped the King's manoeuvres and remained uncompromised in Hamlet's 'heart's core', would in other circumstances have been treated summarily too.

Hamlet's self-justification is portentously inhuman:

'Tis dangerous when the baser nature comes
Between the pass and fell-incensed points
Of mighty opposites

– and Horatio's angry humanity contrasts with it:

Why, what a king is this!

Hamlet restates the righteousness of his mission as if it had taken him the entire play to realise it: [8]

. . . is't not perfect conscience
To quit him with this arm? And is't not to be damn'd
To let this canker of our nature come
In further evil?

But he conspicuously has no plan: Horatio warns that he must act swiftly. Hamlet reassures him:

It will be short; the interim is mine;
And a man's life no more than to say 'one'.

At last he seems to have embraced his heathenish role, having maintained an extraordinary hold on our sympathy despite, not because of, his actions. But he immediately veers away into:

But I am very sorry, good Horatio,
That to Laertes I forgot myself. . . .

This talent for sympathetic identification implies that he cannot kill the King now, any more than he could take him at prayer. Some wild provocation is needed to turn him into the man who stabbed blindly at Polonius's curtain. And in fact it now arrives.

It is heavily disguised as a diversion: a new character entering apparently, like the Gravedigger, to allow Hamlet to score easy points, but at a deeper level to confound him. Hamlet reserves a special venom for Osric, a man formidable enough in fact for Claudius to trust with a crucial mission, that of seducing Hamlet as

8   Indeed the King's design on him is the only cast-iron evidence that he has of his murderous nature, the rest being enthusiastic surmise still.

he himself has seduced Laertes. Hamlet first compares Osric to a waterfly, a brightly-coloured insect of no purpose (in the age of toxicology Shakespeare might have made him something more noxious, a tsetse-fly perhaps). Then he calls him a jackdaw ('a chough'[9]) and advises Horatio that it is a vice even to know such a man. What is it about Osric that causes him to wheel about for damning images? To him the man is the tawdriest side of Claudius's tawdry court, deeply depressing in his time-serving and abuse of language: he recalls Claudius, and perhaps Polonius as well, vexing archetypes whom Hamlet can only deal with either by killing them unjustly or by not justly killing them. The resentment is not expressed very elegantly: he indulges in a silly game as to whether it is too hot or too cold to wear or not wear a hat, and then embarks on a parody of the courtier's speech:

> Sir, his definement suffers no perdition in you, though I know to divide him inventorially would dizzy the arithmetic of memory, and yet but yaw neither in respect of his quick sail.

This naturally leaves Osric stumped. Horatio restores order, possibly rebuking Hamlet as much as Osric:

> Is't not possible to understand in another tongue?
> You will do't sir, really.

Hamlet's humour remains childishly competitive:

> OSRIC: You are not ignorant of what excellence Laertes is –
> HAMLET: I dare not confess that, lest I should compare with him in excellence. . . What's his weapon?
> OSRIC: Rapier and dagger.
> HAMLET: That's two of his weapons. But well.

Sweet prince. As ever, he will take the breath away with some brilliant insight, and then risk everything with morbidity or facetiousness.

The terms of the challenge Osric brings are obscure to us:

> The King, sir, hath laid, sir, that in a dozen passes between yourself and him he shall not exceed you three hits. He hath laid on twelve for nine. . .

---

9   There is another reading: 'chuff', which implies a boorish country fellow who has inherited too much money. This perhaps relates him to Sir Andrew Aguecheek in *Twelfth Night*, and later on to Sir Wilfull Witwoud in Congreve's *The Way Of The World*, though of course neither has Osric's courtliness. Meanwhile the sound of his name connects him to another Shakespearian parasite, Oswald in *King Lear*.

The gist is that there is a sort of handicap: because of Laertes's superior skill, Hamlet only loses if he wins three fewer bouts than him out of a total of twelve: if the result is Laertes seven to Hamlet five, Hamlet wins. (What exactly 'he hath laid on twelve for nine' means we may never know). So the King's wager is that the losing horse won't lose by very much. Hamlet's reply:

How if I answer no?

can have an edge of pique, as well as concern about fighting even a friendly duel set up by an arch-enemy with a man who has just tried to strangle him.[10]

Swallowing the taunt and suppressing the suspicion, Hamlet chooses to believe that the King is on his side:

I will win for him if I can

and the thing is on. Osric has his strength: having held his line despite some gruelling treatment, having insisted on keeping his hat off, having delivered his challenge and had it accepted, he can go back with the job well done. Whether he knows of the plot is uncertain: he will not be exposed after the debacle, but on the other hand, he will have been in charge of the weapons, and Laertes may need guiding to the poisoned sword. Director's choice.

The Lord who follows Osric on is looking for confirmation that Hamlet will fight immediately – Claudius must be sure – and expresses the Queen's hope that the whole event will be done in good humour; he can also make a contrast with Osric, being possibly not another 'waterfly', but an altogether soberer, perhaps older, officer of the court. His further purpose is as a segue, to move Hamlet from Osric mode into a definitive fatalism – the last deliberation, in fact, the play will allow him. From grouchy complaint against Osric, he now deals with the Lord with dignity, quite becoming the prince again:

I am constant to my purposes; they follow the King's pleasure; if his fitness speaks, mine is ready. . .

He complies with the Queen's wish for 'gentle entertainment' to Laertes:

10   Hamlet says that he has been in 'continual practice' since Laertes went to France, rather confirming Claudius's earlier claim that he had been envenomed with envy at Lamord's praise of Laertes. All things in his life considered, this is miraculous. How early in the morning did he get up, and what about his antic disposition?

> She well instructs me

and is ready. It is typical of Hamlet that a sense of conspiracy releases his most beautiful sentiments: just as betrayal by Rosencrantz and Guildenstern moved him to link man prince of the universe with man the quintessence of dust, so now the smell of intrigue behind the duel – it cannot possibly be innocent – produces the most limpid awareness. Something ill's around his heart, but it is too deep for him to allow Horatio to be worried by it. His thought crystallises into:

> We defy augury. There's a special providence in the fall of a sparrow. If it be now, 'tis not to come. If it be not to come, it will be now. If it be not now, yet it will come. The readiness is all. Since no man knows aught of what he leaves, what is't to leave betimes? Let be.[11]

Philosophical apex or absolute negation, this is conclusive, his last bulletin.

From here on everything runs downhill. The court arrives, the duel is fought, the poisoned sword exchanged so that both duellists are mortally wounded, the poisoned drink intended for Hamlet is taken by Gertrude, and Hamlet finally kills Claudius. This last movement – a hundred lines of violence, harsh, improbable and generally lacking in grace – is, like *The Murder of Gonzago*, a ritualisation of the play's violence, and a purging of it. Subordinating character to action, it releases all tensions, and represents a last degeneration, in which human integrity is squandered in 'carnal, bloody and unnatural acts'. However, its perfunctoriness accentuates Hamlet's heroism, and by the end an audience faced with four grotesque deaths should feel their hearts shaken.

Claudius 'puts Laertes's hand into Hamlet's' – forcing the two men into a public gesture of sportsmanship. Laertes will certainly be reluctant, and it seems that Claudius has him by the hand as firmly as he might a stubborn child. Hamlet's apology opens with typical charm:

---

11   The original editors of the play made a great scramble of these lucid lines, unable to decide on one of the play's final chords. The Second, 'Good' Quarto, reads, incomprehensibly: 'Of aught he leaves, knows.' The Folio, edging towards sense, reads: 'Ha's ought of what he leaves', but then leaves out 'Let be', an omission almost as notable as that of 'How all occasions do inform against me' (especially if it was done by the author himself). For once, it is worth favouring later editors, particularly Dr Johnson in 1765, who provides the reading I've used.

Give me your pardon, sir. I have done you wrong;
But pardon't, as you are a gentleman.

He moves on to blaming his destructive behaviour, which encompasses Polonius, Ophelia and the fight in the grave, on his 'distraction'. Faced by the reality of his actions, Shakespeare stops us and him in his tracks with an arresting half-line:

What I have done
That might your nature, honour and exception
Roughly awake, I here proclaim was madness

– and the implied pause brings Hamlet face to face, perhaps for the first time, with the enormity of his career. As if in retreat from this, he embarks on a superficially pleasing string of quibbles, unconvincingly put to the service of self-exoneration, which he concludes, amazingly, by calling the man whose family he has destroyed his 'brother'.[12] It is well-meant, complies with the Queen's wishes, and changes nothing; however, it compares favourably with Laertes's reply, which is completely mendacious. With none of Hamlet's fluency, he draws a distinction between his 'nature' which accepts the apology, and his 'honour' which won't allow him to until he achieves some obscure form of public vindication from 'some elder masters of known honour'. This is purposely opaque: but it must be a relief to both Laertes and Claudius that he can come up with anything plausible at this point of tension. There is an immediate bustle of short exchanges and half-lines while the foils are 'chosen', and Hamlet's fluency allows him a gallantry that makes Laertes obtusely resentful:

HAMLET: I'll be your foil, Laertes; in mine ignorance,
    Your skill shall, like a star in the darkest night,
    Stick fiery off indeed.
LAERTES: You mock me, sir.
HAMLET: No, by this hand.

12   It is exactly the kind of riddling, sophistic speech that led an eleven-year-old friend of mine to despair of Shakespeare, saying that the play had a great story and some good fights, but that there was too much of the sort of 'If true is false then false is true, is it not or is it?' material that adults like so much. The same authority advised me on the doubling of Claudius and the Ghost. How should I make them different, I asked him over a pizza. Make the Ghost right-handed, and Claudius (the villain) left-handed. Make your voice wobbly and high for the Ghost, whispering and vague: then deep and frightening and in the nose for Claudius. Do quick jerks for Claudius, and play the Ghost on tiptoe. I have enjoyed working with Peter Hall, John Barton and Tony Richardson, but I'm not sure that I have got more vivid advice from them.

The alternating of sustained speech with anxious interjections is typical of the scene, and will be most striking when the catastrophe is resolved into final leavetakings. Hamlet is easy in his choice of weapons, Laertes elaborately chooses a foil that is 'too heavy' before taking the crucial one. It is indeed difficult to see how he can do this, and how the untipped sword can remain hidden from the court, except with the help of Osric, who is specifically in charge of the weapons. Whether the poison is administered to the sword now by one of them, or is already congealing on it, is discretionary of course.

So far, so good: everyone is happy, Laertes is safely equipped, Hamlet seems to have found a lightness of spirit, Gertrude must be pleased by that, and the court is anticipating pleasure. Claudius drops a poisoned pearl into Hamlet's cup with the same ceremony with which he celebrated his 'decision' to remain in Denmark at the beginning of the play:

> And let the kettle to the trumpet speak,
> The trumpet to the canoneer without,
> The cannon to the heavens, the heaven to earth. . .

but it is more drawn-out and even coarser. It must be a surprise to the court, and, depending on his fatalism, to Hamlet as well, to hear Claudius celebrating a man he has furiously banished to England and recently been offended by in the graveyard in such hyperbolic style, with a 'union'

> Richer than that which four successive kings
> In Denmark's crown have worn

going into the cup.

The duellists square up. Now it comes to the point, Laertes is nervous: and the sight of him muffing his early chances acts powerfully on the King, making him call after only one hit for his second line of defence – the poisoned drink, which Hamlet refuses. After Hamlet's second 'touch', which creates an advantage for him that, in terms of the odds, no-one could have expected, Claudius, now very concerned, is forced to a compliment:

> Our son shall win

– and the Queen, having first dealt as best she can with the troublesome line

> He's fat, and scant of breath

(fat almost certainly means perspiring here), fatally decides to drink his health. Does she have an instinct, bred of her new apprehension of the world she lives in, that she is sacrificing herself? Claudius has either to watch her do it or give himself away. He seeks to command her vocally:

> Gertrude, do not drink

and is firmly refused by his now independent wife. The director has carte blanche here to finalise Claudius's character: if he is too far away on the stage to knock the cup out of her hand, he is of course helpless; if he is close enough to do it, he is a man who, rather than incriminate himself by such a strange gesture, sacrifices her, this woman who was conjunctive to his life and soul. The actor now reaches a Waterloo of his own:

> (*Aside*) It is the poison'd cup; it is too late.

– it takes a deal of ingenuity to avoid the laugh on this melodramatic line.

Asides are creeping into the action: always a bad sign. Now, in panic, Laertes offers to hit Hamlet when he is not looking, Claudius refuses, and Laertes confides in the audience that indeed it wouldn't be *quite* right:

> (*Aside*) And yet it is almost against my conscience.

This is followed by Laertes's wounding of Hamlet and the exchange – 'in scuffling, they change rapiers'. In sword and dagger fighting, as opposed to glove and sword, the initial disarm that allows this to happen is quite difficult to do – the dagger has to twist the sword out of the opponent's grip: but the incensed Hamlet achieves it either as a legitimate manoeuvre, or by sudden violence. Laertes may even drop the weapon in shame, though this is probably a soft option. Hamlet wounds Laertes, and only then Gertrude, who has presumably been discreetly queasy, falls: and the play turns into its final straight.

The Duel has been a tawdry event, full of crude mechanisms, disguised by the sheer skill of the two swordsmen. It has to be fully staged, heroic and exciting, despite the waning energies of the Hamlet, or else a theatrical catharsis doesn't happen: yet, however long, it will still seem afterwards that the catastrophe has happened in a flash. Laertes is a very good fighter, and Hamlet is unexpectedly good, the charm of watching him nearly win by fair means finally sealing our emotional bonds and creating delight for the disinterested spectators: Ophelia's hero is at last before us. Watching, we know that the actor, as well as Hamlet himself, is pulling his last reserves out of the bag, and we urge him forward.[13] Through him, Shakespeare transforms bathos into romantic tragedy, drawing a continual contrast between him – witty, light-spirited and gallant at the last – and the debased nature of the set-up.

Suddenly, with the Queen's collapse, it is all over. Within a few moments they are all down, all victims of Claudius, of the malevolence and misplaced ambitions that disposed of old Hamlet. Laertes manages a metaphor:

Why, as a woodcock to mine own springe, Osric

– Gertrude dies without summary, and Laertes blames Claudius, but himself only a little. With the news that there is fast-acting poison in him now, the weeks of delay concentrate into lightning impulse: Hamlet turns on Claudius as he turned on Polonius, and kills him comprehensively for the unexpected reason that Claudius has tried to poison him. The court – so conditioned that even after the weight of suspicion falls on the King they shout: 'Treason! Treason!' as Hamlet cuts him down – becomes once more a dumb force, ready to be turned to advantage by the unappealing Fortinbras.

Polonius, Rosencrantz, Guildenstern, Laertes, Gertrude and Claudius have died, like Hamlet's father, unhousel'd and unannel'd; the Gravedigger will bury them all. None of the victims makes a final account of themselves or really summarises their fate, unusual in Shakespeare and a particular horror to the Elizabethans, who believed passionately in the speech from the scaffold.[14]

---

13   In both of fight director William Hobbs's recent versions (in fact he has done the duel in *Hamlet* over twenty times, all of them as different as his stars – among them Maximilian Schell, Klaus Maria Brandauer, Peter O'Toole, Ralph Fiennes) he has one point in common: that Laertes has Hamlet at his mercy very early on but can't bring himself to finish him off.

14   The sequence breaks every law of probability – Gertrude has a good swig of poison and lasts for twenty lines; Laertes is scratched with the poisoned sword and lasts for thirty; Claudius, attacked by the sword and then made to drink the poison, dies instantaneously; Hamlet is scratched but survives for fifty-five lines. In the absence of realism, Hamlet should not play the action of the poison too clinically – it will get in the way of the text. But unless an audience sees something of the effect that

swift as quicksilver [it] courses through
The natural gates and alleys of the body

they will feel cheated. Split the difference.

And in his last breath the hero escapes our grasp as well. The moment Laertes is gone, and he alone waits for death – or rather races to get everything said before he is overtaken – the language shifts from rhetorical clatter to valediction:

Heaven make thee free of it; I follow thee

– and then, uncannily, to a comment on the entire action that implicates all of us who have watched the play as much as the dumbstruck court:

You that look pale and tremble at this chance,
That are but mutes or audience to this act,
Had I but time – as this fell sergeant, death,
Is strict in his arrest – O, I could tell you,
But let it be.

There is more that Shakespeare could say: but the hour is late. The words embrace Hamlet himself, the theatre act, we who look for meaning: and they conclude with Hamlet at his best, the man who, with nearly the same words – 'Let be' – calmed Horatio before the Duel. He is duly anxious to be understood after death: he insists that the distraught Horatio not kill himself so that he can be his representative, expressing this requirement with a mythic beauty:

If thou did'st ever hold me in thy heart,
Absent thee from felicity awhile,
And in this harsh world draw thy breath in pain,
To tell my story.

With innate musicality, Shakespeare brings in the sound of the outside world at this plangent moment ('A march afar off and shot within') and a drumming begins which should be sustained through Hamlet's death to the arrival of Fortinbras – the hero does not die in a theatrical vacuum, but in counterpoint with continuing life of a sort. He lends his formal voice to Fortinbras – there is not in fact going to be an 'election' – and then goes with a riddle, 'the rest is silence', as teasing as his first line in the play, striking out of two nouns multiple meanings: nihilistic, romantic, heroic, humorous, restrained, defeated and triumphant at once. Glimpsing the undiscovered country at last, literature's most loquacious hero promises 'silence': and the 'rest' is both his and our release from his efforts – it is a more enigmatic version of the leavetaking of Puck, Prospero, Feste or Rosalind. This heroic and poetic tragedy is also one of the world's great ironic parables: and its gifted hero, cruelly wasted, leaves us with both benediction and emptiness.

Fortinbras's takeover is professional, swift, unquestioned and unquestioning, only delayed by a metaphorical reaction

This quarry cries on havoc. . .

which compares very unfavourably with the style of the protagonist we have just lost; by the formal regrets of the ambassadors who have arrived at the same moment from England; and by a longish general summary by Horatio, in which he does his best to encapsulate the play's bewildering events and to do some right by his friend – the true extent of the mayhem, however, must wait for a longer 'audience'. The Norwegian doubtfully claims 'rights of memory' and nobody is arguing. His tribute to Hamlet, perhaps well-meant, is ludicrously inappropriate:

The soldiers' music and the rites of war
Speak loudly for him. . .

– having perhaps known nothing about him, he certainly misunderstands his talents, but at least he gives him dignity.

Nothing is resolved: there has been only prodigal death, of which the required one – Claudius's – is without catharsis. We do not know who the Ghost was, or whether he is now at peace, or whether Gertrude knew about her second husband, or how else Hamlet could have fulfilled himself – only that we could have done no better with his difficulties than he has. Denmark, once powerful, has been reduced to a client of Norway – largely through the activities of Hamlet. But of course his meaning is not contained by these circumstances, far from it. His body is to be taken, in a final pun, to 'the stage', a place of display and honour, with a sense of permanence, facing the sky. As the play closes on a single half-line of practical instruction and the lights go down on Hamlet, probably on the soldiers' shoulders, the frailty of his life, the permanence of his spirit, and above all his extraordinary enquiries, begin their long ringing in the ears.

3
THE CHARACTERS

3

THE CHARACTERS

The Royal Triangle

King CLAUDIUS is a thief: nothing he has is earned, and for that reason he is damned. He has stolen both his woman and his crown: he will never know if Gertrude is with him for his sake or because she wanted to remain Queen. She has a natural gift for the job after years of experience, but he is a maverick dressed in a little brief authority. Like Macbeth, he has no children. Perhaps he hopes for them with Gertrude, who may well be less than forty when the play begins (no younger, for Hamlet's sake), and Gertrude's fertility may be one of Hamlet's anxieties. Claudius seems to have been a career politician, a sensual bachelor; he is old enough to call Hamlet 'our son' but there is no evidence of an earlier marriage or any family ties. So he has the insecurity of the childless step-parent, and the play aggravates it: he is frustrated by everything motherly in Gertrude, her preoccupation with Hamlet, her sympathy for Laertes, the nonsense about Ophelia marrying her son. *The Murder of Gonzago* may be only a public version of an enactment he knows well: he may have spent nights recalling the murder while Gertrude slept peacefully, and that is why he drinks and copulates so much, to get some rest. Watching the Play, he feels more of a fraud than any of the Players: it shows in a mirror the fidelity that he has violated, and he fears the meaningless collapse of love that surely enough follows for him. He obviously has a capacity for repentance: but regret and loss of self-esteem don't inhibit his forward drive very much.

Alcohol is important to Claudius.[1] He is a man who has murdered to get what he has and prospered without apparent effort:

1 That doesn't mean that he has to be 'bloat' as Hamlet says – though he probably shouldn't be too skinny either: skinny kings don't inspire confidence. Only republicans like Cassius are skinny.

but in fact he is running very fast to keep still, his brain ever more active as he is sucked by his coat-tails into retribution. How does he sustain himself? I think he is a progressive alcoholic who draws creative energy from his habit at the outset; but he is weak over a long distance, and as Hamlet gradually encroaches on him and when he loses Polonius (an indispensable ally), his political judgment, as opposed to his operating skill, begins to fragment. He hatches with Laertes a foolhardy plot against Hamlet's life which has to be doomed at its moment of success, even if he were to turn against Laertes and repudiate it, as he presumably would have done. The poison in the cup and the poison on the untipped sword: how were they ever going to get away with it? It is a piece of recklessness, an addict's fantasy of short-term gratification.

Nevertheless, Hamlet's 'treacherous, lecherous kindless villain' demonstrates throughout the play abundant talents – even a provisional humanity. His motives for murder may have been blatant:

My crown, mine own ambition and my Queen[2]

and he certainly doesn't offer a political justification, though no doubt he would were he ever to be found out; but his usurpation could have been be a blessing for Denmark, if it hadn't been for Hamlet – the old King's regime seems bleak, unprofessional, too full of unregulated loyalties and unreliable transactions. But human justice demands that Claudius be brought down, wounded and gurgling like a baby on a poisoned bottle, and with him tumbles the court of Elsinore.

The part is a good one, as long as the plotting scene with Laertes is left in. In fact, if it wasn't for Hamlet, it would be as good as Macbeth. But of course Hamlet pushes everyone aside in the last stages, and Gertrude, Claudius and Laertes tail off. Many of Shakespeare's plays are predicated on the confrontation of two big figures – Othello and Iago, Richard and Bolingbroke, the meeting of two lovers. Hamlet too promises mighty opposites, and demands that theatrically Claudius should be as strong as Hamlet: after all, the working world of the play is his. But because the part doesn't fully deliver, it is quite difficult to cast: a producer can often not quite get a 'leading actor', much as he is wanted, and in a seasonal

---

2   Since he is speaking alone, he is telling the truth – no character in Shakespeare tells lies to the audience.

repertoire company like Stratford-upon-Avon, he may need to offer a Lear, a Prospero or a Timon to such a man, who may then accept Claudius as a side-bet. Consequently it's rare to see a real battle of the giants. On industrial dilemmas like this does the welfare of a great play depend.

THE GHOST of Claudius's victim is not some mountain in the mist, but a man with a point of view, urgently participating as far as he can: in a very short time he brings on a picture of utter torment and tells the most important part of the story. Still, it is a little difficult to talk about his character, because it has been altered by death from something we can only dimly sense in any case through the testimony of others. He has been a man of action, austerely military and, at least in Hamlet's emotional hindsight, a loving and attentive husband who inspired Gertrude's devotion and desire. Hamlet doesn't really say what he was like as a father, though his hyperbolical comparisons of him to classical figures like Hyperion, Jove, Mars and Mercury are rather chilly. He may or may not have been in life what he is now: a little immodest, humourless obviously, proud to a fault and obsessively verbose.

His words in the Closet Scene have only a formal humanity; but the scene with Hamlet alone is a set piece for the Ghost. This is not a character in relationship to others or to present events, but rather creating the play's future: and since his world is outside everybody's experience, the actor is imaginatively on the wing, free-associating to show something he has no clearer idea of than any live person. The following is therefore highly subjective, some notions I had while preparing to play the part, and images that flew in in the nightly effort of performing it – where, as always, your mind is simultaneously in control of pace and form, and wide open to impressions. It certainly is a hell of a ten minutes to play.

Mark me. How easy is it for a ghost to speak? Perhaps he hasn't used his voice since life. I have a recurring dream of talking to my dead father, and it always costs him the greatest effort to make a sound.

My hour is almost come like a tolling bell, and then an image from Hiëronymus Bosch: *When I to sulphurous and tormenting flames Must render up myself* – the victim given naked to the furnace, like an undead body cremated. The pain is unimaginable to Hamlet, who can only manage 'Alas, poor Ghost': but the Ghost *knows* it.

Pity me not, but lend thy serious hearing To what I shall unfold. The father is angered by his son's helpless remark, mistaking it for sentiment or flippancy.

I am thy father's spirit, Doom'd for a certain term to walk the night, And for the day confined to fast in fires Till the foul crimes done in my days of nature Are burnt and purg'd away. The Ghost's sins, to be cauterised by flame, are those of all of us, not some special transgressions of his own. He has been in purgatory, with who knows what effect on his body – but anything you do mustn't be so showy as to distract from delivering the narrative.

But that I am forbid To tell the secrets of my prison house, I could a tale unfold whose lightest word Would harrow up thy soul, freeze thy young blood. . . The Ghost forbears to cause Hamlet this pain not from love of him, but because he is forbidden. By whom? He is standing there with his son – why can he not open his mouth and tell him? (Perhaps even Shakespeare couldn't do it justice.) There is something pagan here, a sense of arbitrary rules which, broken (like Orpheus looking back at Eurydice), condemn you to final torment.

Make thy two eyes like stars start from their spheres, Thy knotty and combined locks to part, And each particular hair to stand on end Like quills upon the fretful porcupine. The father threatens a bogeyman. The picture is nearly comical, like Strewelpeter (Gertrude paints it again in the Closet when the Ghost reappears), resolved by the beautiful reality of the porcupine, a homely beast that can do you a small harm. The delivery could be sincere, even tender, quiet.

But this eternal blazon must not be To ears of flesh and blood. List, list, O list – all consonants at the end, the few vowels short ones: not a sweet sound.

If thou didst ever they dear father love. . . Revenge his foul and most unnatural murder. Everything preceding this moment needs to be held on a tight leash, straining towards it.

I find thee apt, And duller shouldst thou be than the fat weed That roots itself in ease on Lethe wharf, Shouldst thou not stir in this. The picture is classical – Acheron, the pool of Avernus: Hamlet inherits his father's taste for mythological comparison. To the point:

Now Hamlet, hear: 'Tis given out that, sleeping in mine orchard, A serpent stung me; so the whole ear of Denmark Is by a forged process of my death Rankly abus'd; but know, thou noble youth, The serpent that did sting thy father's life Now wears his crown. A King's concern for his country: a wrong done to his people is a wrong done to him. The nation's ear is as infected as his.

Ay, that incestuous, that adulterate beast, With witchcraft of his wits, with traitorous gifts – O wicked wit and gifts that have the power So to seduce – won to his shameful lust The will of my most seeming virtuous Queen. The Ghost shows the ugly face of human jealousy. He must believe that only a brew of beastliness, witchcraft and treachery could have taken Gertrude from him – it was not a woman's free volition, and it meant she was not virtuous, and could never have been virtuous, only seemed it. His language inflated by resentment, he mistakes obedience for virtue. So may we all, when these things happen.

O Hamlet, what a falling-off was there! From me, whose love was of that dignity That it went hand in hand even with the vow I made to her in marriage, and to decline Upon a wretch whose natural gifts were poor To those of mine. . . Yes, of course. The audience has watched this 'wretch' displaying a number of natural gifts. Is the self-righteous Ghost going to hell because his pride won't let him understand the world? Will revenge really free him?

But virtue, as it never will be mov'd Though lewdness court it in a shape of heaven So lust, though to a radiant angel link'd, Will sate itself in a celestial bed And prey on garbage. A real reef-knot of antitheses: *Virtue* has to be counterpointed with *lust; never will be mov'd* with *prey on garbage; lewdness* with *a shape of heaven; lust* secondarily with *radiant angel link'd; sate* with *a celestial bed; a celestial bed* with *garbage.* And if you miss any of them it won't be understood.

But soft, methinks I scent the morning air. Brief let me be. The feral Ghost has the scent of day in his nostrils. After fifty-nine lines he decides to be 'brief', but he will continue for thirty-two more, so brief he's not, though now he must be quick: it is the moment before light that birds can sense, and he may at any time be cut off.

Once again, the point: *Sleeping within my orchard , my custom always in the afternoon Upon my secure hour thy uncle stole With juice of cursed hebanon in a vial And in the porches of mine ears did pour The leperous distilment.* A quaint setting, as in a Book of Hours. The picture is nostalgic, an old family routine that Hamlet remembers, don't disturb your father. The murderer is recklessly operating in broad daylight.

Whose effect Holds such an enmity with blood of man That swift as quicksilver it courses through The natural gates and alleys of the body

And with a sudden vigour it doth posset And curd like eager droppings into milk The thin and wholesome blood; so did it mine; And a most instant tetter bark'd about, Most lazar-like with vile and loathsome crust All my smooth body (a hint of vanity?). With delighted detail, the Ghost relives his agony. 'Swift as quicksilver' is a good guide: without skimping the changes, the whole passage must be kept moving because it sways into rhetoric, which clogs good acting, like lumps of meat in the throat. This pain is not the worst for him, there is a deeper loss:

Thus was I, sleeping, by a brother's hand, Of life, of crown, of Queen at once dispatch'd; Cut off even in the blossoms of my sin, Unhousel'd, disappointed, unanel'd, No reckoning made, but sent to my account With all my imperfections on my head. O horrible, O horrible, most horrible! The Ghost is riven with the knowledge of his unshriven sins. Don't cheat this final big line; mean it, but don't make an *effect*, or the whole performance goes down the chute. It may be different every night.

If thou has nature in thee, bear it not; Let not the royal bed of Denmark be A couch for luxury and damn'd incest. But howsomever thou pursuest this act, Taint not thy mind, nor let thy soul contrive Against thy mother aught: leave her to heaven, And to those thorns that in her bosom lodge To prick and sting her. The King's care for his country again, a piece of impossible advice for Hamlet, whom he clearly does not understand, and, pitifully, spare your mother, who in fact shows no sign of remorseful thorns at all. His only small tenderness is reserved for her, whom he overestimates, not Hamlet, whom he takes for granted.

Fare thee well at once; The glow worm shows the matin to be near And 'gins to pale his uneffectual fire. The scent of dawn has developed into a low mist over the marshes, like an Essex fog in Dickens perhaps, or the magical morning mists in Andrei Tarkovsky's films *Stalker* and *Nostalgia*: a disorientation in which you can pass from one zone of existence to another without knowing it. It is dank and uncomforting, overtaking the night lights; we must *see* this from the voice. These are beautiful lines that must not be spoken beautifully: it is cruel for the Ghost – he is leaving his son and going back to the unthinkable.

Adieu, adieu; Hamlet, remember me. This is how the performance will be remembered. The words can be an appeal, or furiously mandatory, or they can be spoken very simply. All the Ghost's qualities jostle behind the four final syllables. If pain isn't in it, you may get a laugh; if firmness isn't, it will be sentimental. If it isn't simple, the audience will soon forget it.

And – he could be the devil all the time.

GERTRUDE has attracted and then disappointed many leading actresses. The interest would seem to be: to find the emotional cast of a woman who remarries within a month a man whom she at first does not know to be her husband's murderer; who loses the affections of her son (who takes every opportunity to crucify her); who then realises too late the rottenness in her situation, and sacrifices herself emotionally – and perhaps physically – for him. But most of the part depends on unrealised hints: that she is sexually infatuated with Claudius, although she never speaks about it; that she may come to know his real nature; that she rejects him and is reunited with Hamlet after the Closet Scene; that she may have wished Hamlet to marry Ophelia; even the hint, beloved of a certain kind of realist, that she lets Ophelia drown for the sake of a pretty descriptive speech. The trouble is that hints are what they are, and every case is open: the actress's and director's decisions are bound to be a bit arbitrary. To explain her early lack of suspicion of Claudius, we make her vague, ditsy, gullible, but without much chance to tie these qualities to the lines; to show her desire for him we have them jumping on each other in public in a most unstatesmanlike way; and later we invent gestures of physical rejection between, around and across the lines. In fact, these lovers have three moments alone together in the whole play: they are always on duty, meeting for narrative purposes, never for themselves, and in the end, Claudius lets Gertrude die and she bids no farewell.[3] *Hamlet* would gain much if Gertrude expressed her feelings about her old and certainly her new husband; like so much else the matter is sacrificed to the central character.

As far as the relationship with Hamlet goes, in the big scene between them the bewildered and negligent mother says very little, and less to him thereafter:[4] so this is a second interesting relation-

3 It is sometimes argued that Shakespeare has restraint in sexual matters on the stage because his women were played by boys. It is nonsense: think of Othello abusing Desdemona, Troilus and Cressida coming together under the eye of the obscene Pandarus, Romeo and Juliet in the morning, Antony's rage at Cleopatra.

4 Interestingly enough, one of the most successful recent Gertrudes was Glenn Close in Franco Zeffirelli's film: once she was reconciled with Hamlet the director insisted on regular

ship implied but not really delivered. In the vacuum, unhelpful worries arise: working-class actresses are troubled about being queenly enough (irrelevant), regal ones feel decorative only. But there *is* something to play: Gertrude as a professional. She is more experienced than Claudius, with a greater natural authority. She handles Rosencrantz and Guildenstern with skill and diplomacy, has the accent of command with her son, she is witty and perceptive about Polonius ('More matter, with less art'); and she has an inspired comment when Hamlet, in front of the court, demands her opinion of his shocking play:

The lady doth protest too much, methinks.

This is her superiority and strength. However hopeless and profligate in her life, she is not stupid at her job: there she gives out and reserves herself in good proportion, while Claudius develops a habit of confiding his troubles in the wrong people.

Gertrude achieves a humanity, rather like one of Shakespeare's kings stripped of power, after the Closet Scene and then after the death of Ophelia: she begins to understand other people's pain, some of it caused by herself. This is expressed with sympathetic lyricism: her accounts of Hamlet's madness have real beauty, her description of Ophelia's drowning famously so. There is tenderness towards Hamlet in the Duel Scene:

Come, let me wipe thy face.

When she drinks the poisoned cup she refuses the King's desperate plea with real dignity:

I will, my lord; I pray you, pardon me

– and this latter maturity, more than her melodramatic dying lines:

No, no, the drink, the drink; O my dear Hamlet;
The drink, the drink; I am poison'd. . .

is her epitaph. She may have been vain, capricious, culpable, and have lived a destructive life; but in the end she gets the Shakespearian gift of grace.

---

reaction shots, perpetuating an illusion of contact between them, free of the confinement of the lines.

The Prime Minister's Household

The ambiguities in POLONIUS's family are vexing but extremely playable: the group is by turns attractive and slightly repellent. In Polonius the Elizabethans would have immediately recognised William Cecil, Lord Burleigh, one of Queen Elizabeth's principal and foxiest advisors. Recently dead, he had been a man of circuitous style who, apart from his public activities (he had drafted Mary Queen of Scots' death warrant) had been well-known for promoting his daughter's interests at court and for having written a list of moral precepts for his son and then spied on him in Paris. In other words, a very topical satirical portrait inside an epic tragedy, and certainly not one of a fool. As the picture lost its meaning over the next three centuries (there was always a handful of perceptive actors who played him as much fox as fool, but their names mean little now, since history has a way of enshrining the stars and ignoring the character men), Polonius's effect perhaps became a purely theatrical one, as comic relief; now, when we want some kind of political reverberation from the play, we expect Polonius to be a large part of it. The role can even be over-interpreted: perhaps he was instrumental in 'the election' of Claudius – who says to Laertes 'I lov'd your father'; he might even have had an inkling of the old King's murder, though, knowing him, he would probably hint at it in the course of the play if he did. He may even, in his zeal for separating Ophelia and Hamlet, really be testing them: establishing what is wrong with Hamlet and curing it might prepare the ground for an advantageous alliance.

Whatever he is politically, Polonius is a bad parent, no doubt about it, bringing the manners of his working life home with him, egotistical and untrusting as men alone with their children can be. He clearly doesn't listen to his daughter at all, and there is nowhere a single word of affection from him towards either her or Laertes. Even the small formal apology to Ophelia for having misread Hamlet sounds like regret for a professional mistake. The restraint that he might have felt as a father doesn't prevent him exposing Ophelia to the ordeal of the Nunnery Scene; and quite possibly it is Hamlet's awareness of this trick that makes him torment her. Polonius takes no step to protect or comfort her either then or after the Play Scene, but is immediately bustling about and intriguing once again, planning to hide behind Gertrude's arras. His brusqueness might accord with a certain kind of dumb male love: perhaps the 'slow leave' wrung from him by Laertes to go back to Paris shows real reluctance, perhaps the bustling advice that he gives him bespeaks a camouflaged affection, perhaps his over-solicitude to Ophelia masks real protectiveness. But Ophelia's obvious repression and Laertes's failings as a human being give the lie to any idea of family health. Both son and daughter seriously lose personality when their father is present, Laertes disappearing behind formalities and Ophelia losing her mischief. Meanwhile Laertes is not much good with Ophelia, mad or sane. Yet Polonius's death (together with Hamlet's rejection) is enough to send Ophelia mad, and it brings Laertes hotfoot back from France, ready to 'take both friend and foe, Winner and loser'. The son's feelings towards his father may be compensatory – his pain is much to do with Claudius's having given him only perfunctory obsequies – but his grief at Ophelia's death is deep; and Ophelia's lament for Polonius:

> His beard was as white as snow
> All flaxen was his poll

is intimate and familiar, her sorrow for his coldness in the ground very moving. Love from the children seems to coexist with all the emotional suppression.

Polonius's incompetence as a parent in turn invades and destroys his success as a politician – the pawns that he is playing with are his own. Spying may be a legitimate weapon of government, but there is a strong streak of prurience undermining his efforts. Whenever Claudius is ready with a decisive political action, such as sending Hamlet away, Polonius intercedes, insisting that the whole problem is to do with love, and that he needs one more opportunity to prove it. His zeal for eavesdropping, going beyond the professional, is the end of him. The diplomatic skills that he does have are of the secondary kind, such as making Claudius wait for his disclosures about Hamlet until the ambassadors have been interviewed.

Shakespeare being Shakespeare, however, having created this unsavoury man he then makes him enjoyable company in the theatre. Just as Claudius is redeemed by self-knowledge, Polonius is made palatable by the fact that he is funny – or at least the cause that wit is in other men. He rouses Hamlet to some fine improvisations, and his garrulousness and pedantry are turned into more or less innocent comedy. So the part has to be played by an actor who is a merciless character man but also has the gifts of a stand-up comedian – otherwise the Reynaldo scene and the long sequence in which he brings Hamlet's poem to the King and Queen become impossible.

Between knave and fool, most performances fall to one side or the other, and it has to be said that a Polonius who gets no laughs at all, so pregnant is his every move with political meaning, is no better than a Polonius who does nothing but. One thing is very surprising – at his wretched and unexpected death we are more shaken than we ever would have thought, and feel some of the perverse love of his unfortunate children. A man whom it would be abominable to know in life is mourned in the theatre.

Given his parentage, what chance in life has LAERTES? His father's tones, sententious and rather sleazy, ring out in his advice to his sister at the opening, and his language when he returns from France is ugly and fascistic. He completely lacks the self-criticism of Hamlet, whom he does not remotely challenge for our sympathy. Also, he has no humour at all – not even his father's gift for arousing a sense of fun in other people.

This is not an accident, of course. Laertes is, like Fortinbras, an invention of Shakespeare's: in none of the sources dogging the play, he is part of an inspirational design, a triangle of young men contrasting with and reflecting each other in their capacity for useful or destructive action. In the play's second scene, Fortinbras, Laertes and Hamlet – or their stories – follow each other into the plot in procession. Later, the counterpoint ticks unobtrusively away: Laertes looks to revenge his father with none of Hamlet's hesitation; Hamlet is the bogeyman to Laertes as Claudius is to Hamlet; Laertes is frustrated by the machinations of Claudius as Hamlet is by his own introspection. In the amoral bloodbath that closes the play, both men kill their fathers' killers.

Laertes is both influential within his family and independent of it. His life in France is important enough for him to petition the King for a return to it at the earliest opportunity. As Polonius falls behind the arras Laertes rises to life in Paris, and a parallel revenge story begins. As an instrument of action, he gains in energy but loses in personality. This is a fair burden on the actor, who has to come back at full pressure, ready to carry the rest of the play, providing the pulse that Hamlet has given it in the middle area. Laertes works off the kind of unrelieved heroic attack (like parts of Coriolanus and Henry V) which is the most tiring thing to play and the most difficult to vary. As his character becomes less distinct, it is hard to distinguish between Laertes as rightful avenger and Laertes as potential killing-machine:

> To hell, allegiance; vows, to the blackest devil;
> Conscience and grace to the profoundest pit;
> I dare damnation.

The worst and best sides of him co-exist in the big temptation scene with Claudius; his behaviour in the Graveyard is perfectly understandable and even splendid. But his end does little to redeem him. He tells Hamlet he is dead, quite dead: he explains the reason, briefly condemns the plot, confirms that he is dying himself, and blames the King, only managing a perfunctory settling of accounts himself:

> He is justly served;
> It is a poison temper'd by himself;
> Exchange forgiveness with me, noble Hamlet;
> Mine and my father's deaths come not upon thee;
> Nor thine on me.

This is more of a farewell than that of Claudius or Gertrude; but Laertes doesn't fully acknowledge his part in the plot even now, and there is no particular grace or self-knowledge in him.

Full of blind energy, impassioned responses, and a sort of benighted self-confidence, the role is not exactly thankless: it just looks thin next to Hamlet. Still, Laertes suffers much, and deserves a luckier life; and there will surely be a tide of sympathy for him – to watch two fundamentally good young men, first cast against each other by fate and then manoeuvred into nose-to-nose enmity by a devil, is to feel the play's tragic accumulation. In many ways Laertes works best in productions where totalitarianism shadows the work, and the image of an heroic revolutionary corrupted by a dictator has a special chime. Otherwise he has a big responsibility and not that much reward, as well as a sword fight to learn (with a colleague who has much else to learn) and survive. An ambitious young actor will be glad to get the part and may end up, as frustrated as Gertrude, over-elaborating it. He won't understudy the Hamlet, because if he were to go on for him there would be two understudies fighting the duel that night, and this is generally regarded as daft.⁵ He may be asked to double as a Player these days, which at least keeps him in the play and out of the pub; and the audience will sympathise with him as he struggles with those grotesque exclamations in Ophelia's Mad Scene. He won't win any prizes, and may get laryngitis. Handle with care.

In the early stages, OPHELIA is hardly there at all. With Polonius she seems almost offensively mute and compliant: 'I shall obey, my Lord. . . no, my good Lord, but as you did instruct. . . . I do not know, my Lord, what I should think', rising in protest only as far as

My lord, he hath importun'd me with love
In honourable fashion

– and in the Nunnery Scene she becomes bewildered to the point of stupidity. Only when Hamlet leaves her does she begin to wake up: her idealised description of him is interrupted by the sudden sound of sweet bells jangled;⁶ and from here on, as the character looks down her abyss, the part looks up. However, this startling image is not the first hint of a talent gasping in an airless household: her description of Hamlet's visit to her 'all unbrac'd' is famous because of the descriptive power she brings to it, and in her first scene she shows a brief sense of humour – and a delightful turn of phrase – with Laertes:

Do not, as some ungracious pastors do,
Show me the steep and thorny way to heaven
Whilst like a puff'd and reckless libertine
Himself the primrose path of dalliance treads. . .

She is not afraid of her brother – she understands him and tolerates his pompous advice with love:

'Tis in my memory lock'd
And you yourself shall keep the key of it.

This is the woman she might have become – warm, tolerant and imaginative. Instead she becomes jagged, benighted and imaginative:

5   As a matter of fact it is no easier to play the other part in a fight than it is to do a completely new one, and perhaps more difficult.
6   Quite what his 'music vows' were of which she 'suck'd the honey' we have no evidence of at all, rather the reverse: he has written a feeble poem and she has rejected him by not standing up to her father.

They say the owl was a baker's daughter. Lord, we know what we are, but know not what we may be. God be at your table!

Ophelia is made mad not only by circumstance but by something in herself. A personality forced into such deep hiding that it has seemed almost vacant has all the time been so painfully open to impressions that they now usurp her reflexes and take possession of her. She has loved, or been prepared to love, the wrong man, her father has brought disaster on himself, and she has no mother: she is terribly lonely. Her existence has been all restraints, and when they are removed, a secret life rises up and floods her.

Madness is the safest place for Ophelia: it is where she expresses herself. She may not be a particularly good singer, but she responds to the sounds, voices and pictures jangling in her head. She remembers folk-songs she didn't know she knew. All the channels blocked by 'sanity' open wide, her skin becomes super-sensitive, her glands secrete. She can hear the passage of time like a synaesthetic. She can read people's minds, and sees a grimacing villain when she looks at Claudius, and a nymphomaniac greed behind the Queen's sympathy. She knows somehow that Laertes is on his way to right her wrongs – in fact to reclaim her – and she addresses him momentarily as a lover. She calls everyone 'ladies'. She may be incontinent. Silence dins in her ears as loudly as the waters she will eventually sink into. She is knowing where she was innocent, astute where she was helpless, satirical where she was bland. In spite of her disorders, there is not a line she speaks which is not humming with meaning, warning and portent. She is not so much mad as unacceptably sane. Hamlet and Polonius and Laertes (by his absence) have ruined her life, and her spirit takes flight in a one-winged, raucous trajectory before dropping like a stone to the ground.

Her dominant theme is her father's death (in production, Ophelias very typically wear a garment of Polonius's, so he is back among us), but her imagery tangles him, Hamlet and even Laertes together in a brilliant psychological displacement. Hamlet appears in the scene as the young man in the Saint Valentine's Day song that tells of a virgin who comes to his window – he promises to wed her, and then rejects her exactly because she sleeps with him. In Ophelia's case it was the other way round – it was Hamlet who visited her chamber, partly naked – but the young man's dirty trick in the song matches the bleak cruelty of Hamlet's verbal games: 'I did love you once. . . I loved you not. . . get thee to a nunnery'.

As always with mad scenes, what matters is not the twitches, but the superior logic in the brain. Ophelia looks people straight in the eyes, and speaks naturally to them. The common trap is to do only an interesting pathological study, with the benefit of modern research. The First Quarto's stage direction runs 'Enter Ofelia playing on a lute, and her haire down singing', and is presumably, like the Ghost in his night-gown, a memory of stage practice. Harley Granville-Barker, writing in 1937, saw its value:

> The dramatic point of the lute is that you must stand – or better, sit –
> still if you are to attempt to play it. Modern Ophelias have an
> ineffective habit of drifting vaguely about the stage. A lute is at least an
> admirable anchor...

He was clearly afraid of a drifting, loopy Ophelia. He didn't live to see the new cliché, the sexually rampant one ('by cock they are to blame'), suiting the action to the word. Obviously, sexuality is in it – how could it not be? – but too much of it, like whimsy and neurasthenia, makes the scene monotonously opaque.

Even the sturdiest intellects seem to come over a bit sentimental when it comes to Ophelia: this is because of the flowers. I think they should be real – though a list that includes fresh rue and columbines as well as rosemary, pansies, fennel and daisies is certainly a headache for a prop buyer, and no doubt they will end up being made, making that unconvincing dry slap on the stage when dropped. But, apart from the pleasant incongruity of Laertes, Gertrude and especially Claudius having to hold the flowers Ophelia gives them, the truthfulness of their colour and texture and the girl's precise knowledge of them is very moving; they are beautiful things withered by the fetid air of Elsinore. Her understanding of them is sane and exact: I have seen Ophelias holding weeds and grasses and imagining them flowers, even holding nothing at all and doing the same thing – both these solutions draw attention to her derangement, which we know, and her imaginative gifts, which we also know. The reality is much more powerful.

At first blush, Ophelia is not a patch on her predecessors – Juliet, Rosalind or even Anne Page – and less still on what followed: Viola, Perdita, Cordelia, Miranda. With the special exception of Viola, sitting like patience on her monument, these women stand up to their fathers, and if necessary to their lovers. Ophelia, doing neither, describes the oddest arc, finally winning the right to say anything she likes to anyone, but at the cost of her foothold in the world. The last we see of her, she is being thrown about in a grave, just as she was thrown about in life: shouted over by two assertive young men vying with each other over who loved her more, when there is no great evidence that either of them did very much. Rest in peace.

The Court

VOLTEMAND (the name, slightly corrupted, of a number of Kings of Denmark) and CORNELIUS (a Dutch name) form the foreign policy arm of Claudius's government. Courteously dispatched by him to Norway at the outset, they are 'You, good Cornelius, and you, Voltemand', which makes Cornelius sound senior but is in fact the only way the metre will work. On their return, they are 'good friends'; and it is to Voltemand that Claudius turns – Cornelius may be just as ready with the news, but this time it is he who is defeated by the metre –

Say, Voltemand, what from our brother Norway?

Voltemand has rehearsed carefully. His message is simple enough, but starting with Norway's pleasant salutation:

Most fair return of greetings and desires

he takes sixteen lines over it, larding the news with emotional material about the King's disappointment in his nephew and his subsequent relief – he is 'overcome with joy' that Fortinbras has not argued with him.

The speech builds to an euphoric climax – there will be general amusement that it is Poland, the territory that Fortinbras was pretending to attack before, that he is now being paid to invade – at which point Voltemand slips in the bad news: the request for 'quiet pass' through Denmark. This is what Alfred Hitchcock would have called the McGuffin – the small detail triggering a big story. It shows that Voltemand's work has not been an unqualified success – in fact, he is typical of Claudius's court, a skilled diplomat who hasn't quite dotted the i's. Should he not have questioned this detail? How much authority did he have? When Claudius dispatched the two of them there was a touch of distrust, as if they would be making side-deals – he gave them

> no further personal power
> To business with the King, more than the scope
> Of these dilated articles allow.

In fact he has inhibited them: the result is that Voltemand, going no further than his brief, has not argued a crucial point, and now draws no special attention to it, although it is obviously the weakness in the whole arrangement. Claudius unwisely lets it through in the general good cheer and Voltemand gets off with a clean record. He and Cornelius are characteristically rewarded for their 'well-took labour' with the promise that 'tonight we'll feast together' and, feeling they have done their job, go out of the play. If Claudius had given his diplomats more authority or been more alert himself, if Polonius had demurred instead of maintaining an untypical silence, or if Voltemand had underlined the potential problem instead of keeping his own nose clean, Fortinbras would have been an even smaller part, Horatio might have ended up as King and Denmark would have stayed Danish.

OSRIC is a sign of the times. According to the ever-critical Hamlet,

> he hath much land, and fertile. . . Thus has he, and many more of the same breed that I know the drossy age dotes on, only got the tune of the time and outward habit of encounter. . .

In other words, he is a shallow man of private income, and he has, like James Harthouse in Dickens's *Hard Times*, 'gone in for politics'. In order to fall into step, he may have modelled himself on Polonius, using more art than apparent matter. In fact he has no art, and his language is tainted: he is a measure of how far Claudius's court has lost even the illusion of moral authority since the beginning of the play – new men are coming to the front now, with a mountebank whiff to them, and a style *à la mode*. It may be that Osric has been visible in the previous court scenes, and so the audience will have sensed this degeneration from his progress to the front. If Polonius is Lord Burleigh, Ronald Reagan or Harold Macmillan, Osric is a young Spiro Agnew or John Redwood, with a bit of Sir Fopling Flutter mixed in. But between him and Polonius is a big difference. Polonius's prolixities and paradoxes nevertheless reflect an intelligence that may 'by indirection seek directions out' – but Osric's 'golden words' only gild the lily, obscuring actual meaning by lavishing attention on a small component of a man's sword-belt:

> Three of the carriages, in faith, are very dear to fancy, very responsive to the hilts, most delicate carriages, and of very liberal conceit.

Even Hamlet doesn't know what he's talking about.

The business with his hat, whether he should wear it or not, and the state of the weather:

> HAMLET: Put your bonnet to his right use; 'tis for the head.
> OSRIC: I thank your lordship; it is very hot.
> HAMLET: No, believe me, it is very cold; the wind is northerly.
> OSRIC: It is indifferent cold, my lord, indeed.
> HAMLET: But yet methinks it is very sultry and hot for my complexion.
> OSRIC: Exceedingly, my Lord, it is very sultry, as 'twere – I cannot tell how

is often played to show foolish confusion in Osric, but is more fruitfully (and no less entertainingly) sardonic routine subservience on his part. He and his colleagues have come to expect this sort of thing from Hamlet – and in fact Osric wins the battle, calmly insisting in the end:

> Nay, good my lord, for mine ease, in good faith.

In fact Osric's frivolity masks a certain determination: he is not a fool, but a reliable functionary whom Claudius has chosen for a ticklish job. In the duel, complicit or not, he is the acknowledged master of ceremonies: though Claudius refers to other 'judges', Osric adjudicates alone on doubtful hits, and calls attention to the Queen's plight, so he has a certain public authority. In the last moments of the play, he moves, as the bringer of news, into a subdued, easy verse:

> Young Fortinbras, with conquest come from Poland,
> To the ambassadors of England gives
> This warlike volley

– becoming a part of the play's final chorus, simple, plain, emotion contained by form. If he was in on the plot he is undiscovered and re-shaping himself for the future. Perhaps he is stunned by the scale of the disasters, and it has turned him into something human – he was not up to all this villainy, after all. Or perhaps, like Rosencrantz and Guildenstern, he was simply caught for a moment in the crossfire, and, more fortunate than them, has got away with it.

As for THE COURT at large, there will not, in these pinched days, be much to it. The sense of bustling activity, an ongoing life that even has nothing to do with Hamlet's adventures, is available only on film: to Olivier, to Kozintsev, to Zeffirelli, to Branagh. It is difficult even for the national theatre companies in this country to afford, and perhaps this has always been the case since the end of Herbert Beerbohm Tree's spectaculars at Her Majesty's at the turn of the century. Even so, when I was in my first RSC *Hamlet* in 1965 there was a cast of twenty-five principals, and a further twenty who never spoke at all, and as if that weren't enough, many doubled to swell the overall effect: you may recall that Fortinbras was the Ghost's legs, and he was also a clerk in the court up until the Play Scene. In 1980, on the other hand, there was a total of twenty-one all in. In the commercial production of 1994 the barely economical cast was eighteen: Claudius's court had their hair-raising quick change to become Fortinbras's army, and attendance at the duel dwindled as courtiers slipped away during the exciting bits to become the English Ambassadors and Fortinbras's army once again. Probably it was like this in Shakespeare's company: the assembler of the Bad Quarto had played three parts by the time of the Play Scene alone.[7]

This straitened condition puts a certain responsibility onto a handful of actors, and it is quite a creative one. Every face will become familiar, and everybody will surely have something to say at some point, either as Voltemand, as Reynaldo, as a Gentleman, or as the important Lord who forms a contrast to Osric – a completely mute part is unusual in Shakespeare nowadays. The handful has to be chosen well, with regard to age and as much personality as can be expressed without speaking: they are telling us vital things. Are they all like Osric, or very unlike him? Just as a film director will change his shot for reactions, an audience's roving eye is always checking the responses of the onlookers to events, and what those onlookers are like. The business of courtly sycophancy is certainly more complex than the wearing of a crooked smile and a darting eye: at each moment in the play there will be an appropriate general response and a private reaction more or less suppressed. So everyone in the group has to be able to answer confidently, if a director should suddenly stop and ask: What do you feel, officially

---

7   Thomas Platter, a Swiss visitor, reported in 1599 that he had seen *Julius Caesar* at 'the house with the thatched roof' (the Globe) with a cast of fifteen and dancing at the end. What happened to the crowd in the forum?

and unofficially, about the remarriage of the Queen, about the derangement of Ophelia, about the fight in the grave? Are you convinced by Laertes's accusation against Claudius: there is a cry of 'Treason!' as Hamlet kills him, but is this because everyone believes the King innocent or because regicide is treason come what may? Finally, what is the nature of the silence as the court falls in under Fortinbras, keeping its head down, trimming to survive?

In return, a director has to establish a vocabulary by deciding on the production's 'givens' – whether Claudius's announcement of the remarriage is a surprise, or a celebration of what everyone knows already; whether the court is used to seeing travelling actors in plays; when the last big duel was. A Danish courtier may not have the right to bring a rehearsal to a halt to establish his personal feelings at a given point, but he or she should have material to chew on rather than being used as all-purpose toady or unpaid stage management.

There is a famous trade story of a director trying to sell a non-speaking part in a Shakespeare play to an actor who expected something more substantial: this, the director insisted, was to be the character who becomes irresistibly intriguing to the audience because he is always *there* and *refuses to speak*. Had the offer been taken up, the ensuing performance might have been a dreadful thing. No-one can truthfully make great claims for the rewards of being a supernumary in *Hamlet*; but there is at every moment a discreet job to do.

The Soldiers

Likewise, it would be an affectation to pretend that the parts of MARCELLUS, BARNARDO and FRANCISCO are ultimately rewarding. But within his five lines Francisco sounds the play's first quiet tocsin:

> For this relief much thanks. 'Tis bitter cold,
> And I am sick at heart

and has his beautiful, practical observation about the motionless mouse – so half of his lines are quite famous, and the casting should not to be negligible.[8]

---

8   If Marcellus and Barnardo have told him what has happened on the previous two nights, he will of course be nervous of what he might see; but in fact they have imparted their news

It falls to Marcellus to introduce the awesome idea of the Ghost, to Barnardo to do the build-up to its appearance, and Marcellus has the beautiful speech at the end of the first scene about Christmas. Neither says anything much while Horatio then recounts the story to Hamlet, but to be convincing in support, they must decide how they stand in relation to the Crown Prince – which of them is senior, and have they met him before. Barnardo disappears, and Marcellus is deeply involved in the toing and froing with the Ghost, before presumably, like him, becoming a Player or part of Fortinbras's army.

Above all, the three of them form an important opening picture: Claudius's military in a state of high alert. They are decent and humane, but they should be tough: they protect the castle, looking out for signs of an invasion by night from the north, and any other emergencies. They feel weakened and confused by the incursion of the supernatural. If one of them is to be young, the other two should have the weight of some years and experience, both as soldiers and actors. Best to cast them with as interesting personalities as possible, hoping again that what Shakespeare has left unexpressed in lines may be made up for by a degree of charisma.

The Commoners

The PLAYERS are professionals: if anyone is the ham, it is Hamlet, not they. In Elsinore, everyone either plays an artificial part to survive (Hamlet, Claudius) or deceives themselves (Gertrude) or performs for an audience (Polonius); the real Players provide the quality, bringing true feeling to remote, invented situations. It is only their repertoire that is old-fashioned: they are, like us, modern actors doing the classics, and their approach is as contemporary as the Method.

The First Player is an admired older actor, and perhaps the manager as well. In the seclusion of his study, Professor John Dover Wilson decided in 1918 that this was a satirical portrait of Edward Alleyn, head of the Lord Admiral's Men, Shakespeare's company's main rivals, a 'robustious, periwig-pated fellow', all

to Horatio 'in dreadful secrecy'. So Francisco is in the dark about this Ghost, but he is uneasy in a way many people in Denmark are uneasy.

bombast and rhetoric. Why such a figure should have so deep an influence on Hamlet he doesn't explain. This chimes with the bad stage tradition (now mercifully on the wane) of playing him well over the top: an insult delivered to the theatre by the theatre itself. He strikes deep truth out of fantasy: like all good actors, he can live intensely in the moment, then hold his hand out for his fee.

In a period production of *Hamlet*, the Player Queen might well be a boy player, as in Shakespeare's own company, even if Gertrude and Ophelia (the 'real' people) are being played by women. Shakespeare's boy players are difficult for us to imagine.[9] We may feel a point of contact with the whole remote tradition via the *onnagata*, the female impersonator of Japanese kabuki theatre, and it may be this that has led to kabuki-ish versions of the Play Scene, which is rather confusing. Really it is not the same thing: the *onnagata* is an adult, and may be middle-aged. Splitting the difference, our male Player Queen nowadays is likely to be a young, reasonably delicate actor, and he certainly doesn't need to be effeminate. Rather, he is a trusted specialist, like a counter-tenor; and he has, like all sex impersonators, a certain amount to put up with, not least Hamlet's condescending play on his insecurities:

> By'r lady, your Ladyship is nearer to Heaven than when I saw you last, by the altitude of a chopine; pray God your voice, like a piece of uncurrent gold, be not cracked within the ring. . .

This is like meeting a theatregoer who tells you you're older these days and wonders if you can still cut the mustard – you smile, but you'd rather kill.

The actors come into the court with the odd mixture of contempt, genuine awe and childish mockery the 'entertainment' always feels in grand venues (I know: I've played Buckingham Palace). It is only the First Player and the boy that Hamlet greets: the rest are simply 'masters', but among them is one who will play the villain Lucianus, a small part only because Claudius stops the show. Lucianus presumably had a scene of seduction after the murder; so he could easily be (and sometimes is) played by the leading First Player, releasing a substantial (but less sexy) part, the elegiac

---

9   Even if we can conceive of the Rosalinds and Juliets, it takes effort to imagine Mistress Quickly and Juliet's Nurse, parts which must have called for the skills of an adult (perhaps on occasion bringing with them the knowingness of the drag artist), rather than the delicately ambiguous juveniles.

Player King, to another weighty actor in the troupe. There will be those in the company both learning from and vying with these principals. In *The Murder of Gonzago* they don't have much to do apart from stage management, setting up the orchard and so on, but the normal contours of a theatre company – internal cliques, poker players, the earnest and the ambitious ones, the emerging stars and the skivers – can be discreetly played. Some admire the First Player, some think he was better last night, some think he's had his day. The main thing is that they should all be good at their job and wary for their livelihood. Of the various clichés that have sprouted around the Players because of the innate oddity of a Prince (who may be being played by the most striking actor on the stage) advising professionals on how to act, with demonstrations, one of the least helpful is when they all laugh at Hamlet behind their hands or become obviously impatient at being lectured on their own business. Royal patronage is crucially important to these people: they have to put up with all the rest, just as professionals these days have to put up with corporate sponsors or endure being cornered by a zealous (and always ungenerous) amateur actor at a party, who wants to talk as one pro to another. It comes with the territory.

The two nameless figures who look at Ophelia's death down the other end of a telescope were simply described as 'Clownes' in the early texts; and sure enough, they are there to make you laugh. Nowadays, as realistic GRAVEDIGGERS with mattocks and spades, they bring a daunting comedy into the play; if they were originally done by Shakespeare's cap-and-bells men, Robert Armin and William Kempe, the creators of Touchstone, Feste and Dogberry, his audacity in bringing them into *Hamlet* becomes even more extreme[10].

10. In Peterborough Cathedral in Cambridgeshire is a portrait of Old Scarlett the gravedigger, a man who, born in 1497, (incredibly for the time) lived into his ninety-eighth year, burying two generations of each Peterborough household, and in addition two Queens: Katherine of Aragon (1536) and Mary Queen of Scots (1587).
      Second to none for strength and sturdye limm
      A scarebabe mighty voice with visage grim. . .
he is formally dressed in the round-shouldered, high-waisted Elizabethan tunic that makes men look slightly hump-backed, and his ruff and his beard join together in a kind of curly grey penumbra round his head, topped by a scarlet skullcap. The soles of his surprisingly courtly black shoes with their long blue laces are scarlet as well, so he is, cap-a-pe, as his name implies. He carries the keys to the graveyard and a spade, and a pickaxe and a skull are set beside him against a rather formal classical pillar. His weatherbeaten face contrives to

Certainly, their naturalistic roles as master and apprentice parallel their function as comic and feed. The apprentice starts strongly, but is soon worn down by his mate's remorseless Socratic dialogue, and he takes himself off to the pub, from which in fact he never returns. Dealing with a colleague who has to be right about everything, he hasn't done at all badly – faced with the riddle about 'the mason, the shipwright and the carpenter', he has been in the right general field, near to 'the gravemaker'; but he feels as if he has been run over by a slow steamroller, and that is the end of him:

> SECOND GRAVEDIGGER: Marry, now I can tell.
> FIRST GRAVEDIGGER: To't.
> SECOND GRAVEDIGGER: Mass, I cannot tell.
> FIRST GRAVEDIGGER: Cudgel thy brains no more about it. . .

The wiseacre First Gravedigger is a saloon bar philosopher (specialities: the law, including Latin, local history and ethics) who will go at his own pace and in his own time in pursuit of his own circular conclusions – and he will brook no interruptions:

> FIRST GRAVEDIGGER: . . . argal, she drowned herself wittingly.
> SECOND GRAVEDIGGER: Nay, but hear you, goodman Delver –
> FIRST GRAVEDIGGER: Give me leave. Here lies the water – good. Here stands the man – good. . .

He has no sympathetic emotions, though he seems roused to something close to a feeling by his memory of Yorick:

> A pestilence on him for a mad rogue! 'A poured a flagon of Rhenish on my head once.

(Why the court jester was pouring wine over a gravedigger is hard to imagine: the latter seems to have become somebody else for the moment, another clown at the court.) This is a man who, asked how long he has been working, will stick his spade upright in the ground, lean on it, say he 'came to't' on the day the old King beat the King of Norway, then tell you you are a fool if you don't know that was the day the King's son was born, and make some jokes about the son's madness and the madness of the English before answering the question: he has been sexton, man and boy, for thirty years. Beyond this, he has no biography: we know no more of him than of some self-appointed expert met on a bus.

---

look both threatening and humorous: its practical gaze, combined with the slight flamboyance of his scarlet trim -- not to mention a hint of immortality -- make him at once a man of death and a clown.

The Gravedigger's victory in his contest with the Prince, coupled with the sense that he has a significance to the play beyond himself, makes his a very good part, often doubled with the Ghost and/or the Player King or even Polonius – a senior actor's job, small as it is. He has to have an absolute reality, absolute detachment, unnerving humour. Like Abhorson the executioner in *Measure for Measure*, his is 'a mystery': he knows the survival rates of flesh. His jokes are good, but utterly negative. He makes nothing, apart from holes in the ground. He is not exactly sinister; but to see him confound Hamlet at this stage makes him, subtly, a symbol of the very thing he deals in.

The PRIEST has an impossible job. He has been forced to do something against his conscience and the law: to bury a suspected suicide in consecrated ground. He has to go ahead with it, and his explanation, that he is forced to 'by great command', has a suppressed fury: there is no greatness in the order, just totalitarian force. Attacked by Laertes, he is eloquent on the limits of what he can do, and what should, in his view, be happening to Ophelia until the Last Judgment, describing it with surprising violence:

> Shards, flints and pebbles should be thrown on her

– and he defies this aristocrat, the next-of-kin, without respect or quarter. So in his tiny part there is a glimpse of a larger, undeveloped theme – the Church disenfranchised by the secular arm; and Claudius knows, for what it could ever be worth to him, that he has an angry pastor against him.

Norway and England

When it comes to FORTINBRAS,[11] the third corner of the play's triangle of young men, Peter Hall may have been right the first time. The Norwegian is an important innovation by Shakespeare: in his brief but sharply-drawn figure the dramatist crystallises the play's political struggle, at the same time amplifying its central theme of filial revenge.

---

11   The name would have been recognised by an Elizabethan audience as a translation of 'strong-arm', a pun on Armstrong of Gilnockie, the border Scot whose raids threatened the peace between England and Scotland in the 1530s; in our time he has become the protagonist of John Arden's play *Armstrong's Last Goodnight*.

His two entries are perfectly timed: first at the end of the pur-
gative sequence running from the Play through the Closet to
Hamlet's banishment, and then to summarise the sickening helter-
skelter of the climax – both times he brings in the cold actuality of
a different, still more northern sensibility. For long before his first
arrival, Fortinbras lightly shadows the play: once established, he is
never mentioned again (though his father is, by the Gravedigger)
until his final appearance.

Half of his significance is political. His father's crown has
bypassed Fortinbras as Hamlet's father's has him; politically em-
bittered (unlike Hamlet) he is empire-building on his own account,
waiting for the passing of a weak King, his uncle. The combination
of a self-confident Claudius and this compliant uncle is, for the
moment, too strong for him; so he turns his eye to Poland, where
he conquers, seemingly without effort, returning by the same route
to converge with the ambassadors from England on a Danish court
now completely decimated from within: a bonus indeed. He closes
the public area of the play rather as Claudius opened it, with the
assurance of a new ruler, as yet uncrowned in his own country, but
uncontested here.

The other contrast he provides is poetic and imaginative: he
links us with the awesome old world of his father and King Hamlet,
evoking memories of single combat, heroic deeds on the ice, the
matrix of young Hamlet's nostalgia; this, in contrast to Claudius's
Realpolitik, is the epic sound in his voice, austere and rhetorical, at
the end:

> This quarry cries on havoc. O proud death,
> What feast is toward in thine eternal cell
> That thou so many princes at a shot
> So bloodily hast struck?

His shortcoming is imaginative: his is a controllable world, and he
interprets everything according to his own code, so the civilian
destruction that he finds now may genuinely shock him – it is the
kind of thing he is used to at work, but here it 'shows much amiss'.
Hamlet must have a soldier's funeral because that is what Fortinbras understands – though Hamlet's military prowess is perhaps his
most unsung virtue. The Norwegian's final tribute to his Danish
counterpart is, of course, a little bit for the cameras; it is also, for us
who have watched the Dane all night, highly ironic.[12] Of the three

young men intent on avenging their fathers, Fortinbras is at once the least attractive, the most successful, the least haunted by the other two and the most limited.

He also belongs to a group in the play, as does the Ghost, whose characterisation is severely abbreviated by Shakespeare – not that they are not striking figures, but they exist on their own terms only and don't undergo any refining interaction with other characters. Their nature is more or less fixed: Fortinbras sees the dead body of Hamlet, of course, and is affected by the sight, but he can only pay tribute to him according to his own, very un-Hamletlike values. In this sense much of Shakespeare is epic theatre: as opposed to that of Chekhov, for example, which exists uncompromisingly in terms of character. For the Ghost and Fortinbras, and indeed Voltemand and Cornelius, the actor brings on his own qualities, having been cast as close to the part as possible: impact is everything. In this particular case, what is called for is a young actor with vocal timbre and few doubts about himself.

Similarly the ENGLISH AMBASSADORS, who arrive at the same moment as Fortinbras. They are strictly unnecessary. We could have taken it for granted that Rosencrantz and Guildenstern were dead from Hamlet's account, and in fact it could have been confirmed by letter – were there anyone left to read it. But Shakespeare needs to hear their music, developing Fortinbras's reaction to the deaths he sees around him. So they must strike the same bell of formal regret, and not do the obvious, react with violent amazement. They are the English equivalent of Voltemand and Cornelius, professional diplomats; but their Englishness needs no special emphasis, and a wrong note here will spoil the play at the eleventh hour.

Hamlet's Friends

HORATIO is perhaps not so much a friend of Hamlet's as an innocent bystander who gets cast in the role.

He is the hero of the first scene and of the end of the last, and between falls back into the Horatio position: Hamlet's ear,

---

12   The question of whether Hamlet would really have 'prov'd most royal' is an open one – he might be too much his own man intellectually to be a good King. Certainly of Malcolm's long list of 'king-becoming virtues' in *Macbeth*, Hamlet has about three.

Hamlet's rock, only the faintest sound of remonstrance or scruple intimating a break into individuality. The part thus looks most unrewarding indeed, barely 'fifth business' in the play: a confidant used by Hamlet when the emotional need arises but never really consulted, an intimate who risks offence at every step. When Horatio brings the first news of the Ghost, Hamlet and the production depend on his handling the business sensitively, but the responsibility is more than the reward. Apart from one felicitous line which has passed into quotation:

A countenance more in sorrow than in anger

Horatio behaves here more like a servant or messenger than a friend ('Hail to your lordship . . . your poor servant ever. . . my honoured lord'), and the self-contradictions that will dog the part begin to butt up against each other – Horatio saw the old King 'once', but twenty-five lines later claims to have known his face so well that the Ghost's was as like it as his two hands are to each other.

After this early sign of bad construction, Shakespeare seems unable to decide whether Horatio belongs to Elsinore or Wittenberg, how close he is to Hamlet or how well anyone else knows him. In the first scene on the battlements, he seems to know Danish history intimately: in the second, he needs to have Elsinore's drinking traditions explained to him by Hamlet. Though a poor scholar, by the beginning of the fourth day he seems to have become a central figure in the court, advising the Queen against her wishes to see Ophelia: later he is 'good Horatio' to Claudius. Yet when Hamlet writes to him he seems so solitary that he knows of no part of the world he should receive a letter from if not from Hamlet. A literary critic might regard all this inconsistency as unimportant, because our gentle poet had his own way; but a certain biographical logic is much appreciated by actors and audiences. The difficulties presented by Horatio really are a mark of failure – as ever, there is a price to be paid for the playwright's absorption in Hamlet himself.

In practice Horatio is unlikely to get warm reviews even if he is good; but if he is bad, particularly at the end, he will be spotted. He is a base colour for Hamlet to stand out against; at the same time Hamlet's tribute to him is a tangible ideal which he somehow has to live up to. The part is important, but it makes no-one's name.

For all that, there is something there. For one thing, Horatio's deference and modesty could mask an intellectual's pride. And the opening scene gives him a development which can be missed in all the excitement of the Ghost. Appointed as a scholarly leader of the team by the nervous soldiers, his approach is utterly sceptical and blunt:

What? Has this thing appear'd again tonight?

– this is an intellectual who plays the plain man. His Wittenberg University background would not make him a disbeliever in the supernatural – not at all, since metaphysical speculation and independent thought would have been his daily bread: it was here that Faust reputedly tinkered with the devil, and Luther nailed his thesis to the church door. Rather, the disrespect of 'this thing' may be a sign of familiarity, not disbelief. It is followed by what seems like further scorn ('Tush, tush, 'twill not appear'), but is perhaps Horatio's judicious opinion, based on his trained instinct in these matters. So, between knowledgeability and scepticism, there are two separate tones for the actor to strike.

However, the actual encounter with the Ghost leaves him stuck for an answer, and he fears the supernatural upheavals preceding the death of Julius Caesar – something cosmic, not just political change. When the Ghost reappears Horatio shows real courage, and an ingenuity in his four questions which, if it were to answer, would surely prove the thing either a devil or an 'honest ghost'. Finally he modulates into the untypically lyric tone of the scene's end – no longer a speculative scholar, but a man stripped down to common sensitivities, released into articulacy. From detached observer to engaged protagonist, Horatio has reinvented himself in a hundred and fifty lines.

At the other end of the play, it is he who takes charge: stoic, authoritative, and with a new voice that is the more moving for its unexpectedness. The beautiful requiem to Hamlet:

> Goodnight, sweet Prince;
> And flights of angels sing thee to thy rest

comes from this surprising quarter – it is the same voice that gave us the russet mantle at the opening. He deals with Fortinbras with a dignity and political sense (tactical circumlocution too) that Fortinbras immediately respects, accepting Horatio's advice to get on with the funeral arrangements 'lest more mischance On plots and errors happen'. The play and the audience need this firm authority of the veteran – certainly not sentiment or emotionalism – to bring the play to its grave, uneasy, musical end.

These days, ROSENCRANTZ and GUILDENSTERN would be sent back to the author for further work, perhaps with a suggestion that the two parts could be combined into one. Why two salaries? If Shakespeare wanted a friend for Hamlet as corrupted as Horatio is loyal, how about Rosenstern?

Is there really any difference between these two? It is difficult to see it as you watch.[13] Without the complementary feed-and-punch rhythm of the true double-act, they are more a duet for perfectly matched voices, and something about the hapless pair invites facetiousness. There is no shortage of meaningless small partnerships in Shakespeare, names at which professionals sigh and the public snigger, thinking of department stores or solicitors' firms: Angus and Menteith in *Macbeth*, Longaville and Dumain in *Love's Labour's Lost*, and worst of all, Salerio and Solanio (or is it Salarino – even the names are editorially uncertain) in *The Merchant of Venice*. Perhaps the point of such pairings is that the two will speak to each other, confidingly, about what is going on. But Rosencrantz and Guildenstern never do, not once; they only mildly qualify each other while addressing other people.[14] Even their names are metrically identical (Shakespeare saving himself trouble: each is two-fifths of a blank verse line, *prêt-à-porter*) – at least Voltemand and Cornelius have different stresses. This is a single atom whose fission has produced little energy.

They start as they mean to go on, introducing themselves with the same voice and in the same rhythm:

13 For mnemonic help I have noticed designers inclining towards colour-code: red or brown for Rosencrantz and green or grey for Guildenstern, which is certainly more helpful than the other way round.

14 Until Tom Stoppard came along. *Rosencrantz and Guildenstern Are Dead* starts as an inspired *jeu d'esprit* and becomes an existential comedy of such depth that it is a nutritious study for actors playing the Shakespeare parts. Giving the two men distinctive characters (or at least contrasting moods at any given moment) in a way that Shakespeare would have done well to consider, makes it possible for Stoppard to make comic capital out of their interchangeability:

GUILDENSTERN (*turning on him furiously*): No wonder the whole thing is so stagnant! You don't take me up on anything – you just repeat it in a different order.

ROSENCRANTZ: Both your majesties
   Might by the sovereign power you have of us
   Put your dread pleasures more into command
   Than to entreaty.
GUILDENSTERN: But we both obey
   And here give up ourselves in the full bent
   To lay our service freely at your feet
   To be commanded

– whereupon the Queen makes a joke about their identity. It is not a promising start for two hopeful young actors anxious to prove their distinctiveness.

When they report back things are little better:

ROSENCRANTZ: He does confess he feels himself distracted
   But from what cause he will by no means speak.
GUILDENSTERN: Nor do we find him forward to be sounded
   But with a crafty madness keeps aloof
   When we would bring him on to some confession
   Of his true state.

Then they plunge into the action, to be whirled about by it until they are dead, getting all the worst jobs and being blamed by everyone, ever less distinct from each other: it seems that their purpose is purely antiphonal, one voice split into two. Certainly some of Shakespeare's concerns were only musical – his interest in what we call character, when it wasn't astounding, could be extremely moderate. He is casual, too, about provenance, and Rosencrantz and Guildenstern belong in the same limbo as Horatio: student friends of Hamlet who are nevertheless quite at home at the court, and known to the King and Queen, even if Claudius's enthusiastic greeting

   Moreover that we much did long to see you

can be taken with a pinch of salt. But whereas Horatio is a completely loose cannon in the play, there is a tension in the position of Rosencrantz-and-Guildenstern, precisely caught between two mighty opposites. So there is throughout something for the two of them to play; it is just that it is usually the same thing, and the same for them both.

It is of course an unenviable position in any time or culture to be plucked out to help in some domestic crisis affecting the Royal Family: and Rosencrantz and Guildenstern suffer a more or less permanent anxiety. Their formality when brought face to face with the monarch contrasts well with their easy prose rhythms with Hamlet, the only other character they speak to for more than a moment: there's a deal of undergraduate silliness in their first encounter with him, but they do at least sound like human beings. However, they will never be able to relax with Hamlet either, since, apart from his justified mistrust, he may at any moment sell them a dummy – a great wrong-footer, he pulls rank on them, judges them mercilessly, and finally destroys them. To this sense of inevitable casualty the actors have to hang on tight, through their various protests, acquiescences, uneasy perceptions of divided loyalty; above all the two of them are not silly, certainly not campy, but decent men in over their heads. The news of their deaths:

HORATIO: So Guildenstern and Rosencrantz go to't.

should carry a reproof from Horatio and bring a silence to the theatre.

Scouting about, the actors may turn up the following: in general Rosencrantz initiates while Guildenstern qualifies – though there is no special timidity or shyness about him. Although Shakespeare often alternates their order of speaking, it is with a sense of weary routine: Rosencrantz leads in the discussion of the Players with Hamlet, and Guildenstern has his turn with the recorders after the Play Scene. On the whole, Rosencrantz seems to be the leader; but then at one point, after the Closet, Claudius calls 'Ho Guildenstern!', following it with 'friends both' – but on this occasion neither of them gets to speak. The name Rosencrantz sort of means 'red coronet', Guildenstern sounds like 'golden star'. There was a Rosenkrantz at Wittenberg University a few years before the play; both names would have registered as typically Danish.[15] Rosencrantz is the bigger part, almost twice as big: by way of compensation Guildenstern may be offered the understudy of Hamlet (much to the disgust, at Stratford in 1965, of Fortinbras).

---

15   Shakespeare made no secret of his models. He got into trouble with Falstaff, whom he originally called Sir John Oldcastle after a companion of Henry V's, overlooking the fact that one of Oldcastle's descendants was now Lord Chamberlain. He changed the name, offending the Fastolfe family instead. He was surely on safer ground with a humble student of Wittenberg.

Hamlet

> It really boils down to symptoms. Pregnant replies, mystic allusions, mistaken identities, arguing his father is his mother, that sort of thing; intimations of suicide, forgoing of exercise, loss of mirth, hints of claustrophobia not to say delusions of imprisonment; invocations of camels, chameleons, capons, whales, weasels, hawks, handsaws – riddles, quibbles and evasions; amnesia, paranoia, myopia; day-dreaming, hallucinations; stabbing his elders, abusing his parents, insulting his lover, and appearing hatless in public – knock-kneed, droop-stockinged and sighing like a love-sick schoolboy, which at his age is coming on a bit strong. . .
>
> Tom Stoppard, *Rosencrantz and Guildenstern Are Dead*

In the English theatre at least, a director who decided to do *Hamlet* and then started looking around for a Hamlet would be an oddity. There are a lot of good actors about, and you might embark on a *Merchant of Venice*, an *As You Like It* or a *Henry V* with the confidence that someone would turn up out of the great British repertory company to play the leads – but not a *Hamlet*, or a *Lear*, or an *Antony and Cleopatra*. These are the 'specials': the motive is the actor who's ready, the actress at whom the blood quickens. As Max Beerbohm said, Hamlet is a hoop through which every eminent (let's update him: every dangerous, marketable 'hot') performer must sooner or later jump – if he wants to. And since this is an unforgiving contest, he has to strike exceptional fire or not do it at all – a middling Prince is no good to anyone. The interesting player is thus taken to the part like a match to the touchpaper: you retreat and wait for the bang.

Hamlet is perhaps the cleverest hero ever written, the subject of the first European tragedy worthy of the name for two thousand years: a form of genius, as Orson Welles observed, akin to Mercutio and Richard II (I would add Berowne and perhaps Richard III), and a type that Shakespeare despaired of writing thereafter, having perceived that the heroes of tragedies must be sublime idiots (Lear, Othello). Among actors, the role is supposedly the object of much professional rivalry; among those who have played it, it is the source, surprisingly often, of regret, and occasionally of real self-definition. It's also said that nobody can quite fail in it, because Hamlet becomes the man (or woman) who plays it. By this reckoning, Shakespeare's character could be almost anything, and it certainly has been a garment pulled in all manner of directions. Such infinite variety does make it difficult to define the man in the usual terms: but of course there are some practical rules. Any lack of vitality in the actor translates into a sluggish Hamlet. A lack of generosity makes his Hamlet mean: only a true breadth of spirit, embracing fatalism and aspiration at the same time, will do. Most cruelly, any lack of 'personality' in the player makes for a dull Prince.

But for all his resonance beyond it, Hamlet is a character in a play, confined by the play, bound by the same rules therefore as Osric; and to serve it, he must be certain measurable things. There are mileposts all the way through that the new candidate is checked off against: 'O what a noble mind is here o'erthrown / The courtier's, soldier's, scholar's eye, tongue, sword' grieves Ophelia, and the audience checks back – is it so? The Players arrive and Hamlet is carried away with excitement and pleasure: can you believe he is brainy enough to remember certain of their speeches by heart? He certainly knows what acting is about and what it is for: does he personify those standards himself? Claudius says: 'How dangerous is it that this man goes loose': so is his personality a real threat to the King, and are they 'mighty opposites'? As well as the capacity for threat, has he a talent for lethargy ('I have of late, but wherefore I know not, lost all my mirth'), and plain silliness ('that's two of his weapons; but well')? Is he enough of a clown for Polonius, Rosencrantz and Guildenstern, and at the same time a sort of romantic lead? Is he ruthless enough to switch the packets on shipboard, sending Rosencrantz and Guildenstern to their deaths when all he strictly needed to do was save himself? Is he a good fencer, able to run Laertes close, even though he has lately 'forgone all manner of exercise'? Does he have the vision to crystallise 'To be or not to be', the childish cruelty to say to his mother 'at your age The heyday in the blood is tame', the recklessness to make a joke in front of his father's Ghost? Sufficiently wise to say 'The readiness is all', and existential enough to declare that Polonius is 'Not where he eats but where he is eaten'? And what of his own estimate of himself, making allowance for his pervasive irony (he has to have that too): 'I am very proud, revengeful, ambitious, with more offences at my beck than I have thoughts to put them in, imagination to give them shape, or time to act them in'. And in the end, when he lies dead, does he meet the final tests (the critics are very hot on these): Horatio's 'Goodnight, sweet prince And flights of angels sing thee to thy rest', and

Fortinbras's 'He was likely, had he been put on, To have proved most royal'. Was he, will they, and would he have?

To deal with such a mass, what is the state of the actor's equipment? Is the voice strong enough to do perhaps eight performances a week? Does his stage personality have both a smack of the classical ('My father's spirit in arms? All is not well') and the provocatively modern ('In heaven, send thither to see; if your messenger find him not there, seek him in the other place yourself')? Is he mercurial enough to keep an audience interested for four hours or so? Is he a wise enough performer to know that he is not a one-man band, and that if the play is to work, he must balance himself against Claudius, Ophelia and Gertrude, with all of whom he has relationships, albeit in decay? Is he sexually attractive, since the making of honest love between him and the audience is vital to the play – though the sexuality of the part is not so much a matter of lineament as of emotional candour and Hamlet's skill, at the last moment, in mythologising himself:

> And in this harsh world draw thy breath in pain
> To tell my story

– with its overtone of a unique solitude, uniquely borne.

If the answer to more than half these questions is yes, play on.

Rehearsing

There have been one-off *Hamlet*s put on because someone, not necessarily a 'Shakespearian', is bursting with the readiness to do it. There are others, specially at Stratford-upon-Avon, where the logic of that almost outmoded thing, a 'classical' career, has developed in a stately way towards the *moment juste*. Whatever the angle of approach, all new Hamlets go into rehearsal with a mixture of fright and assertiveness. For those aware of history, every choice thumps with significance: intimate voices within whisper Garrick and Gielgud, Rylance and Charleson. The 'innocent' actor, enfranchised from all that, may still feel he is in blind flight from imagined precedent, a whole host of nameless voices chattering. How can he know if his instincts are clean? Under these equal pressures, no actor wants to do the obvious, and may determine *not* to watch the King in the Play Scene; to take hold of the Ghost and shake him; to fight not in the Grave but outside it – and may bravely conclude in the end that the obvious is right. Like Hamlet, he feels set apart, like someone working deep in a mine, and finds it quite difficult to join in normal rituals like lunch in the pub:[16] he feels a constant need to be working, taking decisions. Like Hamlet, he will start out surrounded by good will, and then, at a certain stage of desperate self-definition, may intensely irritate his colleagues: 'What's he doing *now?* ' mutter maddened Gertrudes and Ophelias as their man improvises like a jumping jack. Other colleagues who have paid out a lot of rope may haul it back in as their own needs sharpen. On every side are the old sticks who have played Hamlet themselves or were in a *really* famous one, gazing balefully (he thinks) on – they have accepted Claudius or Polonius or the Gravedigger as an inevitable rite of passage. To the paranoid Prince, these are like Ingmar Bergman's figure of Death haunting the Knight.

In due course, the relationship with the director may become complicated as well – many Hamlets are, frankly, determined to do it their way.[17] It must be very difficult to direct a Hamlet. First of all, you must know your man well, not only that he is exciting casting, but that he is interested in the play as well as himself, and prepared to give his time – his life, in fact – to the full range of it. Then you need to exploit his exceptional gifts, giving him carte blanche to explore their recesses, but still be able to pull him back into the ensemble where necessary, or you will have no production. To some degree, you get what you buy – you are backing a very wild horse indeed here, with the ultimate scent in its nostrils, and it is liable to gallop off in any direction. I daresay I was more violent and unruly as Hamlet than John Barton would have liked; Stephen Dillane, more recently, may sometimes have substituted his personal style for Peter Hall's approach to the verse: both received equal acclaim. Because of the inordinate demands of the part and its great self-defining significance, discussion of any given scene may be distorted by the Hamlet's feeling that it is his ideas that should be specially indulged, and that a colleague with one big moment – the Nunnery, the Closet – should necessarily defer to

16 Some kindly people in Stratford have since told me that they would see me wandering around the town and be afraid that I would absent-mindedly step into the path of a bus.

17 John Gielgud has said that a Hamlet needs a strong director to keep him under control, and he should know: he has twice directed himself in the role.

someone who has nine or ten, and several laps of the track to get round. I am not saying that things have to get difficult in this way: only that if they do, this may be the reason.

The part is much more tiring to rehearse than to play. At this stage, it can be a desperate business, calling out everything you know, not only about your job, without yet the reward of sharing it. Every emotion has to be gone through, and, alongside, the knowledge is dawning of how much it is all going to cost physically. Structurally speaking, the part condenses from a series of ensemble set pieces (the first Court Scene, the Play Scene and the Duel) in which there is a powerful frame to operate within, into a group of essential interviews in freer form (with the Ghost, Ophelia and Gertrude) with much less distinct parameters, which form the gruelling meat of the part: and these are further refined, at four crucial points, into the distinctive encounters with the audience, with whom Hamlet has his most confidential – and unstructured – relationship. These last are the most instinctive and passionate areas, and the most invigorating to play.

A certain kind of analysis can be helpful. Once when rehearsing Hamlet and perplexed, I sat me down, devised my own account of the play, wrote it fair – and strangely, it helped me climb back on the horse:

> The external world is proceeding smoothly. The society is attractive, warmhearted, congenial: they all understand one another. The really difficult thing is to stand apart from such a seductive place. Nevertheless, one man, bereaved and prey to morbid reflection, has a nightmare in which he receives a message, supposedly from beyond the grave, declaring that the external world is in fact corrupt, its leader a murderer and adulterer, and his wife guilty by implication. It is inconceivable. The benighted dreamer looks around for corroboration of his fantastic dream and finds none. Everything is the same as before: nobody acknowledges even the possibility of guilt. To them he becomes like a madman at a chamber concert, dressed tastelessly in black, white with tiredness and a grinding grief, speaking in riddles: worms and skulls, inappropriate things often uttered in even, normal tones. This is a damaged animal they would go a long way around rather than take a step to save: perhaps he will go and die in a ditch. A carefully prepared entertainment devised to expose the guilty is taken simply for a social indelicacy. The man must be mistaken, and his dream truly a nightmare. He persuades himself otherwise, his reason totters and he begins to despair. Events move too fast for him and he finds himself caught up in an adventure story that overtakes him. Before dying he does in fact destroy his enemy, though still without

having any conclusive proof of his guilt or of the woman's involvement. By the end the man has killed three people and indirectly caused the death of two others. He has not exposed the original crime to the eyes of the world. He has only trusted his instinct and his dream, and by a deep irony, his instinct was true.

To objectify the part as you are about to climb inside it might seem a silly arabesque: but it may ease a certain pressure, as content begins to be reconciled with form. Similarly, Hamlet's character can only be defined by the action of the play, not by importing a quantity of neurotic or emotional baggage, let alone by a determination to speak for the times; in a sense you have to enter the action naked, with a kind of sweet optimism, and allow the story to be written on you. Although you are confronting all sorts of things – your sexuality, your relationship with your parents, alive, dead, troubled or well, your competence and usefulness – it is the story, one step after another, that defines the effort. George Bernard Shaw said of Johnston Forbes-Robertson's Hamlet that he played 'as Shakespeare should be played, on the line and to the line, with the utterance and acting simultaneous, inseparable and in fact identical': definitive advice and the key to survival. Hamlet thinks and speaks at the same rate: every line is the necessary funnel for a spontaneous feeling, which requires those words and only those words – it is all one thing, the emotion, the pressure, the need to speak, the image that defines. It can be like pressing a tornado through the eye of a needle; it also, in the midst of turbulence, keeps you afloat.

Opening

> The noise is stilled: I come out on to the stage
> Leaning against the doorpost
> I try to guess from the distant echo
> What is to happen in my lifetime. . .
>
>   Boris Pasternak , 'Hamlet',
>   trans. Max Hayward and Manya Harari)

The sound of a first night audience, filtered through the relays into Hamlet's dressing room, is like the baying of wolves, and to some extent that's what they are. There will be excitement in the air, good will in little pockets, and no quarter – Hamlet makes every man a critic. This is a *corrida* in which the part may well gore the man, and since it is your very nature as much as your skills that are being assessed, it follows that you are unlikely to enjoy it unless you are extraordinarily self-confident, too self-confident probably to play the part. However, if you are well cast, you have active intelligence, a blessed gift for thinking on your feet, and a range of emotions on tap: from this combination the anarchic energy of the part flows – in some sense, you make it up as you go along. So in fact you are well equipped for a night like this, when anything can happen: carefully-planned moments will go awry, then something quite fresh will offer itself, and of course you must swing with it. Whatever your doubts, by the end your Hamlet will already be one of a kind. Some great wave, more true than the press, the agents, the ill-wishers and friends, may pick you up within an hour or so and fill you up with Shakespeare's spirit. Do it for the bust of him in Stratford Church, for your mother, your lover or whoever told you you shouldn't go on the stage. And remember to *breathe* steadily: fear hits the diaphragm first.

Playing

If you survive this hysterical ceremony, then you can get to work again and resume where you left off in rehearsals – either with a fixed run of days or weeks ahead of you, or secure in the knowledge, if this is the RSC, that you have a long job ahead, perhaps two years of it; or otherwise hopeful, in a commercial setting, that you have left enough of a marker on the night of nights not to get two weeks' notice to quit.

The assembling customers are no longer vulpine analysts of uncertain quality but, generally, decent and well-disposed types looking forward to perhaps their favourite play. Don't be deceived, though: every night is a needle match, and it is a hunger for disclosure that brings them in and keeps them there. Of the play of course, but 105 per cent of the man. Nobody wants a Hamlet who's conserving himself, or tired, or unwilling to offer everything, all the time, every time. This is very hard to do eight times a week, or even six.

My own first night at Stratford I played in a dull daze, as if all the expectation had worn me out, making me long to be shot of it. Then, indulgently nursed by the repertoire system, I played the part for two years – but three or four times a week, rarely more, in which time it weaved in and out of my life and I suppose announced it. Repertoire is a blessing, and it wasn't always there. We have to thank Shaw's hero Forbes-Robertson (a great actor who hated acting) for the fact that the uncut text is now accepted in performance; but he did say it could only be done occasionally. Since then, Hamlets have either faced a full-length version or the task of playing every night, but rarely both. A straight run is always daunting: all actors know the fearful moment when, with nightly repetition, each performance becomes an imitation of the last one, real thought and feeling a sound pattern accompanied by the making of appropriate faces: in John Osborne's words in another context, such an evening is a pretty long chew on a very dry prune. In such a run as Hamlet, the problem is more likely to be exhaustion than staleness: the part more or less forces you to think freshly. In repertoire, on the other hand, you can ponder it all at leisure. I changed my mind about many things many times – whether I mourned or condemned Rosencrantz and Guildenstern in the end, in what way I loved Ophelia, whom Yorick's skull reminded me of – life moved on, and I didn't always give the performance that had been reviewed. This is as it should be, but not always to the liking of a proportion of the Stratford audience: those who are recording history. I had a furious letter from a fan who complained that on her second visit I had given Ophelia back her letters in the Nunnery Scene on a different line, so that she, the fan, no longer knew what I meant by my Hamlet: she illustrated the point with diagrams, the arc of the gesture in each case underscored by the line of text, very much like the song sheet that asks you to sing 'Fo-ogg-y day i-in Lo-ondon T-ow-n'.

Whatever their frequency, performances can vary from intense exhilaration to four hours of the most dreadful toil – except that the text is so fine a medium for the personality that something good will always happen. When things go sweetly you can do two a day and still be the last to leave the party; other times, the part shakes you like a rat. On any given night, the cure is to give yourself to the action, so that the part begins to play *you*. Character in motion is not tiring to do. If you dredge up wedges of primal emotions and *apply* them to the lines, you start worn out and get worse: if you commit yourself to speaking and demand that the feelings catch up with the words, you should be all right.

In the end the experience of Hamlet qualifies you for nothing except going out the next day and doing it again. The director will presumably have left after the opening, returning only, as they say, to take out the 'improvements'. This leaves you self-critically alone, assessing all the time, post-morteming, keeping in working order. However self-scathing that may be, the audience will never desert you, bringing you every enthusiasm for the event; and you now learn everything from them. You and they are carried by the prevailing winds: everyone wants it to be special, and everyone, including you, waits for lightning to strike. This animal relationship is a wonderful thing, like champagne to tiredness, and more than makes up for the sniffy reservations of a hundred experts.

In return for huge efforts, the part will verify you: you will never be quite the same again. By one standard or another, we all fail – and succeed. Years later some middle-aged person will greet you and declare, with a curiously confidential air, you were his or her 'first' Hamlet – which is very nice. In this part you have the inner ear of the audience like no other character in literature. Good luck.

4

CONCLUSION

State of Play

4

CONCLUSION

State of Play

Later in 1994, at the newly-renamed Gielgud Theatre in the West End, Peter Hall's third *Hamlet* settled in to become one of the winter's successes. The new front-of-house looked splendid; in the auditorium there was, usually, rapt attention; meanwhile whores worked the doorways behind the theatre and at regular intervals three or four fellows in the street would unhesitatingly use the emergency exit doors as a pissoir. These exit doors are not flush to the ground, and there is a slope inside them downhill to the stage. A rat or two was sighted (not behind an arras), and one night Voltemand inadvertently sat on his costume and rose to find a mouse squashed inside it. This theatre used to be called the Globe; we could almost have been in Elizabethan London, except that we all went home to Camden and Wandsworth afterwards.

Shakespeare and his audience, on the other hand, wore the muddy vesture of decay and never escaped from it. Disease, dirt and powerlessness formed a sludge from which Shakespeare's, Jonson's and Marlowe's dramatic imagination flew: it is as well to remember the feculence in which the jewels are set. Shakespeare may be part of our national heritage and all that, but it is the besieged and incarcerated who often hear him best. Many European audiences have understood why Denmark is a prison better than we do, and why a little patch of ground may have no profit in it but the name. Out of terrible constriction comes Caliban's glorious adaptability:

I'll show thee the best springs; I'll pluck thee berries. . .
Prithee, let me bring thee where crabs grow,
And I with my long nails will dig thee pig-nuts,

Show thee a jay's nest, and instruct thee how
To snare the nimble marmoset.

As anyone who has worked on a text with the guests of Her
Majesty knows, the long-term prisoner often seems the perfect
Shakespearian actor. Cut off from past and future, the one tainted
by some act against life and the other a seeming joke, he lives
heroically in the moment of speaking, linking heart and head and
tongue without caution. Just as even a bad production cannot
prevent an actor being ravished by a text, the action of speaking
Shakespeare brings to the dispossessed a power that no screw
can take from him. When a professional actor works alongside a
prisoner, his task may well be to raise rather than lower his own
standards.

Free men at the Gielgud meanwhile, we laboured away amidst
the rats, the tarts and the urine like self-important priests, religi-
ously tuning and tuning as we approached the two hundredth
performance of our work of art. The critic of the *Sunday Times*,
John Peter, was such a champion of this production that each week
he took time in his column to discuss an individual performance
within it – to the chagrin, perhaps, of whoever was opening a new
show that week and wanted all the space. I used to wonder if it was
he who kept us on. He wrote one day that

> 400 years ago this play was what we now solemnly call New Writing,
> and it had to pay its way in a large commercial theatre engaged in cut-
> throat competition with other large commercial theatres. . . . behind
> *Hamlet*, the play of grief, darkness, self-searching and dreams, there is
> *Hamlet* the political thriller and commercial crowd-puller flexing its
> muscles.

Quite true. Shakespeare's company worked for survival in the
earliest commercial playhouses, of which Shaftesbury Avenue is the
heir: for the first time, as opposed to witnessing free performances
in innyards and market squares, people paid money in advance to
see the play. Distant as we are in other ways, we can well understand this theatre's competitive and threatened nature. The original
Globe was an open public stage, built in 1598 by James Burbage,
who with his actors is said to have dismantled overnight another
venue, The Theatre, to construct it. It was to be played on in
modern dress, with minimal settings and props – though there was
some machinery, a trap for example, and there must have been a
cannon too, as a spark from it burned the theatre down during a

performance of *Henry VIII* in 1613. Before that, in 1609, the company, now the King's Men under James I, took possession of the indoor Blackfriars Theatre and played there too, especially in the winter. Significantly, when the company moved inside, the pricing structure was reversed so that those nearest the stage paid the most and those furthest away the least, as they do now: the clientele became more elite, and the plays a degree more experimental and even esoteric. However, this was at the end of Shakespeare's writing career, and it is the Globe that dominates our reflections on his theatre – a building that, although it was only half the physical size of most playhouses nowadays, nevertheless held at least twice as many people (about three thousand, stacked vertically and less neurotic about personal territory). It is as if we were to play Shakespeare at the Bradford Alhambra or the London Adelphi or the Winter Garden in New York, sold out twice over with unreserved places and then shrunk to half its size, in our civilian clothes, with rehearsal props, against the building's brick walls.

That's the distance between us. As *Hamlet* repeatedly shows, Shakespeare's stage was just a stage, the perfect platform for his intellectual showmanship, allowing him a cavalier approach to time and place and even character – matters that we, as post-Stanislavskians, are obsessed with. In logic too, these plays always depended on a certain indulgence from the audience, just as the actors had to grant the spectators the indulgence to carry on with their lives the while. At the end of *Hamlet,* who should turn up but Fortinbras. The wicked Duke in *As You Like It* is about to attack his banished brother when he meets an 'old religious man' in the forest (so we are told by a character we have never met before), and decides to drop the whole thing. And audiences were familiar with the last-minute letter miraculously dropping into the hand, like Portia's in *The Merchant of Venice* announcing that Antonio's argosies

> Are richly come to harbour suddenly.
> You shall not know by what strange accident
> I chanced on this letter.

No indeed: you can almost feel the writers' cramp. Shakespeare understood a theatre of gesture not naturalism, of poetry not consistency: in a world where the most momentous events are played to an audience talking, buying and selling, intriguing, thieving and barracking, a great paradoxical freedom is possible, and the subordination of all things to broad narrative and arresting theme is urgent. 'Character' in the plays is never separated from some public issue; romantic love is never that only, but an anomaly in a context of rivalry or war; a personal hatred usually rocks the state. This theatre existed in the moment of attention, and, freed from logic, Shakespeare's unmatched realism of feeling and width of imagination took the prevailing winds like a great improvised sail. He brought to his writing an innovative harmony that anticipated both Samuel Beckett and bebop: it has never been so easy since.

The prodigality is in these people's *minds*: they are *all* gifted with tongues.

> BENEDICK (*a professional soldier*): Will your grace command me any service to the world's end? I will go on the slightest errand now to the Antipodes that you can devise to send me on; I will fetch you a toothpicker now from the furthest inch of Asia, bring you the length of Prester John's foot, fetch you a hair off the great Cham's beard, do you any embassage to the Pigmies, rather than hold three words' conference with this harpy. . .

> OTHELLO (*'rude in speech' and possibly working in his second language*):
> Whip me, ye devils,
> From the possession of this heavenly sight!
> Blow me about in winds! Roast me in sulphur!
> Wash me in steep down gulfs of liquid fire!
> O Desdemona! Desdemona dead! O! O!

> MISTRESS QUICKLY (*a landlady*): Thou didst swear to me upon a parcel-gilt goblet, sitting in my Dolphin chamber, at the round table by a sea-coal fire, upon Wednesday in whitsun week, when the prince broke thy head for liking his father to a singing man of Windsor, thou didst swear to me then, as I was washing thy wound, to marry me and make me my lady thy wife. Canst thou deny it? Did not goodwife Keech, the butcher's wife, come in then and call me gossip Quickly? Coming in to borrow a mess of vinegar, telling us she had a good dish of prawns, whereby thou didst desire to eat some, whereby I told thee they were ill for a green wound. And didst thou not, when she was gone downstairs, desire me to be no more familiarity with such poor people, saying that ere long they should call me madam? And didst thou not kiss me, and bid me fetch thee thirty shillings? I put thee now to thy book oath. Deny it if thou canst.

I wish you got stuff like that at the Dirty Duck.[1]

---

1   As soon as this exceptional language arrived, it started to drain away. Many of Hamlet's words and usages went to America with the settlers: 'liquor', 'quit', 'I'll have these players

In 1642 the Puritans closed the playhouses, and locked us out of Shakespeare's theatre for ever: it was two hundred and fifty years before we we started rapping at the Elizabethan door again. When Charles II was restored to the throne in 1660, ushering in an age naturally obsessed with redefinition, Thomas Killigrew, courtier and dramatist, converted a tennis court in London's Vere Street, off Oxford Street, into a 'theatre'[2] – that is to say, a rectangular box with space for an audience at one end. It was a timely initiative that coincided with the new taste for opera travelling across Europe, which required a stage on which the audience could see the singers and the singers could see the conductor, exactly as they do now. So Shakespeare's three-sided public platform represents a short-lived moment in theatre history, between the innyards and the tennis court, and it was succeeded in turn by the horseshoe shape (often combined with a forestage, proscenium doors and audience boxes) of the eighteenth century, by Frank Matcham's great period of nineteenth-century theatre architecture, and then, in the recent age of converted cinemas and civic construction, by the undistinguished shoebox. This is where the rub starts rubbing for us. We can go neither forward nor back – we hope to recapture Elizabethan vitality without quaint reconstructions, but our forward technological thrust takes us away from the very roots of Shakespeare's writing. It would be absurdly puritanical not to do the plays in proscenium theatres, even though their display-case nature places a horrendous burden on designers, who have to find literal pictures for an essentially non-literal playwright: you would have to do without the most popular metropolitan houses and almost all the touring ones, and only go to Chichester (where the audience is very unElizabethan), to the Sheffield Crucible, the Guthrie in Minneapolis or the Arena in Washington. Alternatively you would have to change scale radically and occupy spaces much smaller than the old Globe, requiring a good deal of subsidy to

Play something like the murder of my father' are no longer European English. Viola's '*Make me* a willow cabin at your gate' is an American construction. Words like 'ain't' have endured on both sides, but the English use of English seems rather perishable: 'Ça ne fait rien' survives, 'es macht nichts' too, but not the Shakespearian 'that makes nothing here'.

2   Killigrew opened with *Henry IV Part 1* and soon after presented the first actress to play on the English stage, as Desdemona. (A bit late in the day – there had been professional actresses in France and Italy since the sixteenth century.) He went on to found Drury Lane and set up an acting school at the Barbican. The Vere Street theatre became much later the site of the Stoll Theatre.

survive – either in the indirect form of high ticket prices (the Donmar Warehouse in London's Covent Garden) or in European co-production (the Tramway Glasgow), or both, or into lamb dressed as mutton (the Swan in Stratford and the Royal National Theatre's Cottesloe). In England, where dependable subscription audiences are not pursued much, and box-office patterns are very volatile, the only organisations powerful enough to keep such venues open all the time, more or less absorbing them in a larger operation, are of course the subsidised national companies, where the atmosphere sometimes resembles a reunion of old friends rather than the socially chaotic energy of Shakespeare's theatre. However, when such spaces are really used freely – as in the early days of the Other Place in Stratford or in Bill Bryden's promenade work at the Cottesloe in the eighties, or in that of Peter Brook, Robert Lepage and Ariane Mnouchkine in their overseas counterparts – you sometimes sense the vitality of the medieval courtyard and the Elizabethan playhouse.

Two physical attempts to gain intimacy with Shakespeare by literally recreating the Globe bookend the twentieth century. They may prove that the more structural the experiment, the less it releases the imagination. Between 1895 and 1905 William Poel ran the Elizabethan Stage Society, dedicated to doing Shakespeare on a Globe-like stage which he toured to halls and courtyards. It was of course a step away from the real thing, neither quite using the actual venue nor really re-making the past. Poel's great service was to liberate Shakespeare from the spectacular irrelevancies of Herbert Beerbohm Tree (Richard II on horseback, mini-Malvolios following the principal around) by placing an unsuggestive background behind the all-important language;[3] but in the end his company couldn't be sustained, and its rather narrow academicism defeated itself. However, historical curiosity persists, mixed up with an apprehension that the texts may be best served by recreating their original context. At the time of writing, a fine row is brewing between practitioners and academics over the authenticity and use of the reconstructed Globe Theatre in Southwark, the long dream of Sam Wanamaker finally coming about. Alas, Wanamaker died before he could see it, and since he can no longer declare what he

---

3   Ben Iden Payne periodically did something rather similar (but less pedantically) through the first half of the century in the United States with his modified Elizabethan productions, which aimed to preserve the 'melodic line' of the plays by fluency of staging.

wants for his highly personal vision, a lot of arguments are likely to remain unsettled. The theatre community is divided about the project: everyone who sees the space emerging is excited by it, everyone fears the naffness of Heritage Shakespeare or an unrevealing academicism. The twin pillars holding up the 'heavens' (the roof of the stage) may be correctly placed historically: they may also be impossible to work with in terms of sightlines. Instead of working only in daylight, shouldn't we being taking advantage of electricity and playing in the evenings, when most people are freer to attend? And what about boy players reclaiming all the women's parts in our century?

This rather predictable row may yet undo the making of terms between scholars and the theatre industry which has been quite notable over the last twenty years: a period in which academics have discovered the touchstone of performance with an almost naive enthusiasm, granting us an intellectual credibility we don't always deserve; and, dogs out of the manger, we have straightened our intellectual clothes and started to listen to learned talk about the *ur-Hamlet* and Shakespeare's foul papers. As the latest controversy proves, though, the two parishes still converse mainly with themselves. While recognising the scholar as a species of deep-pit miner, chinking away invaluably for facts even if his judgments aren't particularly helpful, theatre people, often intellectually specious and always taken up with practical compromises, find it difficult to hold still for theoretical absolutes – it is all too much of a movable feast, from show to show and night to night, and the ideas aren't worth a squirt of Irving's water pistol if they can't be transmitted to a large number of people, fast.

In fact, whatever Shakespeare had on his mind in writing such a thing as *Hamlet* – his own father was dying, there was national anxiety about the ageing Queen's successor, audiences had a renewed appetite for revenge plays – we are separated from it by a wide and clamorous ditch, inadequately crossed either by guild memory or academic geiger-counter. Unwittingly built to last, *Hamlet* immediately, in the words of Shakespeare's contemporary Gabriel Harvey, 'pleased the wiser sort' – and not only the wiser sort. A highwayman held up a group of travelling players in 1604 and demanded they perform the play for him; and it was done on board a ship of the East India Company off Sierra Leone in 1607 – according to its Captain Keeling 'to keep my people from idleness and unlawful games or sleep', which apparently it did, in spades. English actors were touring the play, together with *Titus Andronicus* and *Romeo and Juliet*, in Germany in a bootleg version (imagine a still cruder version of *Titus*. . .) within a few years of the premiere. These early stories evidence that the play as much as the hero was the thing: it was certainly written, not for an actor-manager, let alone such a thing as a director, but for a working company of actors, several of them share-holders, who were able co-operatively to put on any play in a short time, with little rehearsal but great practical expertise, and a very good leading man, Richard Burbage.

The Restoration changed all that, just as it changed the venues, and the exhibition of the player soon became the point of the exercise. Thomas Betterton, working with England's first female actors in a very much bowdlerised text at a time when Shakespeare was not popular – John Dryden declared that he was too 'disgusting to be shown in a refined age' – occupied the central role unchallenged from 1661 to 1709, by which time he was over seventy. From 1756 to 1776 (a period in which, conversely, 'classics' were greatly preferred to new plays), the part, like many others, belonged to David Garrick, whose respect for the play was such that, as well as cutting the Gravediggers, he left Horatio and Laertes alive at the end to rule Denmark. The century closed with John Philip Kemble's gloomy, romantic Prince – a low point, according to Leigh Hunt, who compared his vocal delivery to a chemist administering laudanum drop by drop. In the nineteenth century *Hamlet* became Literature, falling under the crippling influence of the Romantic Sensibility. To Goethe, this triple murderer Prince was 'a beautiful, pure, noble and most moral nature, without the strength of nerve that makes the hero, [who] sinks beneath a burden which it can neither bear nor throw off', and Coleridge felt he had 'a smack of Hamlet' himself. These romantic individualists tore the prince out of the play to identify him as the permanent outsider, viewing the other characters either without interest or through Hamlet's twisted lens.

Meanwhile writers from Hazlitt at the beginning of the century to Shaw and Max Beerbohm at the end, described, in detail and with style, stars' performances in a part which by now seems to have existed outside of the play. They have therefore become, progressively, quite vivid to us. In 1805 Master William Betty played Hamlet at Drury Lane at the age of fourteen, and the House of

Commons adjourned to see his performance: apparently on meeting the Ghost his face went as white as his neckerchief. He swiftly disappeared from view, and Edmund Kean and William Charles Macready slugged it out for supremacy: Kean won, as he did with many parts – the most natural, the most dynamic, the most illuminating, the most interesting, surely, to us – but as Hamlet he did sentimental things we might not put up with, like returning after his exit in the Nunnery Scene to kiss Ophelia's hair. Macready, an early Method actor who tried to trim everything out of his performance except pure thought, was permanently frustrated by the part, but played it with success not only in England but in Paris and in New York, where he introduced some business into the Play Scene – the waving of a handkerchief – which was hissed from the audience by the American actor Edwin Forrest, whereupon the show stopped and they argued about it. The hostility between the two men led to a riot in Astor Place in 1849, in which twenty-odd people were killed. English actors are not always welcome on Broadway.

Macready, who disliked his own profession, contributed to it in another crucial matter: he was among the first actor-managers to insist on proper rehearsals (something that had never troubled the wild and dissolute Kean), and the subordination of design to the text, which he largely restored from the ravages of Garrick and his predecessors. In this he was like Samuel Phelps, who, though not a great actor himself, from 1843 to 1862 established Sadler's Wells as a permanent London home for Shakespeare and did virtually all of the plays there. If great stars like Kean cared little for management, acting their way into history on their own terms, some not-quite-so-startling actor-managers arguably nurtured a flame – the text, the spirit of the play – that formed the basis of what we expect now, and implied an horizon wider than the leading player's ego. By the time the Victorian and Edwardian Hamlets arrived – Henry Irving, Herbert Beerbohm Tree (with a chorus for 'Flights of angels sing thee to thy rest'), Johnston Forbes-Robertson and Sarah Bernhardt, the critical celebration of great Hamlets and their Moments (not much about the Claudiuses, Poloniuses and Ophelias) was being balanced by a fuller regard for the play as a whole and some responsible administration.

By some process the disorder of those days has turned into the structured tumult of ours. This is due not so much to natural evolution, but, as always, to the jolt provided by exceptional personalities. Many of these begin to congregate around the turn of this century. Just as Stanislavski and Nemirovich-Danchenko co-opted Chekhov (whether he liked it or not) into the Moscow Art Theatre and a completely new approach to acting, and just as Max Reinhardt and then Erwin Piscator in Germany sequestered playtexts into the personal vision of the director, and just as Balzac and Zola forced the French theatre into a realistic mode, so in England the work of three remarkable figures in particular has signalled the conditions that we now take more or less for granted in our approach to Shakespeare. One was an actor and theorist and occasionally a director who is remembered as a designer; the second a playwright, producer and polemicist celebrated for his critical essays; the third a director with vast pre-eminence as an actor.

Edward Gordon Craig, son of Ellen Terry and originally an actor in Henry Irving's company, revolutionised stage design in this century. He worked not only in Britain, but in Florence with Eleanora Duse, in Berlin, Dublin and Copenhagen – and strikingly in Moscow, where his troubled relationship with Stanislavski nevertheless produced a *mise en scène* for the first Court Scene in *Hamlet* in 1911 in which a huge cloak flowing from the King's and Queen's shoulders covered the whole stage, except for where the members of the court appeared in its gaps: on a forestage separated by a ditch sat Hamlet. However, Craig's practical career was limited, and he was as frustrated by the practicalities of production as producers were by his blithe disregard of deadlines and consistency of idea; rather it has been his theory, expressed mostly from Florence through his self-published periodical *The Mask* (and briefly before the First War in his short-lived theatre school) that has articulated his influence. For Craig, flexible screens and uncluttered architectural shapes with high verticals took the place of backcloths and flats – lit not by footlights, but as by the sun from above and in front, creating natural shadows; he also dreamed of, but never really succeeded in, being able to move the stage mechanically about. Like many modern designers, he was suspected of plotting to reduce the actor to the status of a marionette; really he was only responding to the bad practice of the times when he suggested that, just once in a while, the leading actors should be 'in a corner or under an extinguisher' rather than the focus, all the

time, of all things. (In fact he revered Henry Irving as the supreme
Über-marionette.) Wayward and provocative[4] and way ahead of his
time, Craig was arguing for a form of total theatre undreamed of by
the actor-manager. He shifted our conception of what we should
look at behind and around a play alike away from two-dimensional
illusion and Elizabethan reconstructions, towards the kind of
mobile, expressive style typical of the contemporary stage.

It is a great pity that Craig never worked with Harley Granville-
Barker, combining his iconoclasm with the latter's rigorous regard
for the text. In fact his view of his contemporary was scornful – to
Craig, this was

> . . . a writer of plays and a careful producer of modern plays – which
> made him 'hullo, old chap' to Shakespeare, whose plays he never came
> to care about until it was too late

– but in fact Granville-Barker, scholar, producer, actor and playwright, has emerged as the only commentator on Shakespeare that
practitioners have much time for. His effect on the English theatre
in general before the First World War was exceptional: he ran (with
J. E. Vedrenne) the Royal Court between 1904 and 1907, introducing Shaw, Ibsen and Euripides to its audiences and insisting on
an ensemble acting style – he was in a sense the first 'Royal Court'
director. In fact he was the first English director of any kind: and
the three Shakespeares that he did at the Savoy between 1912 and
1914 – *The Winter's Tale, Twelfth Night* and *A Midsummer Night's
Dream* -- seem to have been works of exceptional beauty and clarity.
Again having no truck with stars, and rejecting the historicism of
William Poel, Granville-Barker's insistence on the pre-eminence of
the text and the concentration of his staging were revolutionary.
However, he is in the history books largely because of his Prefaces
to fourteen of Shakespeare's plays, written between 1927 and his
death in 1946, exceptional works of scholarship and practicality
that can also be exceptionally irritating, cancelling out many of
their own brilliant insights into the nature of acting with a kind of
moral pietism – villains as villains, the good prevailing – that is no
use at all to actors. There is a strong whiff of snobbery in Granville-
Barker's attitude both to the smaller characters, who are too often
'simple, kindly creatures', 'a homespun lot', and – oddly, in view of

---

4 Like Goethe, he thought *Hamlet* unperformable, but felt that if it was to be done not a
word should be cut.

his earlier ensemble achievements – to the people playing them. For instance, he fears for a certain speech of ten lines in *Hamlet* that 'a minor actor might well not do it full credit,' and in the second scene requires Marcellus and Barnardo to stay 'respectfully by the door' while Hamlet draws Horatio away to 'stroll or stand with him, friendly arm-in-arm, while he questions and confides. . . ' He is also distinctly shaky on female sexuality: Gertrude (whose knowing adultery is assumed) is 'the pretty, kindly, smirched, bedizened woman', and his account of Ophelia is hopelessly sentimental, right up to her final exit, when

> she bids them a solemn 'God be wi' ye' and departs, head bowed, hands folded, as quietly as she came. . . [5]

So there is plenty wrong with these Prefaces, and Granville-Barker's achievement is both large and limited: throughout, his progressive instinct struggles with Edwardian sentimentality, demonstrating an exceptional man out of touch with practice.[6] But they are written from a practical viewpoint, and his line-by-line discoveries are more helpful by far than broad abstracts and thematic extrapolations.[7] Even if his position as the first man of practical Shakespearian scholarship is a little romanticised, at least a man of the theatre was writing something useful down at last.

5   In fact, throughout the Prefaces there is a need to see women along a judgmental scale between wantonness and chastity. Granville-Barker is sorrowful about the 'pornographic difficulty' of Shakespeare's bawdry; he believes Antony and Cleopatra should not kiss on 'the nobleness of life Is to do thus' ('this is not the sort of thing [Shakespeare] meant by suiting the action to the word'); in *The Winter's Tale* we meet 'Plucky Paulina – what a good fellow!'. Whatever stage our sexual revolution may be thought to have reached, it has brought us a deal closer to a great writer from 1600 than to the Edwardians, and we have at last become as interested as Shakespeare was in unpredictable figures like Cressida, long confined to the moral scrapheap by literary critics, in the real nature of Cleopatra (particularly as a politician), in Titania and Lady Macbeth and repressed figures like Isabella in *Measure for Measure* – a fascinating mirror-image, in her obsession and blindness, to the corrupt Angelo.

6   For a simple reason. He divorced his actress wife, Lillah McCarthy, married an American heiress, Helen Huntingdon (who, predictably, disliked actors and the theatre) and settled in France to write his Prefaces, untainted either by his own practice or the developing influence of those he had inspired. Like Craig, he left too soon.

7   Literary criticism of Shakespeare was very unhelpful at this time – A. C. Bradley had declared that *Lear* was unperformable in the Elizabethan theatre because it lacked the equipment to make a convincing storm, and T. S. Eliot primly announced in 1919 that more people thought *Hamlet* a work of art because they found it interesting than found it interesting because it was a work of art.

Whatever else, we have inherited, or claim to have, his attitude to the text. Whatever job you do in the theatre, Granville-Barker will call you to heel and you should read him once a year. On designers:

> If the designer finds himself competing with the actors, the sole interpreters Shakespeare has licensed, then it is he who is the intruder and must retire.

On acting Shakespeare (in a blank verse line):

> Be swift, be swift, be not poetical. . .

On directing:

> The text of a play is a score awaiting performance. . . a collaboration. . . if [a producer] only knows how to give orders, he has missed his vocation; he had better be a drill sergeant. . .

On playwriting:

> A play. . . is a magic spell; and even the magician cannot always foresee the full effect of it. . .

Interestingly, Granville-Barker wishes at one point that he could be writing a generation later, since he feels the theatrical basis on which he rests his views is changing fast. He is right. The *Hamlet* Preface is quite late – 1937 – and while it was a-writing, John Gielgud, the least sentimental of men, was taking over the Queen's Theatre in London with a company with real depth of talent and expecting results from them, rather than surrounding himself with Barnardos and Marcelluses who would stay respectfully by the door. This extraordinary third figure (who in fact brought Granville-Barker quietly back into the theatre in 1940 to help him with Lear – the great man declared that the part required an oak, and Gielgud was an ash, but he'd see what he could do) is in some sense where many of us came in. He is now very senior, and for virtually all living actors, has always been there. Born three months before the death of Chekhov, Ellen Terry's grand-nephew (and therefore a sort of cousin to Craig), twice a Romeo and a Richard II before 1930, co-star of Mrs Pat Campbell and the young Gwen Ffrangçon Davies, colleague of Nigel Playfair, Tyrone Guthrie, Fyodor Komisarjevsky, Michel Saint-Denis, Orson Welles and Alain Resnais, champion of Shakespeare in the West End sixty years ago, leading exponent of Chekhov, Coward, Harold Pinter, David Storey, Charles Wood,

Edward Bond and Alan Bennett, you could still hear him on riotous form in his ninety-first year as he recalled playing in his newly-named theatre sixty-six years ago in *Holding Out The Apple* ('You have a way of holding out the apple that positively gives me the pip'). He is a national resource we must cling on to (for time is naturally shortish): his life and presence have answered a deep need in our profession for meaning, dignity and continuity.

He can also, despite Barrymore, Evans, Olivier and Guinness, hardly be dislodged as the Hamlet of the first half of the century: he played the part five hundred times between 1929 and 1944 in five different productions (two of them directed by himself), at the Old Vic, in the West End and on Broadway.[8] Gielgud forms a bridge from the past into the over-populated and chaotic *Hamlet* stage of our times. In a mysterious way, something about his pre-eminence seems to connect us with Shakespeare himself: certainly he possessed this part in a way previously possible only for Garrick, Betterton and Irving, and not likely again. It is easy enough to forget how revolutionary he has been. His first Hamlet, in 1929, owed a good deal of its impact to the fact that he was only twenty-five: the right age of course, but his predecessors had been inclined to be twice that, and to edit the text to cut out the unflattering bits and maximise the sentiment – which Gielgud now determinedly abandoned. It must have been a revelation. At the other end of his engagement with the play, he directed Richard Burton in New York in 1964, boldly presenting it in rehearsal clothes on a blank set: the opening-night audience were bemused, but the production broke box-office records. In between, on his return to the part in 1934 it is highly significant that his production, designed by the Motleys, was hailed as loudly as his own performance – J. C. Trewin called it the 'key Shakespearian revival of the period' – and from here on the strength of his supporting casts is very striking: Jessica Tandy, Anthony Quayle, Glen Byam Shaw, George Devine, Jack Hawkins and the young Alec Guinness (making his debut as Osric) in 1934; Lillian Gish and Judith Anderson in New York in 1936; Peggy Ashcroft as his Ophelia in 1944. The development towards a company style, finally the only mechanism useful for doing the plays, speaks for itself.

---

8   He finally did it a sixth time on an ENSA tour of India, the Middle and Far East: at his very last performance, in Cairo, he reports that Horatio had an epileptic fit in his arms.

Fifty years forward we live in a more muddled and perhaps a more demanding age, both progressing and regressing. Granville-Barker's and Bernard Shaw's dreamed-of national theatre has already a history of its own, subsidy is a precarious fact. Breakaway alternatives also have familiar paths and patterns. Meanwhile official attitudes to the theatre in this country reflect the oddest mixture of contempt and chauvinistic pride, and the idea of continuity is mocked by the wanton neglect by local and national government of funding for training.[9] For all the new legitimacy, the life of many theatre workers resembles a scrabble about in the rubble. Nothing could be less conducive to nourishing a flame.

What Granville-Barker and Craig would not have predicted is the breaking down of theatre vocations into specialities: producers, designers, actors, lighting and sound designers, composers and stage managers now come carefully together out of their own corners and rarely do more than one job. Newly-powerful directors – combining the talents of guru and roadsweeper – struggle to 'unlock' *Hamlet*, to pluck out the heart of its mystery, as if it was a padlocked integer which once picked reveals all laid out to the view, instead of, like all Shakespeares, the magnificent shambles it is, an inviting football whose kicking may end up hurting the foot but won't damage the ball. We now expect a *Hamlet*, as well as holding the mirror up to nature and advertising a favoured actor, to show the age and body of the time his form and pressure. The movies court Shakespeare, abandon him, then respectfully fall in love with him again. Some directors attend to the verse, others throw it around.[10] Some directors cut, some won't. Well-budgeted productions, fearful for the audience's capacity to listen, often exhibit, alongside technical fluency, a coldness of heart and a taste for spectacle worthy of Beerbohm Tree, the balance between what you see and what hearing the words makes you see badly tilted.

9   Anyone thought to be established in our industry is now besieged by requests for help from students who have fought to win good places in drama schools but are unable to complete or even start their courses because of the withdrawal of grants. They are thus auditioning once again, for who can write the most effective begging letter.

10   In fact, blank verse is so simple. It is the form closest to speech, so flexible that it is almost impossible to screw up a line of it as long as you don't miss out any syllables. You can, like a risky jazz player, impossibly stress and elongate the words 'not' and 'that' and 'is' in 'To be or not to be; that is the question', but the verse form will tolerate it, just. The real problem with Shakespeare's verse is the difficult vocabulary, the architecture of the big speeches and the stamina they require.

Where there is no money to achieve that, there can be a haphazard and makeshift air -- no shared assumptions and a feeling of reductiveness. Although it is on Shakespeare that the absurd cliché, beloved of ignorant politicians and essentially bad for us, that British theatre is the best in the world is traditionally based, in the blessed plot itself there is only the shakiest consensus. If you are interested in how *Hamlet*, or indeed any Shakespeare, is to be done, from end to end of the industry you will go, from right wing to left, looking for a taste of what feels right, never finding it in one building, with one leader or under one system. The post-war *Hamlet* is thus a coat of wonderfully many colours: the one thing everybody agrees on is the greatness and pervasiveness of Gielgud. He was the last undisputed king of the road, and a great continuum in himself.

So of course we must play *Hamlet* in his theatre. Sir John's own view is that yes, there is such a thing in our profession as the handing on of a torch: the important thing is not to make too much of it. The idea that there might be a 'tradition' to be carried on and certain people equipped to do it is an off-putting one, pompous and exclusive, but it does give the illusion of history to our diverse endeavours, and in the case of Shakespeare to a barely-definable sense of guild: and occasionally, a circle seems truly closed. One evening at the Gielgud Theatre in 1994, I happened on an account by Alexander Hertzen of a performance of Hamlet by Vasily Karatygin, a St Petersburg tragedian, in one of the earliest Russian productions of the play, in 1839:

> I have just returned from *Hamlet*, and believe it or not I sobbed. . .
> I see a dark night, and a pale Hamlet displaying a skull on the tip of his sword and saying 'Here hung those lips and now ha-ha-ha!' You will be sick after this play. . .

Glad of the sobbing (and marvelling at the sickness), I went downstairs to the stage to do the Graveyard Scene. For the first time, either in rehearsal or performance, Stephen Dillane picked up Yorick's skull on the tip of his dagger and displayed it, with a particularly sardonic laugh. This sort of thing is not magic of course: but it's not quite an anecdote either. The sequence of gestures in *Hamlet* concentrates Russian, English, Xhosa, Italian, Spanish, Albanian, Polish, Swedish, Danish and Marathi sensibilities because of one man's vision – his small, human, detailed vision, not even the grand sweep. We might as well try to package up water as to pin Shakespeare down; but although we are cut off from what provoked this play or what it eased for him, we nevertheless find a hidden continuity linking four hundred years of effort, some inextinguishable fire. Believing they have invented them, actors are led to the same actions, the same improvisations, and the play is a refrain in all our lives.

One's own life may be circular too, a wheel within a very much larger wheel. I have now played in every scene of the play apart from the Polonius-Reynaldo and the small scene of Horatio and the sailors – about six hundred performances, moving towards the hottest spot at the fire and away again. However, at the two-hundredth-odd repetition of the latest, my senses began to play me false: I could have sworn I heard Ophelia describe Laertes as 'a puff'd and reckless limousine' and Horatio say of old Hamlet that 'he was an okay king'. Perhaps it's time to sidestep Polonius, move on to the Gravedigger and out.

INDEX OF CHARACTERS